Wanting Wholeness, Being Broken

Wanting Wholeness, Being Broken

A BOOK OF SERMONS

Marilyn Sewell

FULLER PRESS
Portland, Oregon

ISBN 1-55896-372-3
Printed in the United States of America

Fuller Press
2135 NE 16th Avenue
Portland, Oregon 97212

Library of Congress Catalog Card Number: 98-93031

This volume of sermons
is dedicated to the ones
who have called them forth from me,
the members and friends
of the First Unitarian Church
of Portland, Oregon.

Contents

Introduction

*T*HE SERMONS in this collection represent the best of my work during the first five years of my ministry at the First Unitarian Church of Portland, Oregon. They were selected by a committee of two from the congregation, both women of great literary sensibility and deep knowing: Elizabeth Hirsch and Jane Glazer. I am grateful to them for reading and re-reading stacks of my sermons and then spending hours in the decision-making process.

I am grateful, too, for my fine editor Karen Kirtley, whose subtle sense of language and awareness of detail refined the text. Also I must thank Robert Conklin of Timber Press for his encouragement and advice, and his associate Darcel Warren for her help with the technical aspects of publication. Martin White made suggestions for the format and printing that contributed substantially to the beauty of the book.

And now a word about stealing. All ministers steal material wherever they can find it. We especially love to find a good story or anecdote. And since sermons are generally such transient things, we freely borrow from one another, from magazines, from newspapers, from overheard conversations in supermarkets and on airplanes and in restaurants. We develop the "homiletic ear," as they say in seminary, and no one is safe around us, especially members of our family. I have tried to give sources when I borrowed language directly, but more often than not, I have considered the stories and myths "common property." If you are reading this book and find I have borrowed from you without acknowledgment, I apologize in advance and would be happy to give the appropriate citing in the next edition of this book.

Of course it is impossible to capture the real sermon on the page. The sermon exists not on paper but rather somewhere in that space between the minister and the congregants on Sunday morning. I come with my paltry words each Sunday, fearing that they will not be enough. Literally quaking, I am. After all, these people in the pews have come wanting to hear some wisdom about the deepest concerns of their hearts. And then something magic happens. All ministers know about this magic. I step up into the pulpit, and the sermon becomes suddenly more than it is, refined by grace and the moment into the message that individuals somehow need to hear. My fear leaves me. I know I am not doing this thing alone.

Writing and delivering sermons has been a spiritual discipline for me. I have been forced to examine subject matter that I might have otherwise neglected. More important, I have experienced shifts of heart. When I find myself bogging down in the writing process, I stop and ask myself a single question: "So where is your passion in this topic?" And then I am confronted with my own demons, my own frailties. Only then does the sermon begin to bloom.

The discipline of creating sermons for my people has made me change my ways, ways of understanding as well as ways of behaving. I am reminded of a story about Gandhi. A mother came with her son to Gandhi and asked, "Will you tell my son not to eat sugar? It is bad for his health, and I cannot convince him to stop." Gandhi said, "Come back in two weeks." So, dutifully, the woman returned in two weeks, again with her son in tow. Once more, she made her request, and Gandhi told the boy to stop eating sugar. The mother was puzzled. She asked, "Mohandas, why could you not have told the boy two weeks ago when I first approached you?" And Gandhi answered, "Because I had not yet given up sugar." Sometimes it hurts, but I have to "give up the sugar" before I can stand in the pulpit.

The power of a sermon comes about chiefly through relationship. I stand in great and abiding love. I stand as the carrier of the light that has been taken forward through generations by other ministers, both in my church and beyond. More important, much more important, than what I say is my presence. My congregants must know I love them, before they can hear my words. They must know that I'm giving them the very best that I have to offer. I respect them too much, love them too much, to offer less. Yes, some sermons are better than others, more artfully done. Some Sundays I come with more psychic energy than others. But I always come with the best that I can give. That message of presence and relationship is the heart of the sermon, and as I said, it cannot be reduced to a printed manuscript.

Nevertheless, words matter. And so I offer to the reader if not the heart at least the bones, the structure, of my message. These are not polished essays, there is no room for subtle intellectual meanderings. Sermons are written for oral delivery. Insofar as you can, try to hear them, for they are meant to be shared aloud.

Reading this book is not comparable to being in church and hearing the sermons delivered (and I like that birthing image), but perhaps some of the magic will creep through the printed lines. May these humble words find that place in you that needs healing or hope or inspiration.

Marilyn Sewell
March 12, 1998

Longing for the Way

Beyond Therapy

FEBRUARY 19, 1995

I don't want the demons taken away, because they're
going to take my angels, too.
—Rainer Maria Rilke

*I*F YOU HAVE BEEN FOLLOWING the cartoon strip "Cathy," you know that Cathy's boyfriend has just proposed marriage. Cathy is, as we say, freaked, stunned, overwhelmed. They are talking over a cup of coffee, and he says to her, "Why did you get so weird, Cathy?? I only asked you to marry me. If it doesn't work out, we'll get a divorce. What's the big deal? Half the people I know are divorced. Lots of my friends look at the first marriage as a trial run, anyway! You try as long as you can, but then you move on!" Then we see Cathy's thoughts: "Now it's not, ''Til death do us part' . . . now it's, ''Til couples therapy money runneth out.'"

This cartoon is all too close to the truth. We seem to live our lives awash in a sea of uncertainty. Once people looked to religion to give structure and meaning to their lives—the doctors were shamans and priests. When they had divisions in the soul, the "sin-sick soul," they fell to their knees and sought reconciliation with their God and their community.

It's different today. Freud and his multiple incarnations have joined forces with our scientific, mechanistic view of life, and now there is really no such thing as sin among sophisticated persons such as ourselves. There is only bad parenting. The Menendez brothers had bad, very bad, parents when they were growing up, and therefore some jurors couldn't see convicting them for the planned, overt, gruesome, and confessed murders of their mother and father.

We are increasingly seeing ourselves as victims. Everybody is "in recovery," it seems. Did you see the cartoon of the auditorium with a huge banner reading, "Convention for People with Functional Families"? The auditorium is empty except for two or three people. We are so desperate for some kind of escape from our psychic pain that we go to psychotherapists who charge anywhere from $50 to $120 or more per 50-minute hour. Think about it: $120 an hour to talk to someone. Every week, for months or years, we do it. A lot of us. Astounding numbers of us take psychotropic drugs for chemical imbalances in our brain. There is a new medical model for healing. Something hurts: What clinical name can I give it? What can I do about it? Now I want to be clear that I am not speaking against psychotherapy. I have had a lot of therapy myself, and before I was a minister, I was a clinical social worker doing psychotherapy with children and families. Antidepressants can sometimes make an amazing difference, and therapy can be helpful, can be healing. It certainly has been for me, and I frequently refer people to counselors.

Now there is really no such thing as sin. . . . There is only bad parenting.

I believe that our best psychotherapists, however, move beyond the medical model and see a spiritual dimension in their work. I met with some members of this church's psychotherapy network to talk about this sermon topic, and they reported they often move into this spiritual dimension. They say that when therapy is going well, they feel they get out of the way, there is a mystical connection with their client, they come away from the session with a deep feeling of gratitude, of privilege. I also have that experience often in pastoral counseling. I feel blessed. I feel that the Spirit is at work.

Certain issues move very clearly into the spiritual realm and cannot really be addressed in any other way. There are moral dilemmas, such as a decision whether or not to have an abortion, or the difficulty of forgiveness. And there is the larger question of meaning. Viktor Frankl, a Holocaust survivor, says in his classic volume *Man's Search for Meaning* that the failure of the sufferer is to find meaning in one's existence. To live is to suffer, to survive is to find meaning in the suffering, in life as it is, not as we would like it to be. Frankl further points out the dangerous misconception that we need to be tension-free, with perfectly balanced equilibrium. What a person really needs is not a tensionless, pain-free state, but rather the striving and the struggling to live for a worthy goal. To ask someone else what this meaning is for you is like asking a chess champion, "Tell me, Master, what is the best move in the world?" Meaning becomes specific to each person, specific to the demand of the hour. No master or "guru," and certainly no therapist, can tell you the meaning of your life.

Meaning is difficult to find in our post-modern world. The brilliant Jungian thinker James Hillman speaks of our profound alienation in a telling interview. He says,

> Look, a great deal of our life is manic. I can watch 34 channels of TV, I can get on the fax and communicate with people anywhere, I can be everywhere at once, I can fly across the country, I've got call waiting, so I can make two calls at once. I live everywhere and nowhere. But I don't know who lives next door to me. Who's in the next flat? Who's in 14-B? I don't know who they are, but, boy, I'm on the phone, car phone, toilet phone, plane phone, my mistress is in Chicago, the other woman I'm with is in D.C., my exwife is in Phoenix, my mother in Hawaii, and I have four children living all over the country. I have faxes coming in day and night, I can plug into all the world's stock prices, commodity exchanges, I am everywhere, man—but I don't know who's in 14-B.

Is it any wonder that we pay someone just to be there and listen for an hour? Is it a surprise that we pay for massage so we can be touched caringly by human hands? When I greet people after a worship service, I know this is the only time some of them will be touched or hugged for the rest of the week. In such a world, a world in which our old gods have become obsolete and our community is scattered and without coherence, without tradition, where is it we go for meaning?

I would suggest two places to go. First, to the great wisdom literature of the world and to the expression of its truth through symbolism and ritual; and second, to our own experience.

The purpose of religion, I believe, is to frame experience so that meaning is revealed. The wisdom literature—the Bible, the Koran, the Tao, Native American myth—these are poetic forms that feed the soul, enliven the imagination, and give narratives we can live by, forms that suggest this framework of meaning. They speak of the Mystery, a dimension beyond the secular—and the secular alone, after all, becomes a pretty dry crust. When we come to those times in life that startle us in their suddenness and in the depth of their pain, problems that can't be fixed, no matter how much money or sophistication or intelligence we have, we have two ways to go. We can give ourselves to cynicism (as Job's wife said, "Curse God and die"). Or we can be driven deeper to find meaning. No therapist can tell us why we were born, or what it means to die well. No therapist can say what living with integrity would imply for us. As Hillman says, "The question is not 'How did I get to be this way?' but rather, 'What does my angel want of me?'"

Therapy can help us understand our experience, help us become aware of patterns of behavior. Classically speaking, in therapy the client comes to trust the therapist, and through the phenomenon of transference, the therapist becomes the good father or the good mother. We accept, we forgive, we let go and give our energies to living now instead of somewhere in the past. We take responsibility for the course of our lives. But at the deepest level, therapy is not about change. It is not about casting out demons. It is about accepting ourselves, with all our demons. Robert Bly says, "Wherever the wound appears in our psyche, that is precisely the place from which we will give our major gift to the community."

That is a faith stance. Therapy can go only so far. You see, there are boundaries to the relationship between therapist and client, and there have to be. Ultimately, your therapist is not your friend, nor your parent, nor your caretaker. After all, you can't pay for love, and relationship doesn't stop at the end of 50 minutes. The real teacher is experience. Your own experience in the real world. And the active agent, I believe, is grace. You invite a covenantal relationship with the Mystery—that is, you agree to do this hard thing called life, together. It's really that simple. But it makes all the difference.

Sometimes grace comes in the form of a pastrami sandwich. Let me explain. Not long ago I went to the beach with a new friend, a gay man. I noticed during our time together that he was cynical and critical, all the while lamenting the fact that he did not have an intimate relationship. No one was quite "good enough, smart enough."

On the way home, I began talking, and I began to weep. I recognized so much of myself in him. I told him as much. Oh, I know where it comes from—we're both the grown children of alcoholic parents. But the explanation is not the cure. We have to learn to let people love us, I told him. We have to learn to recognize love when we see it, to know what to expect of love. We don't know what love is, I said. He was angry. He said that sounded like a lot of New Age bullshit to him. He just wanted to meet a special guy. That's not the issue, I told him. What did I mean? he asked.

"Well, it's like this," I said. "After I preach three services on Sunday, I'm exhausted. And every Sunday after the last service, a friend invites me to lunch. When I come into her home, she welcomes me. She asks me to sit down. She asks me if I would like a bowl of soup, and I say no thanks. She asks me if I want a sandwich, and I say yes. What kind of sandwich? she says. And I say, What kind do you have? She says I have bacon and tomato, or shrimp, or pastrami. And I say pastrami. What kind of cheese? I say swiss. And she says, Would you like mustard on your sandwich or mayonnaise, or maybe mustard and mayonnaise? And I say mustard. She makes the sandwich and gives it to me, and I begin to eat and to revive."

Therapy is about accepting ourselves, with all our demons.

"When I grew up, nobody cared whether I had a sandwich at all, much less what kind," I said to him. "And I expect it was the same with you. You see, she's teaching me about love, about the nature and form of love. That's how you learn. You begin to recognize people who know how to love, and you let them love you, you let them teach you what love is."

Grace, I told him, is like a pastrami sandwich. It lights on your plate when you least expect it. And you just accept it.

This is the short version of what was essentially a two-hour monologue during which he looked straight ahead, intent on driving, saying hardly a word. Later he wrote a letter saying he was "devastated" by our talk. He said he knew he was unlovable, and he had decided to become a hermit. Then I got another letter from him this very weekend. He said that just when he decided to become a hermit, he met a guy. Someone who knows how to love. Someone who is teaching him about love. Well, there's the pastrami sandwich.

19

When I think about our church, I think about—well, I think about pastrami. I think about our church as a place where love can happen, where it's taught and where it's learned. It's not taught just by the ministers; it's taught by us all—we all have the potential to do that. I see it happening in so many ways: a lay minister goes for a hospital visit; another person drives by the home of an ailing member and leaves flowers; in long and tiring meetings, we still speak with respect and caring—well, most of the time. And we look at each other, touch each other, cry together, and sing and celebrate together.

Sometimes during my morning meditation time, I think of the coming worship service. I think of light coming from the ministers and the musicians, beaming out over the sanctuary. And I imagine light coming from each of you and joining the light from us and joining the light from your neighbors until the whole sanctuary is filled with divine light. Love light. Here we can bring all that we are, all that we can be. Our roots are no impediment. We think of those connections in our past that were strong, that were good, and we sing, "Roots, hold me close." We think of how freeing love is, and we sing, "Wings, set me free." We are a community. May we continue to hold one another close. May we continue to set one another free.

SO BE IT. AMEN.

Prayer

O Spirit of Life, give us the faith that if we invite your presence, you will visit. Perhaps not in the form we expect, but in your own way, in your own time. Because we are human, we are bound to be wounded along life's precarious way. May we use our very woundedness in the service of the good. May we turn our every grief to praise.

AMEN.

Benediction

Be not afraid of your demons. Go now and be about your angel's business.

Wanting Wholeness, Being Broken

MAY 14, 1995

mother, i have worn your name like a shield . . .
I am not grown away from you
whatever i say.
—Lucille Clifton, "February 13, 1980"

I DARESAY that not a single one of us is completely satisfied with our body. I mean satisfied in the sense that we wouldn't take the opportunity to change something if we could. Some of you would no doubt want more hair, or fewer pounds, or you'd like to be taller, or you wish your shape were somehow different. Some parts of your body don't work as well as you would like, perhaps. You may have flat feet, or a troublesome back.

We typically experience these things as deficiencies—something is wrong with me. Now I'm not against taking care of our bodies. That's not what I'm saying. But seeing ourselves as *deficient* because we are human and vulnerable and particular seems strange—and it seems sad.

Given this way of seeing ourselves, though, we are not very well prepared to see someone who has a visible disability. It is typical for us to feel uneasy, to pretend not to notice, to avert our eyes, to ignore or avoid people with disabilities. I want to examine why this is true in a moment, but first of all, what do I mean when I use the word "disability"? To whom do I refer?

21

I refer to people with a wide range of impairments—deafness, paralysis, mental illness, and learning disability, for example. The extent of impairment differs widely from person to person: the term could mean anything from dyslexia to severe mental retardation. These folks may not share much in common—but the thing they do share is that because of these traits, they are singled out for differential treatment by others. The recognition of this fact has led activists to argue that persons with disabilities, then, are a minority group characterized primarily by exclusion.

Seeing ourselves as deficient because we are human and vulnerable and particular seems strange.

Interesting, isn't it? They are characterized chiefly by how they are treated by others. That is where most of the trouble occurs—not because of the particular body part that doesn't work, but because of the attitudes and beliefs of others. Because of social stigma and lack of access—access to all kinds of things.

Some true stories. Don is a quadriplegic who is a student at Portland Community College. He's looking for affordable, accessible housing for himself and a live-in attendant, but finds that most often he is offered small studio apartments with no space for a second person.

Alice has a severe head injury and because of her poor balance needs a service dog to help her get around. Recently she was put out of a restaurant because the owner would not allow her dog to accompany her.

The Oregon Museum of Science and Industry recently had an exhibit entitled something like "Removing Barriers," but there was no braille so that a blind person might experience the exhibit, and no provision was made for the hearing impaired.

We are not talking about just a few people when we say the word "disabled." Among African-Americans, disability stands at 16.3 percent of the population; for whites, 12.8 percent. We're talking about millions and millions of people. Poverty, as you might guess, is a significant factor. About twice as many people in families with incomes of less than $20,000 a year are impaired. And they are more likely to live in rural areas. In other words, being disabled is connected with being marginalized in other ways. People with disabilities are less likely to be married, more likely to be divorced. Both men and women are perceived as inferior partners, and women are perceived more negatively than men. Given negative sexual stereotyping, it is not surprising that people with disabilities are more likely to be alone than are the non-disabled.

We need to watch our language and not use terms like "handicapped" or "crippled" or "disabled" persons, but rather "persons with disabilities," since no one wants to be defined by a disability. These folks are mostly very patient with us—with the poor language we sometimes use, and with our habit of looking away from them. With the curiosity and sometimes cruelty they experience on the part of children.

I would like to share with you parts of a poem written by one of our congregants who is disabled. Her words show sadness and yet a graceful kind of acceptance:

> My twisted woman's body should house a mind
> > gone wormy with rage.
> But justice, that timeless jokester,
> > granted me a mild and patient spirit
> To compensate for girlish parts crooked and bent.
> Gave parabolic generosity for side glances, averted eyes.
> > And I
> A gentle Quasimodo, swing from the empty bell tower
> > of my long cherished wishes.
> Sweetly, with hardly a trace of despair.

Again, it is the stigma, the discrimination, that is the big problem. I want to share with you the story of a friend of mine, a woman who studied to become a minister. She was born with a malformed spine, and she grew to only about half her expected height. She walks with a single crutch. She has a fine mind, writes really decent poetry, speaks powerfully. She wanted very much to become a minister. But no church, not even the smallest and most desperate fellowship, was willing to call her.

Why? For many reasons. I have mentioned the idealization of the body and the emphasis given to physical perfection in this culture. The controversy over the memorial statue of Franklin Delano Roosevelt is a case in point. During all his years of presidency, he was never allowed to be seen in a wheelchair, nor with his crutches, and few

Americans even knew he was disabled from an early bout with polio. Now in memory he will be standing, though he could not stand in life without others by his side, holding him up.

Another reason, perhaps a more profound reason, for our difficulty with disabled persons is the harsh, in-your-face reminder they are about our own mortality. We ourselves might become disabled one day. In fact, if we live long enough, the chances are quite good that in old age, we will not be able to walk or see or hear as well as we would like. We may lose some of our mental functioning, and we don't like to be reminded of this fact. We are mortal and vulnerable. We will die. Part of our attitude toward disabled persons, I am convinced, is rooted in our fear and denial of death.

Now it is perfectly understandable that living creatures would fear death and diminishment of their powers. But in addition to this biologically rooted fear, our particular culture—steeped in the Judeo-Christian tradition—has framed disability as unworthiness, as sin. In the Hebrew scriptures, disability is often connected with moral impurity. Physical imperfection is seen as marring the divine image of humans.

The New Testament also links sin and disability. In her book *The Disabled God,* Nancy Eiesland makes the interesting point that the image at the heart of Christianity is the crucified Christ, a body that is broken, a side pierced and bleeding. And yet in so much of Christian teaching lies the implicit message that brokenness is a sign of sin, of God's disfavor.

Another theme that has been pervasive in Christianity through the years is the ideal of virtuous suffering. This, I believe, is a perversion of the Jesus story. Jesus didn't want to die on the cross, didn't plan to die on the cross—his glory and his witness are that he accepted his death and used it redemptively. But in Christian tradition, suffering is presented as somehow noble. This is surely part of the reason the Catholic church is so vehemently against the Death with Dignity movement. Jesus suffered, so we should suffer. It is God's will.

These cultural messages are so much a part of our thinking that most people don't even question them. Think about the simple, everyday phrase that many of us use, "No pain, no gain." If it's good for you, it will hurt. Sorry, but that's simply not true. Of course, we must struggle at times, and the struggle can make us stronger. But in fact, most things that bring health and wholeness feel good—things like really nourishing food, and exercise, and love. We are not made for suffering; sometimes we have to suffer, but we are made for joy.

The Biblical picture of charitable giving has also shaped the interactions between able-bodied people and those with disabilities. In ancient societies, almsgiving, or charity, made it possible for the needy to survive. Still today, religious organizations provide benefits to society in the name of charity. Many of our hospitals have the word "charity" in their name. This sets up a "we-they" mentality. We are the able: the strong and secure, and out of our largesse, we deign to help the poor or those with disabilities. This attitude not only separates us as human beings, but it obviates the need for justice. We might *Our particular culture has framed disability as unworthiness, as sin.* take note that churches lobbied for and received blanket exemption from the requirements of the Americans with Disabilities Act of 1990. Maybe instead of thinking of ourselves as virtuous, as beneficent, when we provide food for the hungry or access for persons with disabilities, we should think that this is the least we can do—that justice demands it.

How can we do better than we have done? We can start with a simple awareness of the problem, with listening and learning. Sometimes we just don't think. Molly Ivins, one of my favorite columnists, recounts the following incident in her home state of Texas. She says that as a Texas-based humorist, she doesn't have to have much imagination—that funny things happen a lot in Texas. Anyway, some time back the state legislature had a special day to honor persons with disabilities. They planned to have a ceremony during a legislative session. Well, when a number of persons in wheelchairs arrived, they discovered there were about ten steps to go up, even before they got inside the building. They were lifted up the steps, only to find two more flights of stairs to navigate in order to get into the gallery. It seems that it took the officials all morning to get these folks in place so they could be honored. Then the Speaker of the House began: "We want to thank all you disabled persons for being here with us today. Would you please stand so that we can recognize you." Sometimes we just don't think.

It helps if you have an experience that teaches you how the other person might feel. Last fall I had a small taste of what it might be like to be a disabled person. I broke my left foot and at first couldn't stand on it for long. I wanted very much to lead the church in the march to Pioneer Courthouse Square to protest Ballot Measure 13, designed to remove the civil rights of gays and lesbians, and so I agreed to be pushed in a wheelchair. It was a very unpleasant experience in every way. I hated feeling dependent on others to take care of me. I hated feeling vulnerable when I was pushed up to the edge of traffic, realizing that if a car took the curve too sharply, I could be hit, and I had no way to escape. Worse than this was the social ostracism. I was the minister! I had my red robe on! But nobody noticed me, and nobody talked to me. You see, I was not on their eye level. All this excitement and activity was going on around me, and I was sitting there looking into the eyes of small children and the occasional dog. Then came the big moment when clergy were asked to go down to the podium and speak. Three thousand or so people were listening. Of course I would go! But I couldn't. It slowly dawned on me that I couldn't walk. Thank goodness other ministers from our church were there and able to represent us well. But I felt frustrated and angry that I couldn't speak.

Isn't that what we all want? To be seen as the persons we are?

More than any other single person in the congregation, Lou Hall has raised my consciousness around these issues, so I want to take this opportunity to thank Lou. There were times when I felt Lou was pushy and didn't give us church leaders credit for trying to do better —but without his persistence, we no doubt would not be as far along as we are. Not that we are there yet—much of our facility is still not accessible. But the church board and I are absolutely committed to making our new facility completely accessible. Access to buildings is not the only disability issue, of course, but it is basic.

What do persons with disabilities want? As I read what they have to say, as I listen to them talk, I hear two things. First, the big word is ACCESS. They want to participate as fully as possible with the rest of us in the things that make life interesting and fulfilling. Jobs, for instance. I'm doing this sermon today because this week in Portland a national conference is being held by the President's Committee on Employment for People with Disabilities. These people suffer more

26

employment discrimination than any other minority. Businesses resist employing them because they are afraid of having some kind of extra burden, yet in fact alcoholism in the workplace is many times more costly to an employer.

Persons with disabilities want what you and I want—jobs, affordable housing, relationships. They want to be treated not as superhuman heros—everyone is not a Helen Keller—nor as some kind of inferior beings we have to feel sorry for. They want us to understand they are just regular people, like you and me, and are not defined by their particular disability. The brilliant physicist Stephen Hawking, for example, has shown us that he can do anything anyone else can do, including running off and having an affair with his young student. How ordinary can you get?

Terry Tempest Williams in her book *An Unspoken Hunger* writes about her uncle Alan. A breech-birth baby, Alan had serious seizures all his life. "His emotions were not measured," Williams writes, "his curiosity not bridled. In a sense, he was wild like a mustang in the desert and, like most wild horses, he was eventually rounded up." A few days before his death at the age of 28, Terry asked him, "Alan, what is it really like to be inside your body?" "I can't tell you what it's like," said Alan, "except to say I feel pain for not being seen as the person I am."

Isn't that what we all want? To be seen as the persons we are? To not be pre-judged because of our age or our height or our skin color or sexual orientation or ethnic heritage?

I recently talked to a man in a wheelchair who said he had been placing an ad in the *Willamette Week* personals for a year and a half, with no luck. Then, just recently, he had an extraordinary conversation with a woman who answered his ad. When he revealed to her on the telephone that he was in a wheelchair, he waited for her to say what the other women had so often said: "I'm sorry, I can't cope with that." But she didn't. She said, "I understand, and that doesn't matter. I have a son who's in a wheelchair, too. I would just like to get to know you as a person." *I would just like to get to know you as a person.* What beautiful words.

Sometimes, not very often, but sometimes I have moments of spiritual clarity. In those moments, I lose my propensity to judge and to divide, and I became a part of all that is. In those times, I do not tell myself that I have to lose ten pounds, or I'll be forever unlovable. I do not tell myself that my sermon should be better than it is. I am who I am, I do what I do, and it's enough. And when I look at others, I don't measure and classify. I don't see ill-fitting clothes or noses with rings in them. I don't see age or youth. I see a soul, many souls, on a journey, and it really doesn't matter how far along they are. They are perfect as they are—just now, in the moment.

As we grow more and more able to quiet our fears, we are able to come into the presence of the soul. We can begin to say to ourselves and to others, "You don't have to try any more. Give it up, all this striving. You're beautiful, with all your wounds and scars and wrinkles of body and spirit. Give it up. You're absolutely perfect. And I love you, just the way you are."

SO BE IT. AMEN.

Prayer

O God, you are too often broken with our words and deeds. Forgive us and help us to acknowledge our own brokenness and our yearning for wholeness. Forgive us our fears and give us hope, not in this faltering flesh, but in the Spirit of Life that would open our hearts to love and to justice. AMEN.

Benediction

Go now, and know that you are beautiful, just as you are.

Tears: Cleansing for the Soul

MARCH 24, 1996

We open
and there is that shining inside,
that shining in the broken ones.

—Linda Hogan, "Geodes"

IT WAS A VERY LONG TIME AGO, and I was very young—in my early 20s, in my first job as a high school teacher, in New Orleans. I was dating a medical student who said to me one evening, "Want to see a baby being born? Just gown up and go with me this weekend to Charity Hospital." "Me, pretend to be a medical student?" I asked. "Sure," he said. "Nobody will ever know." Now, such adventure—indeed, such pretense—was not in character for me. I don't know why I agreed to go—perhaps I was drawn by the Mystery.

When we arrived at the ward, I could see why he said no one would notice me. It was a huge open space with curtained cubicles all around the wall, and in most of those cubicles were women about to deliver babies, more or less *soon.* Someone would yell out, "There's one coming in No. 3!" and a team of gowned students and interns would rush over to that cubicle. The next time that happened, my friend and I joined the group. I watched as the baby began to emerge from an African American woman who was yelling, "Oh, Jesus! Oh, Jesus!" I was astounded, I was undone. I felt myself in the presence of the Holy. Thank goodness, I was not the doctor—I could only respond by weeping! My mask was getting quite wet, but the busy team

29

did not notice. They were seeing to the baby and the mother. Then the doctor turned to me and asked for something out of the pharmaceutical cabinet, something with a big, long, complicated name. I went to the cabinet, praying that I could find the whatever it was—and so I did. There was a bottle with that name printed on it. Saved again. I took the bottle back, handed it to the doctor, smiled, and promptly fainted. So much for my foray into medicine. I'm better at doctoring souls.

My response to birth was weeping. Words would have been insufficient. And so it is for us *Homo sapiens*—we talk and talk and talk. But sometimes the talking stops, and we must go deeper, then tears cleanse the way for the buried language of the soul. We weep when a friend dies. We weep when our daughter gets the letter saying the college of her dreams has accepted her. Or when our son is teased at school because he has funny hair, and he does have sort of funny hair. Or when we have a flat tire, we don't have the strength to change it, and the night is dark. Or when we hear Handel's *Messiah* once again at Christmas, and we stand during the Hallelujah Chorus, hopeful, though we are in a season of cold. Or when we are called "nigger" or "kike" or "faggot" or "bitch" by someone who is ignorant and afraid. Or when we hear that the medical test was positive, or negative. Or when we get a note saying, "I love you. I'm there for you." Or when the snow is falling in big, soft flakes, and the earth is perfect, and that moment is perfect, and we cannot imagine wanting anything to be any different from the way it is. Tears of joy, tears of pain, tears of disappointment, tears of thanksgiving.

There is mystery about the coming of tears. Sometimes we think, "I should be crying about this," but no tears come. Other times, we notice that tears are welling up in our eyes, and we think, "Why am I crying now?" The answer does not come. But there is a wisdom in our bodies greater than we can know, and we must respect it. Tears come when they need to come.

Of course, cultural mores determine to some extent the "acceptability" of tears, explains author Curt Suplee. The Stoics believed, "Handle it yourself—and no whining!" The medieval Christian church propagated the notion that mourning the dead showed you had little faith in resurrection. It appears that actual tears are fairly rare in European art, up through the early Renaissance, despite the numerous renderings of the crucifixion. Tears did not suit the Age of Reason, and as early as the 17th century, Locke warned in a treatise on child rearing that crying encourages "those passions, which it is our main business to subdue." The great watershed, so to speak, in the history of approved tearfulness was the Romantic movement, a time when people began to believe that truth could come through feeling and not just through reason. The Victorians actually made a cult of grieving, which Mark Twain parodied in *Huckleberry Finn* with his portrait of Emmeline Grangerford, the morbid young girl whose drawings and poetry are full of tombstones and weeping ladies in black and inscriptions like "Shall I Never See Thee More Alas." When Emmeline finally dies, Huck is sorry, but decides, "I reckoned that with her disposition, she was having a better time in the graveyard."

Tears cleanse the way for the buried language of the soul.

According to sociologist Gordon Blanton, emotional fashions change, just like other fashions. During times of prosperity, we tend to be more expressive, he says. During the 1920s we indulged our feelings, but during the Depression and World War II we reverted to quieter ways. Freedom to show feeling openly returned with the rock-'n-roll of the '50s. The postwar baby boom was entering its teens, and in the words of Blanton, "a vast hormonal stew of sweet pain, young lust and heartache inundated pop music with hot-eyed lamentation." Well, yes, I guess it was kind of like that, come to think of it. And then the Women's Movement came along, and women let it be known that they wanted "sensitive men," so as NFL player Rosie Grier sang in 1972, "It's All Right to Cry." (This cultural history comes from a fascinating article by Curt Suplee, "Why Do We Weep? As Yet Nobody Can Say for Sure," in the June 1984 *Smithsonian*.)

But is it really all right to cry? It's downright good for you—that's the theory, anyway, in the work of William Frey, a scientist who has studied the chemistry of emotional tears, as opposed to tears caused by stimulants such as onions. For five years Frey and his colleagues collected the tears of volunteers from Minneapolis and St. Paul. (Well, what else are you going to do, when you have weather like theirs?) It appears that the volunteers were given a four-hanky movie and test tubes to catch the emotional outpourings. Frey believes that tears remove toxic substances that build up in the body as a result of stress.

Another scientist confirmed Frey's findings in a study showing that people with stress-related disorders are more likely to view crying as a sign of emotional weakness.

Frey reports a huge discrepancy in the frequency of crying for men and women: women cry an average of five times a month, compared with once a month for men. In an interesting article entitled "Can You Stand to See a Grown Man Cry?" (*Glamour*, June 1994), Cindy Chupack challenges women who say they find it touching to see men cry. She says maybe the very first time a normally stoical man cries is OK—but what about the next and the next? She says that many women would agree with her friend Susan, who says, "I like a man who's not afraid to cry . . . but doesn't."

After denying our feelings for years, we don't even know what our feelings are.

One problem is lack of experience, Chupack says: we haven't seen men cry much, so their tears are alarming—*is he cracking up?* She says that women have a double standard: no crisis is too small, no movie too sentimental, to provoke tears for a woman, and those tears are acceptable. Women may be moved by a man who weeps at a wedding or breaks down at a friend's funeral, she says, but we're likely to panic if he sobs over finances or work problems. The message is: it's all right for men to cry when they're happy or when they're sad, but not when they're frightened or frustrated. For women, our taboo is anger. Don't be angry, we're told—smile and make a pretty face: anger is unattractive and unfeminine. But both men and women feel frightened, and both feel anger. Both need the freedom to acknowledge their feelings.

When women move into male spheres of activity, they may feel it's crucial to prove they are strong and in control of themselves. A woman in a business firm is severely criticized at a board meeting; as she leaves on the elevator among her male colleagues, tears begin to sting her eyes, but she bites her lip, thinking, "I *will* not cry, I *will* not cry." At least she knew she wanted to cry. Sometimes, after denying our feelings for years, we don't even know what our feelings are. That kind of repression comes at great cost, for if we are sitting on anger or grief, chances are it will emerge in some destructive way.

One evening a few weeks ago, I was on my way to a meeting with my "ministerial relations" committee. I stopped by my house to quickly check my phone messages and discovered that a dear aunt is not expected to live much longer. She was a mother figure to me—she taught English, and she is the reason I became an English teacher and a writer. So I heard that message and dashed off to my meeting. I hadn't eaten, I was tired, but mostly I was grieving, and I didn't even recognize it. I found myself talking and talking, but not saying much that mattered. My body was tense, I was angry, and I was distracted. Finally one of my committee members came over, sat next to me, put a hand on my shoulder, and said, "How can we help you?" That touch and that question opened me, and I finally was able to cry. I felt my body let go and relax. My committee was there for me in a very loving way. I didn't know, though, until later that I was angry and sad because my aunt was dying. As a minister, I do have to be strong for others. I do have to hold back my own feelings, so much of the time— I don't cry at memorial services, I make space for others to cry, and that is as it should be. But when I begin to deny my anger and grief and longing, I get into trouble.

There are not many places, I suspect, where most of us feel safe being absolutely open, where we feel free emotionally, free to cry if we need to. Work is generally not such a place. Under the guise of professionalism, we play the expected roles and bring only parts of ourselves to any encounter. Many times even with our friends, we don't let our real feelings be known, for fear that others won't understand or will reject us. We all need people with whom we feel safe to cry, when tears need to come.

Tears take us back to those primal moments as infants, when we first learned to cry, and when our very existence depended upon a caring response. Maybe that's when we learn to trust—or not to trust— the sharing of feelings.

I do not have many childhood memories of my mother—she was gone from me when I was nine—but I do have a few. One was the time I got my hair cut. I was eight years old, and I had long, honey-brown hair, halfway down my back. My mother used to braid the sides, bring the ends up on top of my head, and tie them with a bright ribbon. Anyway, about this time, my best friend got her hair cut into a pageboy, the newest thing out. It looked so adorable, the way the edges curved slightly toward her face. So I began to beg my mother, "I want to get my hair cut like Susan's. Please, Mother, let me get my hair cut like Susan's." Mother tried to explain to me that I had curly hair, and that if I cut it short, it would not look like Susan's straight hair. But I wouldn't listen. So she took me to get my hair cut. The long golden locks fell to the floor, and the barber whirled me around so I could see. I looked for all the world like a poodle! I cried, and cried, and cried. That afternoon and evening, I took to my bed, and my mother sat on the bed beside me and stroked my poodle head until I fell asleep.

Sometimes one of you, my congregation, will come to my office with something deep inside you that wants out. Sometimes you will sit down across from me, and before a word emerges, you will reach for a Kleenex, and the tears will flow. And sometimes you will say, "I'm sorry," as though you have transgressed. The truth is that I feel honored that you trust me enough to share your tears. I do not feel any urgency for you to stop, for I want you to let out the fear or the grief or whatever is hurting you. And I will be there with you, as your witness. Sometimes that is enough.

The church should be a place where we feel safe to be who we are. I know many of you do cry when you come here on Sunday morning —you cry and you laugh and you allow yourself to be fully human. I'm glad you feel that free. This is a community where you can bring your authentic self, where you don't have to pretend. Many people have told me they cry every week during the doxology—during "Spirit of Life." For me, too, that is a very moving part of the service. I stand in front, looking out at you all and thinking about your lives. "Roots hold me close." I think of my grandparents and of sitting and rocking on the front porch of the house in Louisiana where I was raised. I think of the prayers at the dinner table, and I think of the good earth where good things grew, the apple tree whose branches I sat under when I needed to be alone. *Roots hold me close.* And I am thankful. "Wings set me free." That phrase becomes my prayer: *Wings set me free.* Let me not be bound by fear. Let me learn what I need to learn. May the Spirit be my guide. Let me fly. Rooted in who I am and where I've been, may wings now set me free to love and to lead.

Like each of you, I am not whole, I am broken. And I need a place where I can come in my brokenness, in my unfinished state, and be enfolded. A place where others come to acknowledge along with me what is real and urgent in their lives, and where we together can hold one another and move to a better place. Where our very tears will cleanse the pain from us and water the flower of our souls. A place from which we can move out into the world with the understanding that we are loved just as we are. When we know that, when we are sure of that, then nothing will stop the smiling, the laughter, the celebration. Nothing then will stop us from loving with our hearts wide open.

SO BE IT. AMEN.

Prayer

"Just As I Am." We thank you, O Spirit of Life, for this our church community, our free faith, where we can come just as we are. May we see the stranger at the door and know it is the stranger in ourselves that we greet. And may the warmth of our love and the joy of our being be shared fully and freely, in keeping with the blessings we have been so lavishly given. AMEN.

Benediction

Know that all life grows in the broken heart of things.

A Community for Life

SEPTEMBER 10, 1995

I take literally the statement in the Gospel of John that God loves the world. I believe that the world was created and approved by love, that it subsists, coheres, and endures by love.

—Wendell Berry

I GREW UP IN A TOWN of 5,000 people in northern Louisiana, a town named Homer, after the Greek epic poet. Homer was right down the road from Athens. It was a community. It was my community, and I knew who I was, because it to a large extent defined me. My family lived on Fulmer Street, named for my grandfather, for he had been the town's postmaster before his retirement.

No one on Fulmer Street, nor on the adjacent street, moved—ever—during the time that I grew up. The Marshalls, both white-headed and reticent, nodded from their front porch as I passed, walking to town. Mrs. Crisler, a widow, lived catty-corner from our house. Her husband Joe was a banker who put everything in order at his place of work then shot himself. She said it was an accident, but we all knew different. I stayed with her nights when she was afraid to be alone. There were the Endoms, who lived next door. Mike was an easy-going man who enjoyed his cigar and his newspaper. Mamie was angry a lot. She could be seen from time to time chasing her older son Charles out of the house with a broom. She gave me a surprise birthday party when I was a teenager.

I knew most everyone in the town, and they knew me. That's the way it was in Homer—everybody knew everybody else, and they even knew everybody else's dog. You see signs up in a city—lost dog, lost cat, followed by a description of the beloved pet. There was no such thing as a lost dog in Homer. Where could it go to get lost?

My Sunday School teacher was Miss Altalene, who worked at White's Dry Goods, which was owned by the parents of my good friend Janet, who lived next to her cousin Brenda, who was also in my group at school, who married Bob, who was the son of the superintendent of education, who later interviewed me for a job in the school system. During my senior year the very successful football coach, a man with a wife and five children, had to quit—quite suddenly—because he had an affair with my father's best friend's son's wife, a really stunning looker, and her husband told the coach he would kill him if he didn't leave town, so the coach had to go. He came in during English class to tell the teacher good-bye. He had the biggest shiner you've ever seen, and all us students knew why.

That was Homer. There was love and there was certainty. And there were secrets, lies, and betrayals. There was complete blindness to racial injustice. There was a stultifying conformity. And there was caring beyond measure. I mentioned interviewing for a teaching job. I had applied for it because I thought I should stay there in town and care for my aging grandparents and my alcoholic father. Mr. Haley, the superintendent, knew my family. He looked across his desk and said to me, "Marilyn, I've looked at your credentials, and you're well qualified for this position. But I'm not going to give it to you. You need to get out of town." I was never so glad to get a "no" in all my life. He wanted me to be what I could never be in that town. He cared enough to send me on my way. This was my community. I don't want to go back. But I know who I am because of it, and I am thankful.

Today much is said and written about community. People are longing for community in their lives and are wondering how to create it. Through almost all the 10,000 years of recorded history, people lived in roving bands, small villages, extended families. But the social revolution in Western Europe during the Renaissance came to dominate and define the modern world as we know it. The focus shifted to the individual rather than the tribe or village. This shift was accompanied by a severing of obligation to others, a desire to accumulate personal wealth, and a philosophy that assumes unlimited need, so that the economy can continue to expand indefinitely. We have evolved into a restless and driven society, where such qualities as kindness, generosity, patience, tolerance, and compassion have little or no value in the marketplace. So we have production, we have efficiency, we have things—but we don't have one another.

I am told there is community in cyberspace. But I am fearful. I see my grown son sitting in front of a computer for hours at a time, just playing games. He refuses to come to dinner when I call. I hear a playwright tell me that he gets ideas from all over the country now that he's on the Internet. I ask him how long he spends with the computer, and he says, "About three hours a day." My unspoken questions are, "When do you write your plays?" and "When do you talk to your wife?" I want a community that includes flesh: bodies that speak so much more than words on a screen ever could; fingers that touch, not just move over keys.

Listen to the words of T. S. Eliot, words from his play *The Rock,* written in 1934:

> We build in vain unless the Lord build with us.
> Can you keep the City that the Lord keeps not with you?
> Where there is no temple there shall be no homes,
> Though you have shelters and institutions,
> Precarious lodgings while the rent is paid,
> Subsiding basements where the rat breeds
> Or sanitary dwellings with numbered doors
> Or a house a little better than your neighbour's;
> When the Stranger says: "What is the meaning of this city?
> Do you huddle close together because you love each other?"
> What will you answer? "We all dwell together
> To make money from each other"? Or "This is a community"?

Eliot's words fall hard on our ears. We are in fact enmeshed in sound and images that constantly invite us to need and to want—is it any surprise that we feel restless and unconnected to others? But his words seem to be addressed to those of us who are able, more or less, to play the economic game. There are those who are falling by the wayside, who seem to have no place at all in the economy. With little hope and fearful for their very lives, they join together in gangs, merely to survive. Yes, even in Portland. We, too, have drive-by shootings. The ministers of this community met with the mayor last week, and she said to us, "Nothing makes me sadder than to visit a school and have a child raise his hand and ask, 'Miss Mayor, what should we do when the shooting starts?'"

We can no longer afford an "us and them" mentality. We are virtuous, we are smart, we are free, we are safe. They are bad, they are stupid, they are lazy, and they deserve their lot in life. Recently I was talking with a woman who said to me, "When I heard about those kids getting shot on the streets, I said to myself, it's because they are from bad families. Then another boy died, this one from a family I knew—from a fine, a loving family. I could no longer fall back on my rationale, a rationale that enabled me to blame the victim." Why do we so easily blame the victim? I believe it is because we feel so overwhelmed by the problems we see, feel so helpless to make a difference. In order to escape the shame and the pain, we say, "They come from bad families. They want to live on the street. They could get a job if they really wanted to."

We have evolved into a restless and driven society.

Instead of allowing our frustration to blot out our compassion, we must act. For eleven years Geoff Canada, author of *Fist, Stick, Knife, Gun,* has taught tae kwon do, a form of martial arts, to poor children in some of New York's most dangerous communities. Through his teaching, they learn order, self-respect, personal power. His way is *his* way—it's not the only way. No one can do it all, but each of us can do a piece. The way back to the open heart, the way back to compassion, is through acting. You don't have to save the world. In fact, it would be arrogant to think you could. But you can act, and you will no longer feel impotent when you do.

The time is over, done with, when we can imagine individual solutions to happiness. We can no longer go to a professional to "fix" our individual wounded psyches. The woundedness is a soul wound, and it has a social context we cannot escape. We can't afford to go to college and think in terms of "my career." We can't look at our schools and say "my children," as in "my children are grown, so it's not my problem."

The Amish are a people known for their simplicity of living and for their deep sense of community. Believing that the values of the larger culture are unhealthful, they adhere to their own. They are considered conservative, and they do value and preserve their traditions, but they are not necessarily opposed to innovation. They simply ask one question when considering an innovation: "What will this do to our community?" "If we don't pass this tax bill, what will that mean to my community?" "If I so much as throw a gum wrapper outside the car window, what will that mean to my community?"

But what about the individual? Certainly individual freedom, the dignity of each individual, has been a theme of Unitarianism since our beginnings back in the Protestant Reformation. I believe we should honor the uniqueness of each individual. The problem comes when an individual seeks personal development as a defense against the larger world. Even spiritual development can be approached as a way of escaping what appears to be a cruel and dangerous world. It is spiritually just not workable to think you can take from the world all it offers but never create anything from what you have received, Robert Sardello reminds us. In his profound book *Love and the Soul,* he quotes from Rudolf Steiner: "The rose adorns herself in order to adorn the garden." Sardello continues, "The rose draws all that it needs from the surroundings and gives out beauty in return. The plant takes in substances from the earth, the light, the rain, the influences of the moon and the seasons, the care of the hands that tend it, and gradually transforms all of this and more into the flower. . . . We could say that individuality is a concentration of the whole world at the site of every person. . . . We are called to [exclude] nothing, taking it all in and transforming it through love."

The time is over, done with, when we can imagine individual solutions to happiness.

But how do we live this way, allowing our individual beauty and power to bless the larger world? Because of the way our society is structured, both socially and economically, we are not led easily along the path of blessing. In fact, intimacy and genuine connection seem ever more difficult to come by. I believe we must be intentional about creating circles of community, creating avenues and institutions where it can flourish. And just what is community? Joanna Macy, ecofeminist, says for her it means, "Not to be alone when I die, and a place where I can tell the truth." That's a good start. I would add, a place where I can be safe. A place where I can be fully and spontaneously myself. And from its members, it requires commitment to the whole.

I started thinking about our church. This is a chosen community. Even if you were born into the faith, you have to make a choice to stay. What kind of community are we creating here? I hope it is a place where no one would ever die alone, or be ill alone, or go through a serious loss alone. I hope it is a place where we can tell our truth, whatever that may be. I hope First Unitarian is a place where all are safe. That is no small thing to say, you know. Last Friday's *Oregonian* carried a story about a young gay man who lost his eye in a gay-bashing incident. I wanted to pick up the phone and call him up and say, "I'm so sorry. You would be safe at our church."

This church community rests upon the traditions and values that we share—religious freedom, tolerance, reason, the power of love. It rests upon our ancestors, those who built this church 128 years ago and those who nurtured it through good times and hard times. They are all still with us here this morning. Now it's our turn to carry on. But it's so big now! How can we create community here? Well, there is a kind of community, a powerful kind that takes place on Sunday morning as we worship together. We join together in ritual that affirms our common purpose, that binds us to one another and to that which is greater than ourselves.

But intimacy and friendship you are not likely to find at Sunday morning worship. For those, you have to find smaller groups—in social justice, or an adult education class, or as a member of the "care and concern" team, or in a choir, or on one of the church committees. Community starts when you blend your voice with 50 others and sing from the deepest place within, or accept a casserole when you can't make food for yourself, or reveal yourself in a discussion group. It is evident when you see your little girl as a heavenly host in the Christmas pageant, and even though you are a godless humanist, you dream of seeing her playing the Virgin Mary 12 years later. It comes to fruition when you begin to think institutionally, and you agree to serve in a leadership position and guide this church to its proper destination. You act with care and patience, for you understand that how we treat one another has everything to do with the power and viability of the institution.

I think back to my roots. My home did provide continuity and

identity. I had a place to sleep, food to eat, a church and a school—
while not sophisticated—that were orderly and decent and caring. So
I am thankful. And yet I did not feel emotionally safe in my home. I
felt frightened much of the time. I did not feel I could speak my truth.
I did not even consider it, for that was not allowed. I experienced daily
the burden and pain of racism and did not even know what to call it.
I just knew it was wrong to treat other human beings the way white
folks treated blacks.

Today, as an adult, I have chosen a new community. Portland
does not offer the intimacy of my small
town—thank goodness! I really don't want
to know if the coach at Lincoln High
School decides to have an affair. But the
anonymity of a city can be cold, can chill
the heart. One can find places of comfort and familiarity, like the corner grocery or a favorite bookstore. But that is still not enough. I need
laughter and singing and tears. I need to be able to share my story—
the real story, the real me—with others, and to hear their stories, so
their lives can lend me courage and hope. I need to feel known and
loved for who I am, not for what I do, nor what I have.

*I need to feel known
and loved for who I
am, not for what I do.*

And I need a place to redeem my history and my family's history
and the history of racism in that little town where I grew up. Homer.
I have my own odyssey. I know that sin begets sin, that violence begets
violence. I have spent much of my life in the process of healing, and I
have had extraordinary healers and teachers to work with. There is
still healing to do. But what remains to be done will never be done in
a therapist's office or somewhere off at a mountain retreat center.
There is no one out there to save me—salvation will come in community, as I give over my own longing in forgetfulness, to care for
the soul of the world; as I understand in an ever more profound sense
that only compassion can fill emptiness.

"We build in vain unless the Lord build with us." We are in the
third year of a planning process now. We will make a place here in this
city that is a holy place. It will be a place of refuge and release, a place
of quiet and rest. It will be a place of learning and of celebration. It will
be a place where our stories can be told, without fear. It will be a place
where the wealthy and the needy, gay and straight, black and white,
Christian and Jew and humanist, sit side by side and learn how much

we all have in common and how much we all need one another. We will not talk much of individual redemption, of being saved, for we will understand that such talk is a luxury when lives are being lost every day. Our hands will extend in love way beyond ourselves, and it is there, in that reaching out, that we will find life. This is a community, you see, for life. Now and forevermore.

SO BE IT. AMEN.

Prayer

Forgive us, O God, for getting lost in littleness, for focusing so consistently on self. We have so much, we are so blessed, and yet the emptiness is there. May we have the courage to both give and receive love, for we know that is where redemption lies. Wake us up! Shake us out of our complacency! Let us live! AMEN.

Benediction

May you see the face of God in every face you look upon.

Hungering for Connection

Friendship: A Journey to Being

NOVEMBER 12, 1995

> *If things are really to exist for us, they have to penetrate within us. Hence the necessity of being naked. Nothing can enter into us while armor protects us from wounds and from the depths they open up.*
>
> —Simone Weil

ONE DAY 15 YEARS AGO I was driving down a highway about 60 miles an hour, and the next thing I knew I was in an ambulance, partly conscious, calling out my children's names. I fell into a black nothingness again, and when I opened my eyes once more, I saw white walls all around me—I was in the emergency room of a hospital. A friend was holding my hand. It was a workday, and she should have been at the office. But she came to the hospital to stand by my bed and hold my hand until I regained consciousness. It turned out I was all right, but I didn't know that at the time. I will not forget her patience, her vigilance, her care. I needed a friend, and she was there.

Friendship is a unique relationship. It is unlike blood relations, for you have no choice over those; it is unlike marriage, for marriage ties you to another with legal and social bonds. Friendship you choose out of your desire and your desire alone, so if a friendship lasts, it must continuously be chosen. Out of that freedom of choice comes the extraordinary quality of friendship. You know that your friend has chosen to be with you because he wants to, and for no other reason. You feel special, and you are. You feel wanted, and you are.

The philosopher Montaigne spoke of a particular friendship this way: "Our souls mingle and blend with each other so completely that they efface the seam that joined them, and cannot find it again. If you press me to tell why I loved him, I feel this cannot be expressed, except by answering: because it was he, because it was I." Why are we drawn to a certain person? It is often a mystery. *Because it was he, because it was I.* We are not compelled to friendship by the perfection of the other party. Not at all. We may be drawn to a person with an ungainly body, or to someone who must always search for the right word, or to someone who has not been particularly suc-

If a friendship lasts, it must continuously be chosen.

cessful according to the world's standards. No, we are not drawn by perfection, but rather by some quality of character that connects to our soul need, some dark, unfinished place within. In each other's presence, we both feel a kind of wholeness that escapes us otherwise.

Friendship, then, is not about self-improvement, but rather about the unfolding of the sacredness at the center of each of us. Self-improvement has to do with analysis and ego and directed action, force of will, whereas the unfolding I mention has to do with a respect for the unknown, and with a faith that the divine potential within us will show itself and make us anew.

What intimacy does for us is simply to make a nurturing space for the natural development of what is already there. Our friends do this by "being with," without judgment. Oh, yes, a friend may disagree or take exception to a decision or to a behavior, but these exchanges exist within a love so nourishing that differences enrich instead of threaten. Nell Noddings in her book entitled *Caring* says that a friend is one who "listens us into being." *Listens us into being.* Do you have a friend like that? One who has the capacity to really hear, to be present in such depth and openness that you begin to say what you never knew was in you to say? You begin to hear yourself being wise or witty, and you marvel at the splendid person you have become in the presence of your friend. In such company, we feel blessed; we feel ourselves like a thirsty plant that has been watered at last, with every pore soaking in new life and vitality.

A few weeks ago a new friend was speaking with me about a painful relationship she was trying to mend. I listened for a few minutes,

48

then pleased with myself for having so quickly analyzed the situation and come up with a solution, I laid it on her. Essentially, her expectations of her friend were too great, I said. Her face fell, and I knew I had done her no favor. She said, "I feel judgment in what you just said." Then my face fell. I had not wanted to judge my friend. I told her I was sorry. She said, "You know, if you can just listen compassionately, I will find the answer within myself." She was right.

In a moving sermon, Paul Tillich speaks of separation and discord within the individual and how it is healed. He says, "The depth of our separation lies in just the fact that we are not capable of a great and merciful divine love towards ourselves. We are separated from the mystery, the depth, and the greatness of our existence." The answer to this separation is love, he says. Tillich continues, "When the old compulsions reign within us as they have for decades, when despair destroys all joy and courage, sometimes at that moment a wave of light breaks into our darkness, and it is as though a voice were saying: 'You are accepted. You are accepted.'" It is that kind of acceptance we find with a true friend, who acts as a way station for the divine, in loving us without judgment.

No, we are not drawn by perfection, but rather by some quality of character that connects to our soul's need, some dark, unfinished place within.

One of the best openings to intimacy and the life it brings is soulful conversation. Conversation is not the same as chatting—chatting is polite talk about nothing, which at best is a social lubricant and at worst is a defense against all that is true within us. Thomas Moore, in his book *Soul Mates,* speaks of "soul conversation." This is conversation with no goal other than relationship. It wanders where it will and is bound by no rules except that the parties must be present, caring, and open. Conversation while walking is an especially restorative practice. There can be long periods of silence while thoughts are filtered through our understanding, and talking is interspersed with reflection. We all need someone to share memories with, someone to trust with our dreams. We often do not know the meaning of these memories until the past is recollected into a coherent form for another. We often do not know our dreams until they manifest themselves in what we thought was idle conversation with another.

I have spoken of the many blessings of friendship. Yet why is it that true friendship is so rare and precious? What is required of us to have such friendship be a part of our lives?

To begin with, we have to make friends with ourselves. Inevitably, parts of each of us lie in the shadow, denied and therefore neglected. Sometimes these various aspects of the self are in conflict, the one with the other. For example, in my own life, the playful child suffers from my neglect. If I keep her in the shadow, she begins subversive activity. She will hide my pencils at times. "How can I write? I have no pencils." "Gotcha!" she exclaims. I glower. "Not funny," I answer. Once in a while when she's really feeling angry, she will touch my brain with amnesia, and I will "forget" a task I promised to do or a meeting I was to attend. How does she affect my friendships? When she is not allowed to play, the adult in me may become judgmental of those who do play. Spontaneous play in others may give rise to anxiety in me.

We feel lonely at times precisely because we've cut off parts of ourselves from our consciousness—the fearful self, the grieving self, the angry self, the playful self. And out of that loneliness comes neediness, not a fertile ground for friendship. When we deny parts of ourselves, we will find ourselves wanting others to make up for what we've held back. They are reduced to a function, and they feel it. So, first of all, to be a friend, you must make friends with yourself.

We all need someone to share memories with, someone to trust with our dreams.

You will discover in every friendship and intimate relationship that this other person is other-than, different-from, not-you. If one of you is a man and the other is a woman, you may be mystified, confounded, incredulous. Scientists are now beginning to discover what we casual observers have always known—men and women really do come from different planets. Biology really does count! If you need someone, of whatever gender, to absolutely confirm your beliefs and behaviors, to see the world just as you see it, then you will be distressed and will begin to withdraw from your friendship. But if you are able to keep your heart open, you stand to learn what you can never learn outside a close relationship. You will be pushed and stretched in ways you never anticipated—and you will allow this, because the foundation of trust is there, supporting the two of you. You are not demanding that the other change—that's not what friendship is about. Rather, you are making a loving space, a holy space, where transformation can occur.

Friendship demands time, something hardly anyone seems to have enough of these days. Often we cruise along in our lives, taking our friends for granted, then we end up in the hospital emergency room or going through a divorce or a job loss, and we understand anew how significant those relationships are. Suddenly we need a place to go where we can feel safe, where our vulnerabilities will be respected and treated with care. We need someone we can call at 4 a.m., whether we actually make that call or not. If we cherish relationships all along the way, when those devastating losses occur— as they do in every life—we will have a refuge, a place to retreat while we are healing. We also need those with whom we can share our triumphs—big people, people comfortable enough with themselves not to be jealous or resentful when we get a promotion or when we are admitted to the college of our choice or when we fall in love.

We feel lonely at times precisely because we've cut off parts of ourselves from our consciousness.

Friendship requires faithfulness, requires loyalty. "Stand by me," we say to our friends, "then I can carry on." Above all, be honest with me, for without that, how can any relationship have integrity? I'm remembering one relationship with a woman friend that went bad for me. It was, alas, over a man. But when I think about it, it was not really over a man. The relationship soured because of dishonesty. Let's call the man Fred. Fred and I were keeping company, and I kept noticing that he and my good friend Susan seemed to be attracted to each other. I asked them both outright—more than once—if they wanted to date each other, and both said absolutely not, they were friends and only friends. Actually, I asked them so often that maybe they began to think it was a good idea to see each other. Anyway, one day I called Susan at her office, and her secretary told me she had gone to Boston for two days. Then I called Fred's office, and his secretary told me he had gone to Boston for two days. So I lost two friends. I was hurt and angry for months and months. Finally I just got tired of being angry and forgave them. It turns out that they really were right for each other, and they're still together after 12 years. But my relationship with Susan was never the same. I didn't have to have the man, but I had to have the honesty. The trust had been broken.

In true friendship, it is fair to expect certain qualities like honesty, fidelity, loyalty, caring. But sometimes our expectations may become demands and may begin to look like control. When that happens, we lose the freedom that makes friendship voluntary and spontaneous. The other party does not feel loved for who he is, but only for what we want him to be. Our agenda becomes changing our friend, and in the face of that judgment, the friendship begins to wither and die. On the other hand, understanding and respecting the limitations of that other person nourishes relationship.

Friends stay with us through good times and bad, then when the time comes, they say good-bye. About this time last year, I lost a good friend to death. We had been close at one time—he was my teacher, therapist, mentor, and confidant. He wanted to be more, but I said no. I had a limitation that he respected. It didn't change his love for me. Then I went off to California, and he went ahead with his work in Michigan. Neither of us wrote regularly, but we sent letters now and then to stay in touch. His never failed to be rich and full and caring. Years passed. I sent announcements to him at watershed moments: graduation from seminary, ordination, Ph.D., the publication of my first book, and then the last, my installation as minister at the First Unitarian Church of Portland.

When I was taking off my robe after the installation ceremony I saw him, standing there in the robing room, grinning broadly. I could hardly believe it! He had come all the way from Michigan to surprise me. I invited him home with me, where he stayed for a couple of days, and we caught up on each other's lives. I knew he had had cancer, and now heart disease, but he still looked good. We talked and talked and talked—about faith, about death, about politics, cities, our children, our abiding love for each other. I still had my limitations, and he still respected them. I knew there was nothing I could ever do to make him stop loving me, and I knew this love had nothing to do with my opinions or my choices. It had to do with the essence of me, with who I was. I was absolutely free, and I was absolutely accepted.

I didn't want to think he would be gone soon, so I denied that probability. "Neil will always be here," I convinced myself. "That piece of my world is secure." But the fact is that he had come to say good-bye. He never actually said the words—but then, that was not his way. Every time we had parted before, it was always, "Catch you later." No big deal.

Sometimes it is only after a friend has gone that you know what you had. I think about him more often now than I did when he was living, so I guess in that sense, he will always be with me. You see, it is so rare, that kind of freedom, coupled with that kind of love. It is friendship of the most profound kind.

Friendship comes to us not because we deserve it, not because we seek it, not because we consciously develop it: it comes to us by grace and grace alone. Through intimate friendship, we enter into the Mystery of being. Where it will take us, we can never know; we can only trust in the goodness of our friend and the sacredness of the process. The path of friendship is like the movement of a mighty river, sometimes smooth, perhaps at times tumultuous, other times blocked, but always moving in depths we never guessed were there.

Friendship, at least in this world, comes to a close, either by death or by circumstance, and even when it has an early ending, we must honor the gifts we were given. We must never say, "That one, she was never my friend, I will forget I knew her," or "He was never a real marriage partner, what a mistake." No, we must go forward in gratitude for what has been. Do you remember the woman I spoke of, the one who came to my bedside in the hospital? She is the same woman who went to Boston with my man. One and the same. Yet I honor her for what she gave me, such as she was willing and able to give. And I love her still.

Friendship, in which we freely choose and we are freely chosen, is of the divine. We taste the depths of it when we lose it. Our longing is not just for the one who is gone, but for the absolute love this person represented, that connection with the everlasting love that holds us secure in the midst of every storm and strife. To enter into this river of being, we give up our ideologies—we cannot say love should be this and this and this. Love is simply what it is. We open ourselves to the Mystery, in gratitude. Our lives sing with thanksgiving.

SO BE IT. AMEN.

Prayer

O Great Mystery, we stand in awe of the gift of friendship. We remember this morning those friends who have blessed us along our way, and we fill with thanks as their names and faces come before us. We acknowledge that we often fear coming close to another—and we ask for courage to be vulnerable, even in the face of certain loss, for through the touch of others, we shall surely feel the touch of God. AMEN.

Benediction

May your friendships bloom and may they brighten even the darkest days of winter.

Making Marriage Work

MAY 12, 1996

When I say "I love," it is not I who love, but in reality,
love who acts through me.

—Robert Johnson

IN THE PAST 25 YEARS OR SO marriage has undergone a profound transformation in this country. Traditionally, marriage was held together by family, religion, and law—but these forms reflected a more elementary grounding: simple economic survival. Since women had few opportunities in the workplace, they depended upon a man for their livelihood. Leaving was unthinkable, since they had no place to go, especially if there were children to be concerned about. As late as the 1940s, some school systems wouldn't let women teach if they were married.

But now it is the rule rather than the exception for women to work outside the home. For the first time in our history, marriage is purely and simply voluntary, and everybody knows that, including our children. And they, and we, have a deep and abiding anxiety about marriage. We know that half our marriages don't last, and the cost of divorce is tragically high—to the partners themselves, to their children, and to their broader community of family and friends. How do we make marriage work, in such an age, in such a time?

Some couples begin by trying to protect themselves in that most contemporary of all ways—with a legal contract. Galen Guengerich, minister at All Souls in New York, recounts the story of Teresa Garp-

stas and Robert LeGalley. Before they were married last year in Albuquerque, New Mexico, they filed a notarized prenuptial agreement
at the city hall. In it, they agreed to each receive an allowance of
$70 per week to cover haircuts, eating out, gifts for friends, and spend-
ing money. They also agreed to spend $5 for birthday gifts to nieces
and nephews, to send each of their parents only a card on their birth-
days, but to spend between $30 and $120 for their parents' Christmas
presents.

A section of the agreement headed "Sex and Child Care" is equally
specific. "We will engage in healthy sex three to five times per week.
Teresa will stay on birth control for two years after we are married
and then will try to get pregnant. When both of us are working,
Teresa can have only one child. When one parent is free, Teresa can
have another child. When both of us are free, Teresa can have one
more child. After the third pregnancy we will both get sterilized."

Then there's the section called "Personal Conduct." "On week-
days, we will turn out the lights by 11:30 p.m. and wake up at 6:30
a.m." (They'll be lucky to sleep that late, if they have three children!)
"When driving," the agreement continues, "we will stay one car
length away from other cars for every 10 mph. We will buy supreme
unleaded fuel (Chevron) and won't let the fuel gauge get lower
than half a tank." Their agreement concludes with a statement of
supreme irony, no doubt lost on these two: "We will provide unconditional love and fulfill each other's basic needs." Good luck, Teresa
and Bob!

I want to grab these two and say, "No, no, you don't understand!
Marriage doesn't have to do with rules and regulations, doesn't have
to do with controlling your partner! It has to do with trust, and it has
to do with faith, and above all, it has to do with mystery, and being
willing to enter into the mystery of life."

I know that now. I didn't know it when I married. I married
because it was time to get married, because I was afraid of being left
out, because I wanted a home and a family, because I wanted love
and security, because I wanted respect. In other words, I married out
of fear and need. I could not bring my self to this joining, because I
was afraid of who I suspected that self was. So I stopped writing in my
journal, stopped praying, stopped teaching, and set about being "a
good wife," the way the books and movies told me to be, the way my

mother wanted. My husband loved me—as much as he could. But mainly, I felt, he needed a wife to make a nest for him and to have his babies. As a young surgeon, he had a plan for his life, he had a slot to fill called "wife," and I was it. I became depressed and began writing again, writing as a subversive activity. Once I began to find my security in myself, instead of outside myself, the marriage was gone. In one sense, it was one of the casualties in an age of transition from old values to new. Some couples made it through this cultural transition, but we did not. I will own my part of it—I think I did not know how to love myself, and therefore was not able to love anyone else, nor even to choose someone I liked instead of someone I needed.

For the first time in our history, marriage is purely and simply voluntary.

And so let us begin by saying: beware of false expectations. Your marriage will not save you from yourself, nor will it solve your problems of being, or of meaning. You don't want to be lonely? Marriage will not take care of your loneliness— your loneliness comes from a place beyond good company. You want a home? Your home is an extension of your heart space, and you can surround yourself with the most beautiful things and the finest books and the latest in cooking equipment and never have a home, a place to receive others. You want a good sex life? Forget technique, forget perfect bodies, forget about somebody else giving sexual pleasure to you. You need to be alive and present in this world, to feel your own erotic powers, then sexuality becomes one expression of that power as you are fully present with your partner.

Marriage is about mutual care and serving. It is often about putting the partner's needs before your own. I hesitate to say this, because women have too often been placed in the dubious position of the "second sex," in the words of Simone de Beauvoir—that is, having the man at the center, and having her life at the periphery, revolving around his. But hear the word "mutual"—in a good marriage, the two partners honor and serve each other, both wishing the other's happiness, both bowing to the other's need. I was struck last year by the Tygres Heart production of *The Taming of the Shrew,* staged by our church's own Jan Powell. I thought to myself, now how is a strong feminist like Jan going to present this play? When Kate is finally "tamed" by being dragged around bodily and half starved, she submits to her husband, only to have him drop to his knees before her and declare his love and absolute service to her. The message for me was that love is mutual devotion, mutual respect.

Author Elizabeth Berg reflected upon her parents' marriage as she prepared for their 50th wedding anniversary. "How did they do it?" she wondered. As she watched them that day, she began to understand that what had kept them together through times not always ideal were their own acts of simple kindness to each other: she pours his coffee; he drops her off at the door of their church on cold winter mornings. Berg says, "The lesson my parents' endurance has taught me is that it is not grand and glorious passion that makes a marriage work but the small daily gestures . . . that say, 'I still care.' And it turns out that those things have less to do with storybook romance than with recognizing the unique individual you married." She continues, "It is wonderful to get a bouquet of flowers from my husband, but it means even more when he gets me aspirin for my cramps. I can take my husband out for a fancy dinner, but it will not give him as much pleasure as my telling him that he looks sexy in his ratty pajamas. In a world that can feel cold and hostile, the value of marriage is that together, you can create islands of comfort that can sustain you. The trick is remembering to do it."

Your marriage will not save you from yourself, nor will it solve your problems of being, or of meaning.

Marriage has to do with trusting. 'Til death do us part. A committed relationship provides constraints that make it possible to explore a much deeper and more profound relationship than would otherwise be possible. John Welwood sees marriage as a "mandala" (which literally means "orderly world"), a sacred context in which a couple set boundaries that keep them safe. Welwood speaks of marriage as a container of trust, in which the two parties can risk being fully who they are. The promise is "I will not go away." This quality of trust is shaken if one of the partners is always using the "divorce trump card" to gain power or advantage.

If a partner has an affair, this container of trust is damaged badly and sometimes broken beyond repair. I have wondered why affairs are so devastating to the parties involved, and I believe it is because our intimate relationships, more than anything else in our adult world, recapitulate the relationship we had with our mother when we were small and vulnerable and unable to live without her protection. So when we allow ourselves once again to be held in somebody else's arms, flesh to flesh, we experience again that terrible and wonderful vulnerability. But we connect it with our very survival. And so if that partner betrays us by lying to us and abandoning us, we experience the most primal kinds of responses of anger and fear and grief. If you're going to be married, you need to wear the ring.

George didn't know that, in his marriage to Betty. He didn't know that a partner needs to be respected and cherished. He was, after all, an important man, a man who made a lot of money and had other people to do his bidding. When Betty found out about George's affair, she confronted him. He tried to explain, to placate her; he told her, "Never again." He might have won her over but for the new car. The next day George came home at noon with a smile on his face, jingling a set of keys before Betty's eyes. "Come and see, come and see!" he said, still smiling broadly. Betty opened the front door and saw parked in their driveway a brand new Mercedes-Benz convertible. "Thanks," she said. She took the keys and drove straight to her lawyer's office, where she filed for divorce. "The affair is one thing— but for him to think he could buy me off, that's just too much."

I would not necessarily say that happiness is the point of marriage.

Marriage is about communication—but let's keep in mind that there are all kinds of communication. And behavior is a better indicator than words. Women tend to be more verbal, and they are dismayed that men often do not talk openly about their feelings. In same-sex relationships, this presumably is not the focus of so much conflict. Lesbians can talk to each other all they want, and gay men can do without so much conversational foreplay. In heterosexual couples, however, it is well to remember that men and women really are very different creatures and to respect that difference. A light bulb came on when a very wise woman once said to me, "You can't expect men to act like your women friends." My aunt who died recently used to tell me how my uncle Len would pass by her chair and just touch her shoulder. He was a gentle man, a Quaker, and he didn't talk much. But in their silence, she felt deeply loved. The promise was there. He wore the ring.

Back to our young couple in Albuquerque, Bob and Teresa. They will most likely discover before too long that they can't control where their marriage goes, that they will in fact be walking in blindness and mystery. In his classic essay "Poetry and Marriage," Wendell Berry tells us,

> The promise must be absolute, for in joining ourselves to one another we join ourselves to the unknown. We can join one another only by joining the unknown. . . . What you alone think [marriage] ought to be, it is not going to be. Where you alone think you want it to go, it is not going to go. It is going where the two of you—and marriage, time, life, history, and the world—will take it. You do not know the road; you have committed your life to a way.

Marriage is a sacrament—that is to say, a way to come to God. A way to realize the self, and a common commitment to a larger good. It is not so much two people staring into each other's eyes, but two people standing together and looking out at the world. And so I would not necessarily say that happiness is the point of marriage. There is a deeper kind of joy and fulfillment, however, in the kind of ripening of the soul that marriage or holy union allows. If you do enter into this relationship fully, you will experience heights and depths of human experience that it is difficult to experience outside of marriage. You will be confronted with your folly, your selfishness, your pride; you will have to deal with depths of yourself that you never suspected were there, and your illusions will fall away. Marriage is not for the faint of heart. It is for people who are willing to be real and have all their fuzz rubbed off, like the velveteen rabbit.

And how do you do this hard thing? Rumi says, "To find the Beloved, we must become the Beloved." We must cherish ourselves, find ourselves precious and beautiful, and thereby allow ourselves to become a conduit for the love that flows through us to another. Love will be different from what the books say, from what the songs tell us, from what our hurting ego wants. Love will be what it is, and if we receive it as a sacrament, we can embody it and it will live through us and bless the world. That is what marriage is about: loving out of the primordial flow of love in the universe and joining that love with a particular other and becoming one in your love, to bless a world that is hungering for it. It is a way of faith, of saying yes to the Mystery, of entering the fire of our salvation.

SO BE IT. AMEN.

Prayer

O Holy One, may each of us here today, partnered or unpartnered, acknowledge that we live and move and have our being in your love. May we embody that love more fully as we seek to be your people. May we not turn from love in fear, but may we walk about with generous hearts and ready spirits. When love seems far away and we long for it, may we know that it is abundant in the universe. Help us to wake, and see. AMEN.

Benediction

May you be brave enough to let love rule your life, for it is love that will open to you the God within.

What Women Really Want

MARCH 7, 1993

*On the day when it will be possible for woman to love not
in her weakness but in her strength, not to escape herself
but to find herself, not to abase herself but to assert herself—on that day love will become for her, as for man, a
source of life and not of mortal danger.*
    —Simone de Beauvoir, *The Second Sex*

G ROWING UP AS I DID in the South, all the usual gender role
messages for girls were delivered to me, only more so. I made
two mistakes in adolescence that I knew would never be forgiven by
the boys in my high school—I was tall, taller than most of them, and
I was smart, smarter than most of them, even in math. I tried to take
the role of the Southern belle but was a dismal failure. Ruffles and
bows never looked right on me, since I was almost six feet tall.

The message I kept getting from the culture all around me was
"get small." Even as an adult. Even from my own mother. I remember our last conversation before her death, some 12 years ago, not
long after my divorce. She was unhappy that I was in school for yet
another degree. She said, "Why do you keep going to school? I don't
care what the libbers say—a man has to feel dominant. If you keep
getting these degrees, you'll never find a man." (What can I say? She
was right!) About a month later, she died. She went to her grave never
understanding my love of books and study. I know she loved me, but
she thought I was pretty weird.

Then there was the man who told me after a relationship of many years, "When I first met you, I thought you were a fragile flower. And now you're more like a tree. It's hard to love a tree." There it is again—"get small," be a fragile flower, if you want to be a real woman, if you want to be loved by a man. Maybe that's part of why I came to Portland—I heard you love trees up here.

"What Women Really Want"—a presumptuous title, for I know I cannot really speak for all women, and my own experience colors all that I will say. In this congregation are women of all ages, women who are wealthy and women who are out of work, lesbian and straight women, single women and married women, mothers and those who have never given birth, women who have chosen traditional paths and those who are changemakers. And yet there are commonalities, and I hope those will emerge, at least in part, in my remarks today.

First of all, as a woman, I want to feel safe—and I don't. After a board meeting last week, an unkempt man followed me into the staff parking lot and spoke to me as I was about to back out. He said he wanted to know if he could leave his motorcycle there. I said, "Well, you can't," and began driving out. He approached my car again as I reached the garage door, and I whipped the car out, almost bumping him as I did. He might have been perfectly innocent, but I didn't want to take any chances. I felt vulnerable. Women are.

One in four women is sexually assaulted in her lifetime—and usually not by a stereotypical criminal. Domestic violence is the single largest cause of injury to women in the United States. There was a picture of a man named Lust, interestingly enough, on the front page of the *Oregonian* last Thursday. He is accused of killing two women, his former fiancée and his former wife. The single most common occasion for female homicide is an argument with a man.

And it's not just the men at the bottom of the economic heap who are violent toward women. In one recent survey, 51 percent of college men said they would rape if they could get away with it. Domestic violence occurs in all social classes. The question we must ask, says Gloria Steinem, is not why women can't escape male violence, but why men do it. Is there something about the way women are denigrated in this society that gives men permission to rape and batter and kill? As a woman, I would like to feel safe, and I do not.

As a woman, I want our political leaders to pass laws that make women and children and families a priority. In the last presidential election, we heard a lot about "family values." I'll say it loud and clear: I'm for family values. I want prenatal care for every pregnant woman. I want to be sure that babies and young children get the nutrition they need—which they don't always, when 20 percent of children are living in poverty. I want quality child care when both parents have to be in the workplace. I want a Headstart program that will serve all eligible children, not just a fraction of them. I would like medical research and treatment programs to pay more attention to women's diseases like breast cancer, instead of their present unbalanced focusing on ailments more characteristic to men.

The message I kept getting from the culture all around me was "get small."

As a woman, I would like to receive equal pay for equal work. Although a number of women have been spotlighted recently as they moved into prominent positions in business or political life, it is a fact that 80 percent of women are still relegated to the "pink-collar ghetto"—they are low-paid clerical workers or sales clerks. Women make 75 cents to every dollar men make, and a man with only a high school diploma makes a thousand dollars a year more than a woman with a four-year college education. In almost every field, men receive higher wages than do women in comparable positions. That's true in the ministry, for example. The other day I was talking to a senior minister in another denomination about his experience in hiring an associate minister. He said the church chose a man, but the man wanted his own house instead of living in the parsonage and he wanted this and he wanted that, so the church decided they couldn't afford a man and would have to settle for a woman. Fortunately, the woman has turned out to be an excellent minister—and for less money. Even in our own denomination, I'm sorry to say, women ministers of comparable experience get paid less than men.

As a woman in relationship, I would want to share equally in nurturing and caring. We know that in dual-career families, the wife generally does a much greater part of the domestic work. We sometimes fall into these patterns without thinking—we have learned our roles well. In my second year of marriage, I became pregnant and continued teaching full-time. I was also doing all the laundry, shopping, cooking, and cleaning. My husband *did* take out the garbage. Finally

I became too exhausted to continue this routine, and I told my husband, "You'll have to help." But it wouldn't have occurred to either of us that this household work belonged to us both, equally. He was helping me with *my* work—even though we were both working full-time outside the home.

As a woman it was important for me to establish an identity aside and apart from my relationship with a man. Although this may sound simple and understandable, it is not always easy to do. Witness the brouhaha around the First Lady's deciding to call herself by her full name, Hillary Rodham Clinton. She's threatening so many people with just that little gesture. Why? Because she's claiming herself, and that is still a radical act in this culture.

After I graduated from college, I became a teacher in a school for gifted children in New Orleans. In six or seven years, I was beginning to write professionally, beginning to do some supervisory work, and I took some pride in my burgeoning reputation. Then I married a surgeon. I left my job, and we moved to a small town in Louisiana where he was to work for the summer. There I was referred to constantly as "the doctor's wife." And that was just the beginning. I had social prestige, I had financial power—but it all rested in my being married to him. It was strange, I thought—I haven't changed: the only difference is that I'm sleeping with a doctor. Instantly, I had disappeared. When I decided—for many reasons—to leave the marriage six years later, I lost the social prestige and the financial power, as I knew I would—but I had myself, or at least the potential to find that self, once again.

I was lucky. Society can be cruel to single women. In college I had a friend whose father was the minister of the largest and most influential Baptist church in town. This minister was suddenly killed in an automobile accident, leaving his widow with three children to raise. She went to work as a secretary to the academic dean at the college. In the past when there was a social event, she and her husband were always the first to be invited. But after he was gone, she became "just a secretary" and was never invited, by the very same people she had socialized with over the years as the minister's wife.

One of the women attending the brown-bag discussion on this sermon topic last week, an artist, told the story of her favorite aunt, also an artist, who came for a visit and asked to see her paintings. She had her work stuffed under the bed or in the closet. She pulled a painting out, and the aunt said, "And what is the title?" There was no title. Another came out, and again the question, "What is the title?" Again, no title. The woman began crying and shaking. She confessed to her aunt, "I think my art is selfish." In that moment she began to understand that she must use her gifts, else they would turn against her. This story is so typical, so understandable: women are acculturated to please others, to take care of others' needs, and we often feel selfish when we move to develop our own talents, to create an identity of our own. And we wonder why so many women take psychotropic drugs to fight off depression.

As a woman, I would like to be judged on my own merits as a human being and not seen as inferior because I am female. I had a lot of new learning as a divorced woman—until then I didn't understand that sexism existed, for I had been so steeped in it, I couldn't see it. When I couldn't get a credit card without my husband's name, though our credit was impeccable, I began to understand. Then there was the day I applied for a communications position at IBM. I had two master's degrees by then, as I remember. They said they had no current openings but offered me a job as a secretary. As a minister, I visited ten different churches before choosing the First Unitarian Church of Portland. In almost all the interviews at these various churches, I was asked, "Do you think as a woman you can minister to men?" I invariably thought it a strange question. When have women *not* ministered to men? I knew that no male applicants would ever be asked, "As a man, do you think you could minister to women?" And I knew that some people questioned, "Is she tough enough?" because they hadn't learned that softness and strength can be combined in the same person.

Women are acculturated to please others, and we often feel selfish when we move to develop our own talents.

As I woman, I want to be valued all the more as I grow older and wiser. I want to deny the message that has been internalized: "A woman's worth is in her youth and beauty." Our most powerful female icon in this culture is Marilyn Monroe. Those of you who have followed her story know that she was sought after and seduced by many powerful men, including the Kennedy brothers, J. F. K. and

Bobby. Her tragic death occurred under mysterious circumstances. A British documentary that was suppressed in this country strongly suggests she was murdered, and implicates the Mafia and perhaps the C.I.A. I recently saw Monroe's film *Bus Stop* for the first time and was taken by a portion of the film in which she seems to be speaking as herself, not as an actress. She's talking to a woman friend about men, and she says poignantly, "You know what I want from a man? Not all that lovin' stuff. I want a man to respect me." What do women want? To be seen and accepted as whole persons, not as something to be used to satisfy a man's needs, sexual or otherwise.

But again, women have internalized cultural messages about our appearance. In a documentary film entitled *The Famine Within,* the narrator reports that about 80 percent of fourth-grade girls have already been on a diet. Says Gayle Greene, in a review of Susan Faludi's book *Backlash,*

> Reading of the self-mutilation women inflict on themselves in breast implants, liposuction and face lifts, I was struck by how numbed we have become to our own pain. Smoking to stay thin, risking [anorexia and] death for thinner thighs, killing the breast as a site of sexual pleasure to make it the object of another's pleasure (which is what silicone implants do) indicate new levels of alienation from our bodies. But such practices also make sense in terms of a culture that values a woman's appearance more than her mind.

At this point, some of the men in this congregation may be thinking, as some of my male friends said after seeing the film *Thelma and Louise,* "I'm glad I'm not like *those* men." But you know, I think we as men and women hardly know how easily we buy into the cultural assumptions. And they are assumptions—the way things are—so they go largely unquestioned. In a recent article on male supremacy, Harriet Gill suggests some questions, a kind of checklist, that men might ask themselves to sharpen their perspective on where they are in relating to women:

> When a woman is raped by a man she knows, do I conclude that that is not really rape?
> Do I think that my work is more important than my wife's work?

Am I uncomfortable in the face of female authority?

Do I monopolize conversations with women, talking mainly about myself?

Do I expect personal service from women, such as housework, valet service, running errands?

Do I expect women to defer to me?

Do I take a woman seriously when she says, "I want to talk about our relationship"?

What is my attitude toward women in the workplace?

Do I give the women in my life the same emotional support that I hope to get from them?

What do women want? It was interesting to me to see that Marilyn Monroe and Chaucer's Wife of Bath had much the same answer. In *Bus Stop* a handsome but naive young cowboy falls for Marilyn Monroe. The trouble is, he tries to wrestle her to the ground the same way he wrestles a prize steer, with brute strength and determination to control her. She pulls back and makes ready to leave; then he becomes tender and gentle and lets her know he cherishes her—and of course she falls into his arms and says she wants to stay with him forever. (I love happy endings!)

As a women, I want to be valued all the more as I grow older and wiser.

In the "Wife of Bath's Tale," if you remember, a knight from King Arthur's Court ravishes a maid and is condemned to death. The queen gives him a way out: she says, "I will grant you life, if you can tell me what thing it is that women desire most." The knight has twelve months to find the answer. He goes everywhere searching for what it is that women most desire, but everyone seems to have a different opinion. Some say honor; others say mirth; some say lusty husbands; others say rich array. He despairs as time grows short, then he comes upon an old, wizened woman. She promises to give him the answer, but in return he must promise to do the first thing she requires of him. He agrees. So he goes back to the court and says to the queen, "My liege lady, over all this world women wish to have sovereignty over their husbands as well as over their lovers, and to be in mastership above them." Consequently, "There was neither wife nor maid nor widow who rejected his answer, but all declared he was worthy to have his freedom."

Now here's the tricky part. The ugly old woman asks that he take her as his bride. "Anything but that!" he cries. But she is adamant. He marries her but is in great distress. She then says, "Well, choose, one of these two things: to have me foul and old till I die and to you a true and humble wife, never displeasing you; or else to have me young and fair and you take your chances." His answer? "My lady and my love, do which may be the greatest pleasure and greatest honor to you . . . ; I care not which of the two, for it suffices me as it pleases you."

"Then I have mastery over you?" she asks.

"Yes," answers the knight. And then—you guessed it—he kisses her *in her present reality, as she is,* and she turns into a fair young woman. And the ending goes like this: "And she obeyed him in all which might cause him delight or pleasure. And thus they lived in perfect joy to the end of their lives."

When his greatest concern becomes to honor her and please her, she gives herself to him without reservation. What would it be like if we decided to partner this way? What if control and dominance of the partner, whether male or female, gay or straight, were given up for respect and love for the partner *as that person is,* and what if the greatest pleasure of each was to please the other?

What does a woman want? In *Women Who Run with the Wolves,* Clarissa Estes gives this answer: a partner who will help her "find her true names, . . . to apprehend and comprehend the numinous substance from which she is made, . . . to stay with it. And to sing out her names over her. It will make her eyes shine. It will make his eyes shine."

SO BE IT. AMEN.

Prayer

Men and women alike, we spend our lives longing for love, no matter what else we say we want. It all comes back to love. May we understand that all love is of the divine, and that it is created when we honor ourselves as a cherished gift and when we are able to give that gift from a heart that is unafraid. AMEN.

Benediction

May we reach out to the other, and in that reaching out, come to understand, and in that understanding, come to love.

Searching for the Holy

Who Is This Man Jesus?

MARCH 27, 1994

*I want God to put His steaming arms around Me
and so do you.*

—Anne Sexton, "Jesus Dies"

*T*HE YEAR WAS 1988, and I was in San Francisco, standing in a long line waiting to buy a ticket for Martin Scorsese's new film *The Last Temptation of Christ*. I had come early because this movie was the film event of the year—not because it was a great film (it was not), but because so much furor surrounded it. Jerry Falwell and the American Family Association, among others, had condemned it, and fundamentalist Christians were picketing theaters all over the country, including the one in San Francisco.

I finally got through the line and the pickets, then I had my purse searched before I was allowed into the theater. Still 45 minutes early, I struck up a conversation with a young man sitting next to me, who happened to be an Italian Catholic. He assured me he was no longer a Catholic, he had given up all that superstitious nonsense years ago, then he proceeded to talk to me for 30 minutes nonstop about the Jesus he no longer believed in. Well, what do they say? Once a Catholic, always a Catholic.

The film follows Kazantzakis's novel of the same name. At the end of the story is a fantasy sequence—the last temptation—where Jesus is invited by an angel to come down off the cross and lead an ordinary life. He imagines he experiences sexual love, he has a family, he earns respect as the best carpenter in Nazareth. Then he rejects this vision and accepts the spiritual calling that leads to his death on the cross.

Why was this film so threatening to so many? I believe it is because many Christians are comfortable with the idea of Jesus as God but very uncomfortable with the idea of incarnation, or Jesus as a human being. You see, if Jesus was a human being—if he hungered and sweated and longed for the touch of human flesh—*and* he carried the divine within, then maybe we do too. Then what? What might be expected of us?

I'm compelled by this man from Galilee. I confess I have kind of a crush on him. If I were in a play about Jesus, I would want the part of Mary Magdalene. Who is this character I see in the pages of the four gospels, and why is he so intriguing?

On the surface of things, we don't know much about Jesus. We do know there was a historical Jesus. He was a relatively unknown Jewish carpenter who was born in Palestine during the reign of Herod the Great, probably around 4 B.C., who never traveled more than 90 miles from his hometown, who owned nothing, was not highly educated, and never wrote anything. In his early 30s for one to three years he went about teaching and healing, mostly in Galilee. His teaching threatened the religious leaders of his day and invited the suspicion of their Roman conquerors, and so he was executed as a common criminal—crucified, which was the punishment of choice for the Romans, in the outskirts of Jerusalem. This is not exactly the biography of a hero. Nevertheless, of all the religions of the world, Christianity is the most widespread, claiming one of three persons as an adherent. That's pretty amazing. And think of the diversity—from the intellectual brilliance of Thomas Aquinas to the mass appeal of Billy Graham; from the stillness of a Quaker meeting to the rousing sermons of a Martin Luther King, Jr., to the elaborate ritual of the Greek Orthodox Church. Yes, Jesus lives.

What was this very human Jesus like? What did he look like? Again, we don't know, but I can't believe he was the blond, blue-eyed, sweet-faced man on the Sunday School walls of my childhood. After all, he was from the Mideast, so he probably had swarthy skin and dark eyes. He was a carpenter: he could lift heavy pieces of wood, and he worked with his hands. I think of him as earthy, intense, funny, brief but to the point in his speech, absolutely in touch with his body and his feelings. As Walt Whitman wrote, Jesus was "turbulent, fleshy, sensual . . . no stander above men or women or apart from them."

We know from scripture that he had easy, egalitarian relationships with women. He was known to openly consort with prostitutes, without condemning them for their impurity. He had many women followers, and there is no evidence that women were in any way discriminated against or seen as inferior or stereotyped by Jesus—in radical contrast to their treatment in his culture. After his resurrection, he first appeared to a woman, Mary Magdalene.

What is most poignant for me, perhaps, is his essential loneliness.

He had a strong sense of humor, often using dry wit to get people to laugh at their own absurdities. For example, he tells the Pharisees, who insist on the letter of the law but miss the spirit of the law: "You strain out a *kalma* (gnat) and swallow a *galma* (camel)."

Jesus felt anger, too, most notably when he chased the hucksters out of the temple. He saved his most cutting remarks, though, for hypocritical religious leaders of his day. He says to the Pharisees, "You can tell a tree by its fruit. You vipers' brood! How can your words be good when you yourselves are evil? Out of your own mouths you are condemned." Or another time, "You are like a whited sepulcher— clean on the outside, but putrid and rotting within." Sweet Jesus? No wonder they wanted him out of the way.

He was certainly no ascetic. Jesus was in fact criticized by his enemies for being a "glutton and a wine-bibber." He enjoyed good company and the celebration of marriage feasts. During his ministry, he was forever eating and drinking in the homes of saints and sinners alike. He was pleased and delighted to be anointed with sweet-smelling oil. He was intensely aware of the natural world: the reaping of grain, sheep in the fold, the sparrows' flight in the marketplace, the wind listing where it will.

How thrilling—and how scary—it would have been to hear Jesus teach! He overturned his listeners' expectations at every hand with his paradoxes and his parables. His message is radical, calling into question our values, our assumptions. Some of you may never have read the Bible. If not, I challenge you to do so, and to begin with the gospels: Matthew, Mark, Luke, and John, four different versions of the Jesus story.

We assume we should seek revenge on our enemies; Jesus says to love our enemies, to bless those who curse us. We assume that adultery is wrong; Jesus says that if a man looks on a woman as an object to use, he has already committed adultery. We assume that good, respectable people will have their reward; Jesus says that the publican and the harlot will enter heaven before many who are outwardly righteous. We assume that we should follow the norm in our society and compete for our share of the economic pie; Jesus says to be as free as the birds of the air and the lilies of the field. We assume that the wealthy and the wellborn are happy; Jesus says that the blessed are those who weep, those who are merciful, those who are pure in heart. Perhaps H. G. Wells was right when he said either there was something mad about this man, or our hearts are too small for what he was trying to say.

Jesus knew what it's like to be despised and forsaken. He knew what it's like to be terrified, trembling at what he had to face.

As compelling as his words are, his person is what ultimately draws me to Jesus—again, his humanness, his frailty, his vulnerability. He became tired and had to disengage from the crowds to renew himself. He needed close friends. In my own life, I know about fear, about loss, about feeling disconnected from those I love, about needing support when I'm doing something hard. Jesus was human—fully human—and as he carried out his mission, he experienced all that any deeply feeling human being would experience. What is most poignant for me, perhaps, is his essential loneliness.

You may think, "Jesus wasn't lonely. He had crowds of followers who listened to his every word. He had faithful disciples who went everywhere with him." But I say he was the loneliest of men. I say this because he was the most misunderstood of men. No one understood Jesus, least of all his disciples.

He took the twelve aside one day and revealed to them his fate. He said he would be given up to the chief priests and to the lawyers; he would be condemned to death and mocked and flogged and crucified, and on the third day, he would be raised to life again. And what was the response after he shared this agonizing secret? The disciples started scrambling for power positions. "I want to be on your right hand in heaven," says James. "I want to be on your left," says John. When the other disciples heard, they were indignant and angry. Here are the chosen twelve, fighting like spoiled children over a piece of candy.

Then Jesus said to them, "You know not what you ask. Are you able to drink of the cup that I shall drink of?"

They answered, "We are able." How little they understood themselves! How little they understood Jesus. So once again, patiently, he tried to explain. "Whoever is great among you, let him minister to you. Whosoever will be chief among you, let him be your servant." His kingdom was not one of power and prestige, but one of servanthood and sacrifice. One not of exalting one's self, but of humbling one's self.

Now let's move to the scene in the garden of Gethsemane. Jesus says to his disciples, "All of you shall fall away this night. The sheep will be scattered." Jesus knew how frightened and bewildered his disciples would be when he was arrested.

But Peter immediately says, "Oh, no—I'll never offend you, Jesus, I'll never fall away." And Jesus answers him, "Before the cock crows twice, you'll deny me three times." Peter speaks even more vehemently: "No, I'll never deny you." And they all say likewise, "No, Lord, no, we'll never deny you!" I wonder if they ever really believed that Jesus would be arrested and led away until it actually happened.

When they came to the garden of Gethsemane, Jesus asked his disciples to sit there, while he went away to pray. He took Peter, James, and John, and he said to them, "My soul is full of sadness." He asked them to wait and watch—to be with him. Then he went on alone and fell on the hard, stony ground, and in his anguish he prayed, "Abba, Father ['Abba' is Aramaic for 'Daddy'], all things are possible unto thee; take away this cup from me: nevertheless not what I will, but what thou wilt." You'll notice he prayed this prayer alone—he was facing the essential aloneness of all human beings in this moment. There are certain things we must all do alone: no one can walk our life path for us; no one can make moral choices for us; no one can die our death. We and we alone are accountable.

Jesus must have been thinking about the physical agony he was to face, but I think his agony was more than physical. He must have felt deep sorrow that his message of love was rejected—that instead of answering love with love, humanity had answered love with hatred, with betrayal and death.

Then, after he prayed, Jesus went back to the disciples and found them asleep. He says to Peter, who is perhaps his best friend, "Peter, Simon, are you asleep? Could you not watch with me one hour?" And Jesus goes again, alone, to pray, and returns to find a second time that the disciples have fallen asleep. Again he asks, "Stay awake and pray," but when he returns, they are once again asleep. "Sleep on now and take your rest: it is enough," he said. "The hour is come. Behold, the son of man is betrayed into the hands of sinners." So Jesus had not even the comfort of his dearest friends on the night of his betrayal.

The Jesus story is about what happens when we put love at the center.

At this point Judas, one of the twelve, one that Jesus loved as a brother, comes forward with a large group of men armed with clubs and swords. He goes up to Jesus and says, "Master, Master," and kisses him, in order to identify him to the soldiers. And the scripture says, "They laid their hands on him and took him." What great irony that one who preached love and compassion and forgiveness is approached with swords and clubs. And what happened to the disciples, who swore they would never desert him? The scripture says, "And they all forsook him, and fled." Peter, who was the surest of them all, ended up denying Jesus three times.

You know the rest of the story. Jesus is tried and condemned. As he is hanging on the cross, he is mocked and derided: "Save yourself, if you can—come down from that cross." When in his great thirst he calls out for water, he is given a sponge soaked in vinegar. And in the end, just before he dies, Jesus in all his pain and anguish cries with a loud voice, "My God, my God, why hast thou forsaken me?" Jesus knew what it's like to be despised and forsaken. He knew what it's like to be terrified, trembling at what he had to face. He knew what it's like to be without any earthly hope. He was the loneliest of men. And because he was, because he knew, we feel less alone. He has shown us a way to be with our loneliness, even the loneliness of death.

He teaches obedience, and he teaches love. Notice that in spite of his despair, Jesus does not ask God to change things: "Let this cup pass. Yet not what I will, but what thou wilt." Obedience. Then Jesus is given the strength to forgive even those who nailed him to the cross, and he is given the strength to minister to the two thieves hanging on either side, one of whom curses him, and one of whom believes. Love. Obedience and love.

At a discussion group one evening, someone, upon hearing I was a minister, asked me, "Do you think Jesus was divine?" I said, "Yes. And by the way, so are you." You see, if Jesus is God and not human, then we're off the hook, aren't we? Jesus can take all the goodness onto himself: he becomes the intercessor, the divine lamb slaughtered for the sins of the world. But if Jesus is human and carries within himself the seed of the divine, then maybe we all do. And maybe we all have the responsibility of owning our divinity and living out of that seed, that center.

The Jesus story is about what happens when we put love at the center. What does happen? We feel our fear of death diminishing. The stranglehold of guilt begins to loosen; our self-centeredness starts to shift, and we move towards love-making, justice-seeking. You see, I haven't told the whole story: the death on the cross is not the end. There's the resurrection. And it matters not to me whether you interpret that event literally or metaphorically. It's about new life. It's about love being stronger than death. And when we know that, deep in our bones, we can give ourselves away. Oh, the joy of that deliverance! Oh, the peace in that understanding. This is my message to you in this Easter season.

SO BE IT. AMEN.

Prayer

We give thanks for the life of Jesus of Nazareth—he taught us how to live and how to die. We confess that resurrection is difficult for us, for the habitual ways, the learned deadness, are more comfortable, and we do seek comfort. So we pray on this Palm Sunday that we might have the courage to seek new life, new ways of being, new ways of loving, as the spring teaches her sweet resurrection story in every new blade of grass, in every bud reaching for the sun. AMEN.

Benediction

May the divine in each one of you blossom and bear good fruit.

The Sacredness of the Flesh

JANUARY 30, 1994

*"Here," she said, "in this here place, we flesh; flesh that
weeps, laughs; flesh that dances on bare feet in grass. Love
it. Love it hard."*
—Toni Morrison, *Beloved* (Baby Suggs speaking)

ONE EVENING A FEW YEARS AGO I attended a reading in Oakland by poet and translator Stephen Mitchell. Stephen is a well-known translator of Rilke's work and the editor of several anthologies of devotional literature as well. He is also known as a devout Zen student, having studied and practiced for years with a Korean Zen master. The reading was followed by a question-and-answer period in which somebody asked Stephen about his sitting meditation. "Oh, I gave that up," he said quietly. There was an audible gasp in the room, for he was known as quite the authority. The questioner then asked, "Well, what are you doing for your spiritual practice now?" And Stephen answered, "Right now I see marriage as my spiritual path."

His answer shook all my assumptions. Wasn't a spiritual path something you essentially pursued alone, even if you were in the company of other seekers? Wasn't it between you and the Mystery? Didn't it have to do with meditation or prayer or retreating to nature or even, for some, becoming celibate and leaving the pleasures and pursuits of the world? *Marriage* as spiritual path, or for gays and lesbians, holy union. *Relationship* as spiritual path. What can that mean? What would it look like in practice?

This is a difficult concept because of the sexual pathology in our cultural history, a cultural history that posits a split between the spirit and the flesh. The spirit—the sky-god—represents all that is holy and noble and transcendent; and the flesh—the earth-mother—represents the earthbound, the natural, the sensual. The body is degraded and dangerous: temptations of the flesh will lead us from our higher natures, or so the argument goes. The woman, of course—earth-bound, nature-bound as she is—is the temptress. Didn't Eve give Adam the apple?

I'd like to give you a quick and dirty history of this cultural split in our Western thought, so you'll begin to see how we got the way we are. Six hundred years before Christ, the Greek god of love Eros was seen as irrational, out of control, foolish. The Greco-Roman world was a dualistic one in which the soul and mind sought freedom from the prison of the flesh. Socrates and Plato agreed that any sexual activity was harmful to the health of the soul. At the beginning of the Christian movement, Stoicism was the dominant philosophy of the Roman empire. The Stoics believed the ecstasy of sex was dangerous to the health of men. Seneca the Younger wrote, "Do nothing for the sake of pleasure." Sexual desire, he warned, is "friendship gone mad." The Gnostics, like the Stoics, in their contempt for the body, went back and forth between asceticism and libertinism.

Now for the Christians. Jesus himself said practically nothing about sex, and he honored woman as equals, in stark contrast to the social structure of his day. St. Paul takes it on the chin, but it is these earlier philosophical teachings that are really to blame. When Paul advises against marriage, he does so because he is convinced that Jesus is returning soon. With the end of the world imminent, he reasoned, there are more important things to worry about than your love life.

The big nay-sayer in Christian history is St. Augustine. A brilliant thinker and writer whose views dominated Christian thought for well over a thousand years, Augustine had problems controlling his own sexual impulses. We know that he had two affairs and fathered one child before becoming a priest. A Christian Platonist until his death, he wrote, "Nothing so casts down the manly mind from its [spiritual] heights as the touching of women." He taught that original sin was passed from parents to children by the passion and desire of sexual intercourse. This view of sensuality and pleasure as sin was voiced by virtually all the church fathers thereafter. The Calvinist overlay in our own country didn't help matters. It is ironical to me that in a religion that has as its central figure one who is incarnated—that is, God become flesh—there is so much fear and hatred of the flesh.

Now we don't have to be Catholic, or Calvinist, or even religious, to be influenced by these destructive concepts. They have become part of our cultural assumptions, part of what *is*. Is there any wonder that it's difficult for us to grow up with a healthy, celebrative view of sexuality? How is sex seen, even now, in contemporary culture?

Sex is seen as sin. Of course, if it is misused, it can be sin; but—and this is my point—it is not inherently sinful. Two extremes are commonplace in our culture: sexual repression and libertinism. These are both sides of the same unhealthy coin—a denial of the body, and a separating of sexual feelings from one's emotional and spiritual life, because we see these powerful feelings as unworthy.

Sex is seen as work. Lionel Lewis and Dennis Brissett, in a wonderful article about sex as labor, point to the language in sex manuals, which abound with such chapter titles as "How to Manage the Sex Act," "Principles and Techniques of Intercourse," and—how about this one—"A Controlled Sexual Crescendo." If you have to talk about it that way, folks, you've already lost it! The work ethic, these authors say, has permeated our sex lives.

The woman, of course—earth-bound, nature-bound as she is—is the temptress. Didn't Eve give Adam the apple?

Since we're so suspicious of play, if we can turn our play into work, perhaps we can justify it. This article reminded me of a man I met on a plane recently. He was a young man, in his 30s perhaps, personable, and we were chatting about this and that. I asked if he had any children. He sighed and said, "Well, we're just beginning to try." "How wonderful!" I said. But he just shook his head. "I don't know," he said. "It sure is a lot of work." "It is?" I asked, incredulous. "Well, maybe I'm just not as young as I used to be," he said.

Sex is also seen as danger. For many, physical intimacy carries a fear of death, as AIDS has come to so powerfully influence our sexual behavior. Right now in the state of Oregon alone, 10,000 people are HIV-positive. Until a cure is found, that is pretty much a death sentence: 10,000 people in Oregon alone, and more to come. The only way to absolutely prevent AIDS is to be celibate—or to be lucky enough to have a monogamous partner you can totally trust. The presence of this disease is particularly insidious in how we come to view our sexual lives. We always knew pleasure was a sin, and now that sin is punished with death.

But that's not the only fear associated with intimate relationship. As marriages break up and sexual mores loosen up, many people move from one relationship to the next. How much loss can a person stand before he or she says, "I don't want to do this again. It's too risky. I think I'll just pass." How does that old country song go? "I'm Down to My Last Broken Heart."

For many, physical intimacy carries a fear of death.

Or maybe individuals decide to enter into sexual relationships with their bodies, but not their hearts and their spirits. And so we objectify our partners and see sex as a kind of consumer item. The world of commerce encourages this attitude by raising our fears about our attractiveness and self-worth then offering to assuage those primitive fears by selling us deodorants or sports cars. Maybe we can buy love. That's what we really want, don't we, in spite of our fears.

This consumer attitude—along with our all-American linear, problem-solving, goal-directed approach—can make its way into the bedroom and lend an atmosphere of, well, *tedium* to the whole enterprise. Recently I was talking with a man who happened to be a sex therapist (I did not meet this man on a plane, but at a conference), and he said things have really changed in his business in the last 20 years or so. He said in the past men would drag their wives into therapy, saying, "Help her, Doctor, she's frigid." Now, he said, women are dragging their husbands in, saying, "Help him, Doctor, he's impotent." "Why the change?" I asked. "The women's movement," he said. "Women are demanding so much more from men." "Performance anxiety?" I asked. "Right," he answered with a big smile. Business is good these days.

Now let's think about this. Where is the relationship? The female tries her best to look like a magazine cover—to be an object for consumption. And the male has been taught by our good capitalistic culture that his body is a machine to be used, so he needs to perform.

Then he needs to evaluate. Was it OK? Was I as good as your last lover? But relationship is not like trading baseball cards, for heaven's sake. And sex is not about goals and achievements. We have been taught otherwise. I'm asking us to consider a new paradigm.

How would our intimate relationships be different if we saw the flesh as sacred stuff, as a conduit for the Holy? Not as something to separate off from our spiritual lives, but as an inseparable part of our spiritual lives? What if every twosome became a threesome—the two partners and the Spirit? What if sex became sacrament?

We must begin by trusting desire. "Desire leads us to the sacred," writes Susan Griffin. What can this mean? Certainly not that we should act on every sexual impulse, but to understand that we can trust the source of our desire, which is the source of life. It comes from a stream beyond our making and connects us with all that lives. We cannot possess it or control it. Listen to the words of D. H. Lawrence:

> Love is no more than the stream of clear and unmuddied, subtle desire which flows from person to person, creature to creature, thing to thing. This subtle streaming of desire is beyond the control of the ego. The ego says: "This is my love, to do as I like with! This is my desire, given me for my own pleasure." But the ego deceives itself. The individual cannot possess the love which he [or she] feels. The individual has nothing, really, to do with love. . . . Out of the deep silence of individuality runs the stream of desire, into the open squash-blossom of the world. And the stream of desire may meet and mingle with the stream from [another]. But it is never [one's] self that meets and mingles with [another]: any more than two lakes, whose waters meet to make one river, in the distance, meet in themselves.

I have mentioned sex as sacrament. I was speaking with a minister friend about this a few years ago, asking her opinion, and she said, using a handy food metaphor, "Well, I think sex can be anything from a snack to communion. What are we talking about here?" Let's talk about communion. A sacrament is, in traditional theological terms, "an outward and visible sign of an inward and spiritual grace." Sex, then, as an expression of our holiness, deeply respectful of the sacred character of the other.

In this sense, sex can be thought of as contemplative activity. Says Alan Watts, "Contemplative love—like contemplative meditation—

is only quite secondarily a matter of technique. For it has no specific aim; there is nothing particular that has to be made to happen. . . . Nothing is merely preliminary. One finds out what it can mean simply to look at the other person, to touch hands, or to listen to the voice. Intimacy just leads to passion; it certainly does not have to be willed." And—here's our food metaphor again—he continues, "But there is all the difference in the world between gobbling and actually tasting food when one is hungry. It is not merely that appetite needs restraint; it needs awareness." At the end of his article, Watts speaks of the height of lovemaking as spiritual ecstasy. He says, "For what lovers feel for each other in this moment is no other than adoration in its full religious sense. . . . Such adoration, which is due only to God, would indeed be idolatrous were it not that in that moment love takes away illusion and shows the beloved for what he or she in truth is—not the socially pretended person but the naturally divine."

How would our intimate relationships be different if we saw the flesh as sacred stuff, as a conduit for the Holy?

In my wide reading on this subject, no message has been more consistent than the critical problem of the ego. Growing spiritually and developing real intimacy in a relationship both depend upon a word that is very frightening to most of us, and that word is "surrender." Freedom lies in surrender, not in conquering, not in gaining power over. Of course, we have to feel safe; we have to build with our partner a mutuality of trust in which surrender is possible.

Krishnamurti understands in a profound way how Western thinking and ego-striving create sexual difficulties. He writes,

Surely the problem can be solved only when you understand the whole process and structure of the "me" and the "mine": my wife, my child, my property, my car, my achievement, my success; until you understand and resolve all that, sex as a problem will remain. So long as you are ambitious, politically, religiously or in any way emphasizing the self, . . . so long as there is this activity of self-expansion, you will have a sexual problem. You are creating, feeding, expanding yourself on the one hand, and on the other [during sexual love] you are trying to forget yourself, to lose yourself if only for a moment. How can the two exist together? Your life is a contradiction; emphasis on the "me" and forgetting the "me." Sex is not a problem; the problem is this contradiction in your life.

A religious tradition I have not mentioned yet, but one that is central to our focus today, is that of praise. Joy, celebration, laughter! These elements should be at the heart of worship, I believe. I would be upset if we ever had a service here at this church in which joy was not audibly present. And if we see our bodies, our sexuality, as connected with the very energy and holiness of life itself, how can we fail to bring joy and celebration to our intimate lives? Once I heard the feminist scholar and writer Carolyn Heilbrun speak at a writers' conference. I don't remember her topic that day, but I do remember that she was advocating a sexual looseness I was not com-

We must begin by trusting desire.

fortable with. I challenged her that day in the question-and-answer session and later wrote to her to elaborate on my views. She wrote back and said simply, "The only sex which is immoral is sex without joy." Well, I can't say I agree—it's a little more complicated than that. But I would agree that sex as duty, sex without celebration and play, would not only be tedious, but might well be considered immoral, since it compromises one's integrity and life energy.

Back to Stephen Mitchell's statement, which has animated this whole sermon: can marriage or intimate relationship be a spiritual path? Yes, I believe it can, but there is a danger. I was talking with woman I know, a very wise and sensual woman in her 60s. She had lost her husband the year before, and I asked her if there was a man in her life now. She smiled and said no. She said, "I realized that I couldn't get what I was looking for from a man." "What were you looking for?" I asked. And she answered, "God." Now this doesn't mean she will choose to be alone forever—and if I know her, she won't. But she will never again substitute a relationship with another human being for her relationship with the divine. Relationship can be path. Relationship cannot be God.

Some things are difficult to learn outside of an intimate relationship. It is here that we are confronted with all our demons in living color—our touchy, vain, self-seeking selves. It is here that we can risk in a safe setting, and therefore we have a personal freedom to *become* that we have nowhere else. If childhood wounds still linger, we have a chance to heal, if we have a patient, committed partner. John Welwood speaks of marriage as "mandala," an "orderly world," a sacred context where boundaries are set and principles agreed upon. Within that sacred context, each partner honors the spiritual dimension by asking, "How may I live most fully and joyfully? How may I soften the drive of my ego, surrender my will? How may I be useful to purposes greater than my own?"

The path I have suggested today is a potentially disturbing and frightening one. I understand that. It's profoundly counter-culture. We'll find little support for it in the world out there. And of course, if we allow another to come so close, to touch us so deeply, we risk the pain of loss. What may be even more frightening is that we risk

Some things are difficult to learn outside of an intimate relationship.

transformation. As much as we say we want it, it scares us through and through. Hey, I'm doing OK—why jump off into the unknown? And we are talking about the unknown, about mystery. About a little death of sorts. "For in love, we surrender our uniqueness and become world" (Susan Griffin).

I'm not saying you can just forget your fears and go out there and do it. You might very well have to train first, to become an athlete of loving (which is different from a sexual athlete), to develop your own spiritual practice aside and apart from relationship, to learn patience and compassion and understanding. Whether you've been in a relationship for years, or you've just lost one and you're in pain, or you've been alone a long time, or you're just getting into a new relationship, remember that the very earth is a vast dance of love and creation and that we all have that dance in common. This flesh that we walk around in is holy stuff, and we partake of the divine through it. Treat it with care and reverence, and share it with presence and praise.

SO BE IT. AMEN.

Prayer

O Spirit of Life, we would invite your presence into every part of our lives, including and especially into our most intimate relationships. We are made in the image of God, just a little lower than the angels, the scripture says. Help us to accept the beauty and the goodness of our flesh. Help us to be free of the lies of this culture, lies that separate us from the earth and from one another, as we seek to compete, to compare, to conquer. Let us instead be thankful each day that we have been given the good gifts of the Spirit through the pleasure and loveliness of the body. AMEN.

Benediction

Go now, and know your goodness. Be not afraid of praise and pleasure.

Is Anyone Out There Listening?

FEBRUARY 7, 1993

I think most people have trouble with prayer because prayer is really an act of love, and therefore demands vulnerability. As with love, the more we try to control prayer, the less prayer can happen.
—Gerald May, *The Awakened Heart*

I MIGHT AS WELL COME RIGHT OUT and say it: I'm a praying person, and I came by it quite naturally. One strong, clear memory from my Southern Baptist childhood in Louisiana is that of my grandmother sitting in her big easy chair in front of the fire, reading out loud from the Bible: "Bless the Lord, O my soul, all that is within me, bless His holy name." And each night when she went to bed, prayers—and lots of them—were part of the ritual that led to sleep.

I used to walk Granny down the hall, helping her to the front bedroom. "Will you pray with me, Dr. Marilyn Jane?" she would ask, and I would say all right and crawl into Granny's double bed with her and listen while she prayed for all her children, each one by name: Varnel and Bernadine and Mellie, and Gene and Ernie and Lemos and finally James, who was my father. Everybody called him "Jim" except his mother. Next she prayed for the president of the United States. Then, to finish off her prayers, she always prayed "for all for whom it is our duty to pray, the world over." Then she would turn to me and say: "Dr. Marilyn, say the Lord's Prayer, honey." Having dropped off to sleep somewhere during the president's prayer, I would wake up and go through the Lord's Prayer with her. Then she would kiss me goodnight, say "I love you," and drop off to sleep.

And here I am today, a Unitarian Universalist minister, and still praying. I have not always prayed however. I've just come back to it in the last ten or twelve years.

Unitarians and Universalists used to pray, too—and we've largely given that up now. In some of our churches that are strongly humanist—those in the West, Midwest, and South—members would be embarrassed to use the word "prayer," much less to actually pray.

And yet when I think about it, I remember that some of our ministers I most admire turn to a devotional life for strength and renewal: ministers such as Harry Scholefield, minister emeritus of the San Francisco church; Laurel Hallman, minister of the Dallas church; and John Buehrens, co-minister of All Souls in New York.

Our denomination has always been involved with social action and humanistic concerns, from the early abolitionist cause to the current battle for gay and lesbian rights. That emphasis is one reason I'm in this denomination. But the gospel of good works has not saved the world, as our counterparts hoped it would in the 19th century. We had perhaps our last cultural fling at salvation by works in the 1960s during the War on Poverty. The real war—in Vietnam—left us no longer naive, without the glowing hopes for transformation suggested in such books as *The Greening of America* and *The Aquarian Conspiracy.* The culture of narcissism in the '70s and '80s has worn thin, and the times now call for a different sort of revolution, one that is grounded in our spiritual lives, one that rests on the Rock Maya Angelou spoke of in her inaugural poem:

The gospel of good works has not saved the world.

> Today, the Rock cries out to us, clearly, forcefully,
> Come, you may stand upon my
> Back and face your distant destiny.

There seems to be an emergent longing for things of the spirit in this country. Maybe it's because we baby boomers have figured out that we are going to die one day. At any rate, we know that sales of books about spiritual matters have been rising rapidly—Thomas More's volume *Care of the Soul,* about cultivating the spiritual in our everyday lives, has been a runaway bestseller, for example; not to mention the several books by Unitarian Universalist minister Robert Fulghum. When I was discerning my call, I visited ten different churches, and universally the search committees told me, "Our people are looking for spiritual growth."

Prayer and meditation seem appropriate—maybe not prayer in the form of my grandmother's nightly vigil, but an intentional opening up to the spirit of sacredness in the world. That's how I define prayer, for now: an intentional opening up to the spirit of sacredness, to the Holy, on this earth and within ourselves.

In looking at the nature of prayer, I'd like to say what prayer is not, as I see it—though I must tell you that even this exercise seems a bit arrogant on my part, for I would not want to second-guess how the Spirit might choose to work in any particular life.

Prayer is not bargaining with God.

Prayer is not magic, not a way of conjuring up favors from an all-powerful being. "Dear God, send me $400 for next month's rent" is not what prayer is about. Nor, as Paul Tillich says, is prayer "intoxication." Emotionalism is an attempt to escape, he says, not an attempt to open. Speaking in tongues, for example, is just speaking in tongues and has nothing in particular to do with relationship to the sacred. Tillich says that prayer is essentially "ecstatic," that is, a unifying activity: it unites one who prays with the spiritual presence.

Prayer is not bargaining with God. When I grew up, my concept of God was that of a stern old man—much like my Victorian grandfather—who could give to me or withhold from me what I wanted most. The first thing I really, really wanted was a pony. If only I had a pony, I would never tell another lie. I would stop punching my little brother. I didn't get a pony, and it's a good thing I didn't, because we had nowhere to keep a pony. That's the tricky thing about wanting: we often really do get what we want. I was lucky.

So prayer is not bargaining or demanding. As Tillich says, it is "bringing one's own personal center before God," or if you will, before the Spirit of the Sacred. Prayer is answered, not by what we receive, but by a new, more caring, more integrated relationship with ourselves and with others. All else follows.

Fourth, prayer is not essentially public, but private. Much public praying ends up being rhetoric intended to influence the group gathered, rather than to bring one's heart, or the collective heart, before God. When I pray at the end of each Sunday service, I am aware that I'm not just offering up a prayer for the congregation—yes, I am doing that. But I'm also praying for myself, that as your spiritual leader, I might be whole and strong and wise and devoted to the good.

I remember my grandfather's prayers at the dinner table. They were always designed to impress us children with his grand and elaborate language—he would always end, "And help us to all walk circumspectly before Thee." It sounded more like a threat than a prayer. On the other hand, when my father was called on to pray, which was not often, his prayer was so very different. He would bow his head upon his clasped hands and ask forgiveness, as he would say, "for every low-down, dirty, rotten thing I did." Usually he would cry. I wasn't very comfortable with this prayer either, but I knew it came from my father's heart, and it was not just a public relations gesture.

What we search for, we find; what we think upon, we become.

Prayer has more to do with listening than with speaking. So often petitioners throw out words, words, words, which can get in the way of prayer. Some people who have richly developed spiritual lives do not use words, but just come into the presence of the Spirit, ready to receive. I'll never forget my five-year-old son's advice when I was going through the sadness and fear of my divorce. Seeing my tears during bedtime prayers one evening, he said to me, "Mommy, I know how God speaks." I listened—maybe this child knows something I don't know, I thought. "How does God speak?" I asked. "Real low," said my son. Yes, he was right. I had to quiet myself to hear.

So, in summary, prayer is by nature unifying, integrating, personal, and receptive. It is not magical, not intoxicating, not given to bargaining, nor to be cried aloud in public places.

All that is well and good, you may say. But the pragmatist in me asks, does it do any good? How will my life be different if I choose to include a regular prayer time or devotional time? The real question is a more dangerous one. The real question is, what if my life becomes based upon, emerges out of, my spiritual nature, that part of me that seeks unity and love?

When I grew up, I was a Southern Baptist, and before that, a

Catholic. As a little Catholic girl, I used to pray to the Virgin Mary, and I remember once when I was in the first or second grade, praying for a dog. Sure enough, a few days later I found a mangy, string-tailed dog in an alley, took him home as my own, and named him Poochy. Now I don't for a minute believe the Virgin Mary goes around finding and delivering dogs to children. But I do believe that because I, as that little six-year-old, turned my whole system of awareness to dogs, I was able to see what I might have been blind to before. It was a kind of intentionality that bore fruit. *Intentionality.* That has become an important word for me: what we search for, we find; what we think upon, we become.

What about prayers of intercession, like praying for someone who's having a bad time, or someone who's ill? I don't believe in a kind of rescuing God, a modern-day *deus ex machina* who arrives in the nick of time and pulls us—any of us—out of the fire. But what I notice when I pray for other people is that I change in relation to them. I think of creative ways to be helpful to them, or my relationship is clarified and made more solid. Praying for someone with whom I'm angry is a particular challenge, but when I can bring myself to do it, the anger doesn't have so much control over me. Revenge seems beside the point.

It is the will, the desire, to reach out to God that's important, not the method.

"Prayer changes things" was a motto from traditional religious folk for a while. I like the comment I heard from a very liberal Southern Baptist minister: "No, prayer changes people, and people change things." That's the way prayer works, I think.

Well, it's one thing to talk about prayer, and another thing to do it. Anyone who wants a regular devotional life must be very intentional—there's that word again—about creating it. There will be little support from our society. Jogging, yes. Aerobics with the stars, yes. Prayer, no. The first barrier for us all in this culture of "doing," efficient doing, is to believe it's all right to just "be" for a while. The Japanese are hardworking and productive, yet their culture allows them to support the tea-master. A tea-master spends 25 years of study in his calling: to learn how to serve tea, to learn how to bring presence to a task.

Suppose you decide that yes, you do want to have a prayer life, or to develop a spiritual practice of some kind. How do you begin? There is no one right way. Even Paul, who had a ready answer for almost everything, says not to worry about how: Romans 8:26 says, "Likewise the Spirit helps in our weakness; for we do not know how to pray . . . , but the Spirit intercedes for us with sighs too deep for words." It is the will, the desire, to reach out to God that's important, not the method. The way for one might be journaling; for another, a sitting meditation; for still another, contemplative prayer.

The three years before I came to Starr King School were filled with self-doubt and anguish—I think I can honestly use the word "anguish." I knew I had to make a move, but I didn't know how or where. Reasoning and good will alone, even with my friends' support and their own best thinking, were not enough to keep me going. I had to open myself to something larger.

Prayer is like any other relationships: constancy and faithfulness increase the pleasure and richness of the experience.

I had left my childhood "man in the sky," who had provided more guilt than comfort and direction. As an adult, in my time of most need, I discovered what I came to call the "God-in-me," which is of divine nature and which wants to be central to me. Since then I have tried—not always successfully—to be faithful to that inner voice.

Once in a great while, the voice speaks plainly, like when I was reading Tillich one time. I was immersed in the reading, trying to be with Tillich, and I heard from inside me a blunt, powerful message: "Stop trying so hard to be good." I searched the page, looking for a reference to "trying" or to "goodness," but found none.

Usually, though, the influence of prayer is much more subtle. Afterwards, I feel clearer and more directed from within. I notice that when my life becomes frantic and pressing, I sometimes neglect to pray. That is a mistake for me, for if I slip out of the discipline of prayer for long, I begin to feel scattered and vulnerable, undirected and susceptible. Sometimes I have felt that my life is going so well I didn't need to pray, and sometimes I have felt so alienated from God that I could not bring myself to pray. But what I have come to see over the long run is that prayer is like any other relationship: constancy and faithfulness increase the pleasure and richness of the experience.

Since I have come to Portland as your minister, I must confess that my prayers have become brief—but very intense, and consistent. I am aware, as I told the search committee, that everything I have to give rests on the basis of my spiritual life. That is the ground from which I must lead, and unless that ground is tended carefully, my leadership will not bear fruit.

When I think about the history of my own prayer life, I realize it has taken various forms from time to time, as my needs have changed. I didn't—and still don't—know how to address the Spirit. "God" seems so blunt and overused, and it has echoes of "man in the sky." "Our Father" doesn't fit any more. Sometimes I say "Father Mother God." It's all metaphor, I remind myself. Other times I say "One Whose Name I Cannot Know"—that puts me in the presence of the Mystery. Sometimes I just say, "Well, there I am," or "I'm available." Then I say whatever is in me to say, the deepest concerns of my heart. If I am dishonest, I hear it in my voice, and I speak again until I find the truth in me.

Praying isn't always so orderly, though. At times I find myself pacing up and down, flinging my hands into the air, pouring out my anger and frustration. Other times, when things are topsy-turvy, I'll just make the offhand comment to my jokester God, "This is not funny." Or maybe I'll be reading the newspaper, as I did a few mornings ago, and read about some child whose face was burned off, and quick tears will spring to my eyes. That's a kind of prayer too. I trust that in all these awkward gropings, God knows I'm trying to get through.

I pray because I need to pray. Everyone may not feel that need. A close friend of mine, a poet, brings the Spirit up in her poems. Her very life seems to me to be a prayer. As for me, the forces working against love in me are great, so I pray.

I don't pray the way my grandfather prayed. I don't pray the way my father prayed. I don't pray the way my grandmother prayed. But it's all the same in the end. You do it however you can do it. And right now what I can say is: "I'm available. Imperfect as I am, do your work through me." You must find your own way, trusting that in your willingness to try, you will be heard. "Seek and ye shall find; knock, and it shall be opened unto you" (Matthew 7:7).

SO BE IT. AMEN.

Prayer

O Great Mystery, we do not know who you are or how to invite you, but we know that we need to open ourselves to your presence. Hear the concerns of our hearts: the sorrows that we bear, the dreams that we dream, the needs we scarcely admit even to ourselves. May we be given over to your spirit, that love and mercy may fill our hearts and lives. May we care for nothing more than to serve you with all we are and yet may be. AMEN.

Benediction

May you go now, with the peace that passes all understanding.

Amazing Grace

It is possible, in deep space, to sail on solar wind. Light, be it particle or wave, has force: you rig a giant sail and go. The secret of seeing is to sail on solar wind. Hone and spread your spirit till you yourself are a sail, whetted, translucent, broadside to the merest puff.
— Annie Dillard, *Pilgrim at Tinker Creek*

"AMAZING GRACE" is a hymn that crosses the boundaries of time, of place, of race, of theological bent. The story of its author, John Newton, is fascinating—amazing, indeed— and bears retelling. Newton was born into an English seafaring family in 1725. He lost his mother at a very early age, and his father helped him get a job aboard a ship. He ran away from that ship and later took part in a mutiny on another ship. He was pressed into the British Navy for a while, but that didn't last either. He turned into a real libertine and ended up in the slave trade: he took manufactured goods from Great Britain to West Africa, where he traded them for slaves.

One day he had an experience that changed his life forever. His ship was in a terrible storm in the Atlantic. Known for having such a foul mouth that he gave new meaning to the term "swearing like a sailor," Newton nevertheless did not swear on this occasion. Instead he found himself saying, "If nothing can be done, then Lord have mercy upon us." Then he went back to his cabin and thought, "What can this mean?" Somehow in the midst of the storm, he realized that he did indeed believe in God, and that God had addressed him. God's grace was working in him, and gradually his life changed.

Lo and behold, he became a minister, and he took his first post as the curate in Olney, England, where he often preached about his own experiences and the working of grace in his life. He and poet William Cooper wrote hymns for the Wednesday evening prayer services, and "Amazing Grace" was one of those hymns.

"Amazing Grace!" The word "grace" comes from an Indo-European root meaning "to lift up the voice, or to praise." So we "say grace" before meals. And to be in a state of grace is to be in a state of primal thanksgiving, one's every gesture and word given over, a thankfulness that comes from a relief of the burden of desire, of ambition, of self-seeking, a thankfulness that comes from knowing that all is unfolding as it should and must.

> *To be in a state of grace is to be in a state of primal thanksgiving.*

We say "graceful," or "full of grace." I think of the athlete or the dancer, beauty in motion. In watching Olympic divers or figure skaters, I see a perfection of composition and form, not a single wasted motion. I feel a sense of wholeness and rightness that warms me and thrills me.

Sometimes we have what we call a "grace period," in which we are given leniency in some way or other—to delay payment of a bill or to be forgiven a library fine. And so grace has to do with forgiveness—we fail, yet we are given another chance: the slate is wiped clean, and we are blessedly free to start over. Amazing grace!

One time I did a very foolish thing. I've done lots of foolish things, but this was a dangerous and foolish thing. When my boys were 10 and 11, they spent the summer with me in Berkeley, where I was studying. They asked to go up on the roof of the apartment building and play. A new friend of theirs was visiting, a little girl about their age, so I told the three of them they could go. I knew the wall around the roof was fairly low, but I reasoned that they were responsible enough to handle being there alone. After about half an hour I called them to dinner, thinking everything was fine. It was two days later that my children confessed what had happened. Their new friend, who apparently was a sort of daredevil, had stood up on top of the wall and walked the narrow rim around the roof garden—seven stories up. She didn't fall—but I still have fantasies about that child and what could have happened and what I would have had to live with. For me, it was a great act of grace that my misjudgment did not lead to disaster.

Grace is a gift, an undeserved gift, that is bestowed upon us out of the bounty of life. It just shows up one day and announces itself, to our astonishment, often when we least expect it. For example, Stephen Hall, writing in the *New York Times Book Review* of August 1, 1993, explains that the "rational approach" to the designing of new drugs has its limitations. He says,

> No breakthrough in 20th-century medicine was driven more by chance than the discovery of penicillin. The first penicillin spore was borne by a random London breeze through an open window and landed in one of Alexander Fleming's petri dishes. Although Fleming displayed considerable genius in knowing what to make of this fortuitous visitation, one is tempted to say that penicillin discovered him rather than the other way around.

Rebecca Parker, president of Starr King School, in a talk called "Grace as Gift" remarked that for Universalists, heresy would be to say that there is no gift, that when I come to the end of my human resources, there is nothing else.

Grace is constant; it is there no matter what we do. We are enveloped in grace, completely caught up in love, in the same way that we are surrounded by the air that gives us life. We are quite literally *in love*. That is hard to understand. This love is unconditional. There is no way we can make it go away. We cannot feel it at times, because we are alienated from ourselves and others and God. Sometimes, as St. Augustine said, our hands are too full to receive the grace that is offered.

Contemporary men and women often experience their need for grace as a kind of vague yearning. After all, they have learned from years of schooling that the way to perceive truth has to do with the logical mind, with the scientific method. Faith may seem like a copout. These people are not by and large moving into institutional religion, because it seems far removed from life—and conventional religion has too often taken the side of oppression, militarism, and

99

exploitation. But the yearning remains. How do we satisfy this yearning? How do we open ourselves to the experience of grace?

It's tricky. In our culture, we tend to be assertive; we get a plan and go after the things we want. Some people meditate, with the goal of being enlightened; others pray in order to catch the ear of God. I just don't think it works that way—we're not talking about being a smart consumer of a quantity called grace. Well, you say, isn't there anything we can do to make it happen? Not really—it's more like cultivating attitudes and ways of being that will allow grace in. It's more like "spread[ing] your spirit till you yourself are a sail," as Annie Dillard says.

Sometimes of course grace strikes us when we least suspect it, as in the story of John Newton, or that of the apostle Paul, who was struck blind on the road to Damascus. Such experiences are sudden and so intense that the individual may be transformed on the spot. Not just good or "holy" people experience grace; it comes when it will come. It cannot be controlled.

Most of us experience grace in simpler, more ordinary forms. People who cultivate a spiritual practice may find themselves in a state of grace more frequently than those who do not. They may feel a kind of groundedness and wholeness and a level of awareness that is very satisfying. Traditional native people who regard every movement, every act of life, as ceremonial practice or right living may experience most of their time as grace-filled.

Sometimes ritual brings a sense of divine presence. One part of our liturgy that is almost always grace-filled for me is the singing of the doxology, "Spirit of Life." As your voices fill this gracious sanctuary, with the sopranos and their descant lifting us ever higher, my heart fills with joy, and I sense a unity and a power that speak of the presence of the divine.

Grace may be found in community. Choir members report an experience of extraordinary closeness and a sense of unity as they become one body, one voice that acts as a conduit for the Spirit. Grace may be found anytime a strong connection is made between one person and another. It can emerge between a therapist and a client, or between close friends who really hear each other, or in the act of making love. You can't make that grace dimension happen, but when it does happen, it comes as a precious gift.

More often than not, grace occurs through our weakness—or at least through our willingness to be vulnerable, for then we allow an opening. It may be more difficult for the rich and powerful to experience grace than for the poor and the humble. It may be easier for women to experience grace than for men, since men are acculturated to be strong and in control. The apostle Paul speaks of having a "thorn in his flesh," and though we never learn what his difficulty is, he tells us that when he prayed for it to be removed, God answered, "My grace is sufficient for thee: for my strength is made perfect in weakness." I find that, paradoxically, my spiritual life gets off track when the rest of my life is going beautifully and I begin to feel that I don't need God—I'm doing very well on my own, thank you very much. It is my felt need, my weakness, that pulls me back to God. Fortunately, I have enough weaknesses that I get pulled back a lot.

Grace is a gift, an undeserved gift, that is bestowed upon us out of the bounty of life.

It's not that I "turn my life over to God" and become passive, waiting for the next set of instructions from the Spirit; rather, I enter into a covenantal relationship, a partnership, in which the Spirit and I are working together for the good. Sometimes that's scary, because the Spirit may lead in directions I never guessed. But it's also interesting and exciting.

I am reminded of the true story of Larry Walters, a 33-year-old truck driver who was sitting in his lawn chair one day wishing he could fly. He had always wanted to pilot a plane, but he had never had the money or the opportunity to take lessons. So he spent a good many summer afternoons sitting in his backyard in his ordinary old aluminum chair—the kind with the webbing and the rivets, the kind you might have in your own backyard. One day Larry hooked 45 helium-filled surplus weather balloons to his chair, put a CB radio in his lap, tied a paper bag full of peanut butter and jelly sandwiches to his leg, and slung a BB-gun over his shoulder to pop the balloons when he wanted to come down. He lifted off in his lawn chair expecting to climb a couple of hundred feet over his neighborhood. But instead he shot up 11,000 feet, right through the approach corridor to the Los Angeles International Airport. When asked by the press why he did it, Larry answered: "Well, you can't just *sit* there." When asked if he was scared, he answered, "Yes . . . wonderfully scared." Larry Walters will never be the same. He'll be able to face almost anything. When we say, "Let's fly!" the Spirit may answer, "Hang on! How high do you want to go?"

Hear me carefully. Inviting grace into your life is risky. It threatens all assumptions, all conventions, all normalities. It particularly risks your idols—or in more contemporary language, we might say it risks your addictions: whatever you won't give up, whatever you put first in your life, whatever you are so devoted to that it comes between you and the Spirit. I remember talking to a young man about his inability to love and to make a lasting relationship. "I want you to consider two words," I said, "vulnerability and relinquishment." He looked at me with wide eyes full of fear. "Vulnerability! Oh-h-h! Relinquishment! Oh-h-h!" He literally shuddered as he spoke.

> *Inviting grace into your life is risky. It threatens all assumptions, all conventions, all normalities.*

I find Unitarian Universalists are wanting more spiritual depth in their lives, for the limits of humanism are becoming clear: no, our dependence on scientific positivism has not fixed things. To the contrary, our desacralizing of the earth has despoiled it. Our fancied superiority to indigenous people has been called into question. Our lost sense of community and responsibility for the whole has spawned violence beyond what we could ever have imagined only a few short years ago. There is a longing for the spiritual dimension to enter our lives and renew us, both individually and as a culture.

But inviting grace is difficult for Unitarian Universalists. People who are addicted to drugs or alcohol can hit bottom and come to understand their radical dependence upon spiritual power. But look at our addictions! We're addicted to success, to perfectionism, to overwork—even to stress. The larger society approves of our addictions and rewards us for them—ask me if I know! If reason is one of our most treasured virtues, we may begin to believe that the mind can conquer any problem. We want to restrict mystery or grace until it's graspable or controllable. We are afraid of that which is not of our own making. It is difficult for Unitarian Universalists to be aware that we are dependent, that we can't handle our lives alone. And that kind of spiritual pride may cause us to forfeit the peace and power of grace in our lives.

Maybe we need to acknowledge that we too have been desperate, have felt alone in the world, have been ashamed and needy. Maybe we need to say to ourselves and to our God, "I'm through going it alone. It's too hard. And that's not working anyway. Come into my life and make me whole. Make me an instrument of your love and your peace. I once was lost but now am found, was blind but now I see." Amazing! Amazing grace!

SO BE IT. AMEN.

Prayer

Holy One, we come this day asking first of all for forgiveness. We let our pride keep us from learning; we let our self-reliance keep us from relationship; we let our stubborn self-righteousness keep us from your good grace. Help us instead to live with humility, with patience and forbearance. Teach us what riches are there for us when we soften, and when we wait. AMEN.

Benediction

May you go forth in grace and beauty, both now and forevermore.

Realizing the American Dream

Who, Then, Is My Neighbor?

NOVEMBER 14, 1993

> *"Why did you do all this for me?" Wilbur asked. "I don't deserve it. I've never done anything for you."*
> *"You have been my friend," replied Charlotte. "That in itself is a tremendous thing. . . . By helping you, perhaps I was trying to lift up my life a trifle. Heaven knows anyone's life can stand a little of that."*
> —E. B. White, *Charlotte's Web*

S USAN STARR, a Unitarian Universalist community minister who worked with the urban poor in Chicago, recounted the following story in a sermon. She said that a homeless woman named Sarah crawled into a demister outside a McDonald's in a futile attempt to keep warm one January night. She was found frozen to death the next day. Those who knew her, said Susan—shelter residents, "street people," various social workers and church volunteers—were shocked and angry and were brought once again face to face with despair. Sarah's homeless friends organized a funeral service, which turned out to be quite a media event. Cameras from the TV stations were there, and newspaper reporters interviewed anyone and everyone.

During the service, a time was set aside for those who knew Sarah to speak from their hearts about her. A man came forward. He stood in front of the group, his head bowed, tears streaming down his face. He didn't speak. He stood and stood, weeping, but still he didn't speak. Some people were embarrassed, wondering how to continue with the service. Finally Susan walked up to him, put her arm around his shoulders, and said, "Was there something you wanted to say?" "Yes," he said. "But I forgot what it was—something about love." Susan said,

> I don't know if that man is still alive as I speak today. But in that one moment in Chicago two years ago, he and I met as deeply as . . . two human beings can meet. For in that one moment, his soul and mine were laid bare—the truth was revealed. I was the same as he. I have nothing to say, and my life is a struggle to say something I have forgotten, something about love.

We come here today as a church community in the heart of downtown Portland for much the same reason—to struggle together to say something we have forgotten, something about love. How can we understand that we are not separate from the suffering? How can we start to *become* love? What if we looked at service to others as a spiritual path, a way towards healing ourselves?

Service as spiritual path implies a lack of attachment to the fruits of our endeavors. It's not that we don't want to be successful in our work of finding shelter for the homeless or working for progressive legislation, it's that we don't want to have our egos bound up in our success. We want to be fully present and attentive to our work, but we don't want to worry anxiously or to compete or manipulate other people to reach our goals.

Before I decided to go to seminary, I knew I sought some path of service, but I wasn't sure what. I thought about pursuing a Ph.D. in social work; I thought about becoming a political activist. I remember one evening I went to a meeting of the Democratic Socialists in Lexington, Kentucky. As you might imagine, any kind of socialist would be pretty marginalized in Kentucky, and maybe that explained the behavior I noticed at the meeting that evening. People were speaking to one another rudely. Women were shunted to the side as important decisions were made. There were raised voices, angry gestures. I thought to myself, "These people want to take over the world? Thanks, but no thanks." I admired the principles in their literature, but they were living out the negative values of their culture—supposedly in service to the good. That's not the way of the Spirit: the process and the product should be congruent. It's not that the end is not important, but the means are more important. It's not that we don't care about a goal, but we care more about obedience, obedience to the spiritual law that sent us forth.

Ram Dass and Maraba Bush in their book *Compassion in Action* suggest a process for service that seems healthy and sound to me. They say we should begin by asking ourselves the question, "What makes me happy?" We know what makes us happy, and we need to bring that joy into any service we choose. They tell the story of a woman, a photographer, who was haunted by the street people she saw constantly. She wanted to do something to help homeless mothers in particular, but she didn't know how. What good would taking pictures do? After getting to know some homeless mothers, she taught them to photograph their children. She made portraits of the mothers to accompany those of their children. The photographs became a gallery show, which raised consciousness about the need. People saw the beauty, the humanity, and the sadness of these homeless people. The mothers had treasured photographs and a new skill, which made them feel a sense of accomplishment.

What if we looked at service to others as a spiritual path, a way towards healing ourselves.

Learning to listen is at the heart of giving. In order to determine right relationship, we must listen to those who would receive our gifts. We must try to see the world through their eyes and to hear what their real wants are.

During the early part of my internship at First Church in Dallas, I received a phone call. It was from a church member who sounded desperate. He said his teenage son had just had a mental breakdown. Apparently the son believed that Satan had him bound in chains and that a minister would come by to release him. Since John Bahrainis, the regular minister, was out of town, would I please come by and see if I could help his son. This was not in my job description! I had never worked with schizophrenics, and I had no idea what to do. But I thought I at least had to try.

When I arrived at the home, the situation was just as the father described. The boy was sitting on his bed, his wrists and ankles bound in imaginary chains. Intuitively, I felt I had to get into his system, rather than trying to bring him directly into mine. I said "Hi" and sat down beside him. I asked him to tell me what the problem was. When he explained about the chains, I said that I could see they were binding him, but that I was a minister, and I could break them and set him free. I reached over and broke the invisible chains, and told him he could get up and walk around. I explained that he had not been well, that we would have to take him to the hospital, and he agreed to go. That was the beginning of a long period of healing for him, which included visiting from time to time with me. The last time I heard, he was in college and doing well.

Not only is it important for us to listen to those we would help, but it is important for us to listen to our own inner voice. In order to do so, we must quiet ourselves. The Chinese book of wisdom the *Tao Te Ching* asks,

> Do you have the patience to wait
> > till your mud settles and the water is clear?
> Can you remain unmoving
> > till the right action arises by itself?

Having a regular practice of reflection, prayer, or meditation is invaluable in discerning right action. It's not as though we are choosing— it's as though a path chooses us. And that path may shift, so we must stop and listen again and again. In my own spiritual practice each morning, I ask for certain things—for healing, for peace. I ask for my heart to open. I pray for individuals. But mainly I simply offer myself. "Well, here I am again. I'm available." I don't know what opportunities the day might bring for service, for loving. But I want to be awake enough spiritually to discern what those are and to respond.

Another principle of helping is to start small. It's very easy to feel overwhelmed by the enormity of the need. Not only do we know about the pain of our neighbors, but modern media show in living color the agony of a train wreck, or the horror of war and starvation abroad. We become numb; we feel helpless. The antidote to that feeling is to act—if we act, the powerlessness will leave. To build, to create, is to feel that yes, I can make a difference.

Some might say, "What we really need is systemic change— enough of the bandaid approach." And I would agree—we need systemic change. We need a more just division of resources in this country. We need to provide jobs for those who can work. We need to spend less of the federal budget on weapons and more on shelter and medical care. But the impetus for systemic change comes most often from people who start small—people who have worked in a homeless shelter and know some homeless people by name; people who have held a tiny crack baby and rocked that baby to sleep; people who have watched an AIDS victim decline and die. Start small, and see where it leads you.

Sometimes people say, "I'd like to do something, but I don't know where to start." Start where you are. Reflection and meditation will help, and something I call *intentionality:* willingness to open your eyes and see what is there before you, asking for attention. You can work alone or in community. One member of our church has chosen to work alone. One day quite by accident, he met a man who was on parole from prison, trying to go straight, but with a lot of his past still gnawing at him. The man needed a place to live, and after getting to know him, our church member invited him into his own home. The former prisoner now has a friend and mentor in his journey towards a different life. I have been a sometime witness to this transformation, and it is gratifying and heartwarming.

It's not as though we are choosing—it's as though a path chooses us.

You might be thinking, "I couldn't do anything like that! I would be afraid." Maybe most of us couldn't, but that's the beauty of it—each of us is different, and each of us can do something. For many of us, working in community is more satisfying than working alone. A few years ago when I lived in Berkeley, I happened to be crossing a street near the university when I noticed a young man bending over a huge scattering of nails that had spilled from a wooden box into the street. I thought to myself, "Well, he's got a job there," then started to pass by, not wanting to become involved. "I've got things to do," I told myself. At that moment a young woman walked over to the spilled nails and without a word began helping the man pick them up. I felt slightly ashamed and realized I really did not have anything very pressing to do, so I too joined the young man in picking up the nails. Shortly after that, another man ventured onto the scene and asked, "Is there any method to this?" "No," I said. "We're just picking up nails. Trying to save some tires." Soon all four of us were earnestly putting the nails into the wooden box. We didn't say much. Working together towards the common task, though, made us feel close somehow, and I suspect, good about ourselves.

It turned out that the nails did not belong to the first young man at all; rather, they had fallen from a truck. The four of us were picking up nails that did not belong to us, dropped by someone we did not know, so that equally unknown motorists would not puncture their tires. Surprisingly fast, the nails were all picked up, and the four of us went our separate ways. But that day stays in my memory. The anonymity of the city usually does not permit such spontaneous happenings, such sudden impulses towards community with strangers. I found myself wishing for more of that kind of involvement, in a common task towards the good. I found myself loving people I didn't even know.

One of the hardest things about helping is to acknowledge the reality of others' suffering.

As I said, start where you are. Miracles happen that way. Do you remember the miracle of the loaves and the fishes? Jesus' disciples came to him saying, "What should we do? There are 5,000 hungry people in this crowd, and we only have five barley loaves and two small fish." Jesus blessed the bread and the fish; everyone was fed, and there were 12 baskets of bread left over. Imagine that! Everyone was fed, and some took home doggie bags. Let me tell you how I think this happened. People brought lunches in their desert robes. And with the blessing of the bread and the fish and the presence of Jesus, people were moved to share what they brought with those around them. Furthermore, they felt so filled, so absolutely satisfied spiritually, that they weren't as hungry as they thought they might be, so they had more than enough. The miracle was not in multiplying loaves, but in multiplying love.

That same kind of miracle occurred a few years ago in the park blocks right here in Portland. A woman named Sharon and her friends were having lunch downtown. They had some food left over, and Sharon said, "Let's go see if there are any hungry people in the park who would like this food." Indeed there were. The next Sunday afternoon she came back with more. Other people started bringing food, they told their friends, and the friends came and brought food. This was not a program—it was more like a happening. And now at 3:00

on Sunday afternoons, 300–400 people are given food. It just happens, and people are fed. And that's a miracle.

One of the hardest things about helping is to acknowledge the reality of others' suffering. "It's dangerous to read newspapers," as Margaret Atwood says in one of her poems. Do you find yourself weeping sometimes when you read the paper? It's perfectly understandable. Do you find yourself not looking at the man curled up in a doorway, trying to keep warm and to sleep? It's natural to turn away. But we must keep looking, keep noticing the pain of others. That was part of the commitment we made as a church when we decided to remain downtown after the fire in 1965. To some extent being an urban church keeps us honest. Human suffering is all around us, and therefore we are constantly led to ask ourselves, "Just what is our reason for existing as a religious institution?" We have a beautiful sanctuary, yes, and at our back door we have the funky mural painted by the Outside-In kids. Some think the mural is a bit of an eyesore. I say, thank goodness we have it. It reminds us that we're not an elegant, comfortable private club. We're a church, and we're here to make a difference in the world.

We could be a little more radical, you know. In fact, we could be a lot more radical. What if a hundred of our members showed solidarity with the homeless by sleeping downtown on the city pavement one night? What if five hundred of us pledged to skip lunch once a week and to give the money to the hungry? What if we dedicated 5 percent of our budget each year to serve the urban poor? I agree with Samuel Miller, the former dean of the Harvard Divinity School, who said, "It is not enough to do everything we have always done. The church cannot amuse itself with the posture of past prestige or present popularity; it has inherited a revolution. It will be judged by the measure of its action in dealing with the radical changes in our world, not by its nostalgic reverence or its sterile respectability. Only one kind of religion counts today, and that is the kind which is radical enough to engage in the world's basic troubles. If it cannot do that, then it can do nothing which merits our concern or the world's respect."

I understand that what I'm saying is scary. It's scary for me too. Go ahead and enter your own fear, and run the risk of transformation. Transformation will occur when we dare to stop talking *about* social concerns and actually move to alleviate real human pain. Start at the beginning, where you don't know anything, where everything you thought you knew about love starts dropping away. Let your heart be broken. Then you will begin to remember what love is about, and love will claim you, guide you, and lead you home.

SO BE IT. AMEN.

Prayer

We come this morning, confessing that transformation is not exactly what we had in mind. We like being comfortable. We would really prefer not to see the suffering of others. And so we ask for courage to take this difficult path of awareness and action. Wake us up, let us see what is before us to do, and let us not fear the touch of your Spirit. For in ministering to others, we heal the wound in our own soul. AMEN.

Benediction

Go now, and know that every man is your brother, every woman is your sister, every child is the child of us all.

Working for Life

APRIL 14, 1996

Work is about daily meaning as well as daily bread. For recognition as well as cash; for astonishment rather than torpor; in short, for a sort of life rather than a Monday through Friday sort of dying. . . . We have a right to ask of work that it include meaning, recognition, astonishment, and life.

—Studs Terkel

SEVERAL MONTHS AGO I had the pleasure of hearing Garrison Keillor interview Studs Terkel—live, right here in Portland. Studs is in his late 80s now, and irrepressible as always, only more so. Early on in the interview, Keillor looked at the audience in dismay and said, "How can I get control?"

Studs has been and still is the friend of the working man and woman. His most influential book, simply called *Working,* is a collection of interviews from a wide range of workers. First published in 1972, it is a testament to their lives and to the lives of all who work for a living. I'd like to begin by reading an excerpt from it. These are the words of Mike Lefevre. Mike works in a steel mill. His wife Carol works as a waitress and when she is at home, cares for their two small children.

> I'm a dying breed. A laborer. Strictly muscle work . . . pick it up, put it down, pick it up, put it down. We handle between forty and

fifteen thousand pounds of steel a day. I know this is hard to believe—It's dying.

You can't take pride any more. You remember when a guy could point to a house he built, how many logs he stacked. He built it and he was proud of it. . . .

It's hard to take pride in a bridge you're never gonna cross, in a door you're never gonna open. You're mass-producing things and you never see the end result of it. I worked for a trucker one time. And I got this tiny satisfaction when I loaded a truck. At least I could see the truck depart loaded. In a steel mill, forget it. You don't see where nothing goes.

I got chewed out by my foreman once. He said, "Mike, you're a good worker but you have a bad attitude." My attitude is that I don't get excited about my job. I do my work but I don't say whoopee-doo. The day I get excited about my job is the day I go to a head shrinker. How are you gonna get excited about pullin' steel? How are you gonna get excited when you're tired and want to sit down?

It's not just the work. Somebody built the pyramids. Somebody's going to build something. Pyramids, Empire State Building—these things just don't happen. There's hard work behind it. I would like to see a building, say, the Empire State, I would like to see on one side of it a foot-wide strip from top to bottom with the name of every bricklayer, the name of every electrician, with all the names. So when a guy walked by, he could take his son and say, "See, that's me over there on the forty-fifth floor. I put the steel beam in." Picasso can point to a painting. What can I point to? A writer can point to a book. Everybody should have something to point to.

You might ask, why does Mike Lefevre continue this work, year after year? He tells us at the end of the interview:

This is gonna sound square, but my kid is my imprint. He's my freedom. There's a line in one of Hemingway's books. I think it's from *For Whom the Bell Tolls.* They're behind the enemy lines, somewhere in Spain, and she's pregnant. She wants to stay with him. He tells her no. He says, "if you die, I die," knowing he's gonna die. But if you go, I go. Know what I mean? The mystics call it the brass bowl. Continuum. You know what I mean? This is why I work. Every time I see a young guy walk by with a shirt and tie and dressed up real sharp, I'm lookin' at my kid, you know? That's it.

Mike calls himself "a dying breed." He is, of course, right. The steel industry has eliminated more than 220,000 jobs, or half its work force, since 1980. Of those who lost their jobs to automation, only a third were able to find new jobs in the service sector, and even those experienced a significant drop in pay. The nature of the workplace is changing profoundly. We are quickly moving into what some have called a third industrial revolution, the Information Age. Blue-collar workers are being displaced by machines and robots. The new computer and communications technologies are already eliminating entire employ-

The nature of the workplace is changing profoundly.

ment categories, such as secretaries and receptionists, sales clerks, bank tellers, telephone operators, wholesalers, and middle managers. We all experience these changes in our everyday encounters. For example, rarely does a real human answer the telephone. We can bank without ever seeing a teller. Although recent government reports state that unemployment has declined only slightly, these statistics cover over an ominous reality: new technologies and corporate restructuring have pushed millions of American workers into low-wage, deadend service jobs, in which they work with little hope of advancement. Many of them are temporary workers with no benefits.

Believe it or not, there are still defenders of the "trickle down" theory of economics who say the expansion of markets and global trading will keep people employed. But companies all over the world are competing for these same markets, and virtually every industrialized nation is developing a two-tier society. The top tier is composed of the "knowledge workers," the engineers, technicians, computer programers, consultants, and professionals who make up about 20 percent of the work force. The bottom tier—the bottom 80 percent—is made up of manufacturing and service sector jobs. The question that governments will have to face is what to do about the millions of workers displaced by the new technology.

Meanwhile, back at the corporate ranch, in the midst of these changes, productivity has risen sharply. And the gains have been used to fatten the checks received by stockholders and to pay for corporate salaries that are 40 or 50 times as great as the average worker's salary. At the same time, Americans who have held onto their jobs are working longer hours, not shorter, because fewer workers at longer hours means that companies will not have to pay out as much in benefits.

The contract between business and employees is changing. The traditional expectation is that if the company does well, so will the employees. Not any more. Business profits rose 64 percent since 1989, while real earnings for workers have steadily declined—to 12 percent since 1979. Look at what happened at IBM last May. After the company enjoyed its best quarter ever, its leaders decided that 120 of their executive secretaries were overpaid by regional standards and gave them cuts of up to 36 percent. Simultaneously, IBM's top five executives split bonus money of $5.8 million, including a $2.6 million boost for CEO Louis Gerstner, which allowed him to take home more than $12 million annually. I think of the Quaker term "right relationship": many companies are not in right relationship with their workers.

Capital enterprise has drawn us headlong into the "work and consume" cycle, and our souls are bankrupt.

This is not the first time in history, of course, that technology changed the course of individual lives. During the Industrial Revolution in the 19th century, upper-middle-class women found they had no work save supervising the servants, and factory labor became the lot of working-class women. In England, children as young as seven worked fifteen hours a day, seven days a week. In the garment industry, women worked grueling hours without relief, and some died of exhaustion. Reforms were made, gradually, but not chiefly by the people controlling the capital. Citizens had to defy, to protest, to reform; and government had to make new laws.

It seems to me that in this country, neither major political party has thought very clearly or deeply about our current economic and social dilemma. Most of the public discourse has focused on "welfare reform." Both parties agree that people should work and not be on welfare, but neither has given a viable alternative. The Republican leadership often characterizes the poor as simply lazy and immoral, so their solution is "get them off the dole," since it's bad for their character. The GOP leadership has descended to scapegoating immigrants, working women, and the poor, and has brought up red-herring issues like school prayer and flag burning and censorship of art in order to exploit the fears and frustrations of a people who sense that the world is irrevocably changing—and this approach certainly worked in the last Congressional election. The Democrats, on the other hand, talk about job training and child care—but nobody has said *what* jobs people are being trained for, and at what wage. The Democrats have been content to promote their party by speaking of falling unemployment figures and low inflation. We need to move beyond politics and talk about people. We need to talk about the pain people are feeling, and why. As a society, we have to have a more comprehensive, more sophisticated analysis of the economic changes that are wrenching our lives apart, and a more just, more ethical response. We need a radical new vision.

Jeremy Rifkin, in his book entitled *The End of Work*, has put forth just such a vision. Technology could free us, says Rifkin, to pursue a different way of being in the world—could free us to rest, to create, to serve others. He proposes a kind of New Deal for the '90s. He believes that state and local governments could provide employment for workers who have been displaced by retraining them and giving them opportunities to serve others in community-building jobs in the nonprofit sector, jobs such as preventive health programs, adult education, building community gardens, organizing neighborhood sports teams. As Rifkin points out, the kinds of nurturing tasks that call for intimate relationships are those least vulnerable to displacement by a computer. Preparing men and women for careers in public service and then paying them would be expensive, but Rifkin says that the revenue could come from replacing current welfare programs, from discontinuing costly subsidies to transnational corporations, cutting military expenditures, and placing a value-added tax on all high-tech goods and services.

Rifkin also believes that we should take seriously the possibility of a shorter workweek, an idea spreading rapidly through Europe. If we had a 30-hour workweek, more people could work, and fewer would be stressed by overwork. There would be longer vacations, six weeks perhaps, which is common in Europe now. The government could relieve the business of workers' compensation in return for the shorter time at work, and the loss of government revenue would be made up by the taxes workers would pay. The government might consider additional tax credits to employers willing to introduce profit-sharing plans, so that workers could share in the prosperity of the company.

All this is interesting thinking. I'm not sure I buy all Rifkin's ideas, but we do need alternatives in a society that has a growing underclass of permanently unemployable people. We may soon have more people in jail than in college—and incidentally, keeping someone in jail for a year costs $30,000. Will we have increasing social unrest, drug use, violence? Or will we understand that people need the dignity of work, and make a way for them to have it.

Let's go back to Mike Lefevre, the steel worker whose words appear earlier in this sermon. In 1970, he had two small children. He wanted them to go to college, to avoid the hard life he had led. Maybe they did go to college—and now they are Generation-Xers, facing a world wholly different from their father's. Whereas Mike worked hard, his children don't want to work the way they saw their father and mother work. They resent the fact that their father was old before his time and came home each night too bushed to really be present for them. Mike's children simply cannot trust relationships with companies, so they can't imagine the kind of blind commitment to a job their father gave. Mike's son is a whiz on the computer, and he hopes his skills will transfer to many different job settings. He wants to work smart, not work long. Mike's daughter is not willing to put up with a job culture that is not changing fast enough for her, so she is starting her own small company. They want to do their own work in their own way at their own speed.

Mike doesn't understand his kids, and he's sometimes critical, but he's beginning to see that they're working their lives out in a new way. The kids haven't developed much of a political conscience yet, but they're beginning to realize that a few can't be successful at the expense of others. They're thinking about children of their own in the not-too-distant future, and they want for those children a kinder world than the one they inherited, a world less given over to the powers that be, a world more open to the human spirit and less driven by material need.

Capital enterprise has drawn us headlong into the "work and consume" cycle, and our souls are bankrupt. The final insult is that we're being told, well, there's no work, or no work worthy of you; but please, still consume. Please buy the Barbie dolls and the $100 tennis shoes. Keep the economic machine going. There must be a better way. Intuitively, we know that. Myself, I keep going back to Freud. He said that human beings need two things: love and work. He's right, you know. We need to know we are cherished, for no reason other than that we exist. And we need to give the gifts that are in us to give.

In fact, if we fail to use those gifts, I believe the natural result is frustration, leading to deep anger, leading to illness. Let me tell you about my long-lost second cousin. I was living in Berkeley, going to school, and out of the blue one day, a young woman called, identified herself as my kin, and suggested that we get together. Would I care to join her and her family one evening for dinner? I agreed, and a few weeks later I found myself driving out to a plush suburb in the Bay area. She had it all—the huge home, the swimming pool, the up-and-coming corporate husband, and three children. She was beautiful. The children were beautiful. The husband and house were beautiful. But her life was not beautiful—she was one of the most miserable people I have ever met. She was full of vague complaints and ill-defined medical problems. She had fallen in with a health-food cult and was eating nothing more than plates of nasty-looking grain, to try and restore her well-being. She began to tell me her story. You see, she never wanted to be married at all. She wanted to be a nun, but her mother wouldn't hear of this. Though the family were good Catholics, it's one thing to go to Mass on Sunday and quite another to take your religion seriously. No, it was out of the question for her to become a nun. And being the good girl she was, she obeyed. What a sadness, to see what she had become!

We need to make work a form of worship: we need to see work as an act of praise.

We need to work—not just at any old job, and not just for money. We need to make work a form of worship: we need to see work as an act of praise. We need to honor our inclinations and aptitudes and desires. For if we deny our own true nature, which has been given us from the beginning, we will inevitably feel a fragmentation of body and spirit. We need always, every day, to ask ourselves what is the ultimate authority in our lives, and surely the answer must come back that there is something higher we answer to than our boss. If we give ourselves in service to the Holy, our work will be "dedicated work" and will bless others and make our own lives good. We work in order to live, but not just physically. We work so that the life of the Spirit might thrive as well. It is not just words that praise God, but the feeding of the baby at the mother's breast, and the careful preparation of a legal document, the crafting of a piece of pottery, the building of a fence, and yes, the cleaning of the toilet. All this praises God.

I have two Gen-X sons who are trying to find their way, and they talk to me about their confusion and their longings. Work and love. It's always the same. I'd like to say to them—and I know I can't use this language, because they would just say, "Oh, Mom"—but I would like to say: Praise God with your body, care for it and honor it. Do no less with your mind. Give your gifts, and do what brings you joy, deep joy. Forget about making money just now—that will come. First find what you love and give yourself to it. Do work that will sustain you through the times when love is gone and the night is long. Do work you will not be ashamed to tell your children about. And do work that, when you come to finish this life, you can look back on and smile at, saying, "I enjoyed that, yes, I did, and I made the way a little easier for others."

SO BE IT. AMEN.

Prayer

O Spirit of Life, wake us up to possibility. Help us not to sleep through the main feature! We have been given so much—each one of us. May we cherish our gifts and inclinations as letters from the divine, instructions from the Holy. May we give ourselves to those endeavors that would lift us up and bless others. And may we help to create a nation in which everyone may find good work to do and everyone may live in plenty from their labor. AMEN.

Benediction

Go now, and work in love—and in astonishment.

Using Power Well

To love without taking possession;
To act without appropriating;
To excel without standing over;
This is called the inward
*   mysterious power*
Of those who live according to Tao.

—Lao Tzu

A STUDENT OF A MARTIAL ART FORM called aikido recounts his experience on a Tokyo subway some 20 years before the telling. Our car was comparatively empty, he says. A few housewives with their kids in tow, and some old folks. Then the doors opened, and the afternoon quiet was shattered by a man who staggered into our car bellowing curses. He wore the clothes of a laborer and was big, dirty, and drunk. Screaming, he swung at a woman holding a baby. An elderly couple scrambled toward the other end of the car as the drunk kicked at them. The train lurched ahead, the passengers frozen with fear.

I was young then, he remembers, and in pretty good shape. I'd been putting in a solid eight hours of aikido training nearly every day for three years. I thought I was tough. The trouble was my skill was untested in actual combat. As students of aikido, we were not allowed to fight.

"Aikido," my teacher had said again and again, "is the art of reconciliation. Whoever has the mind to fight has broken his connection with the universe. If you try to dominate people, you are already defeated." In my heart, however, I wanted an absolutely legitimate opportunity to save the innocent by destroying the guilty. This is it! I thought. People are in danger. I stood up. I planned to take this turkey apart, but he had to make the first move. I wanted him mad, so I pursed my lips and blew him an insolent kiss.

"All right!" he hollered. "You're gonna get a lesson." And he gathered himself for a rush at me.

A fraction of a second before he could move, someone shouted, "Hey!" I remember the joyous, lilting quality of it. Both the drunk and I found ourselves staring down at a little old Japanese man, sitting there immaculate in his kimono. He beamed delightedly at the laborer, as though he had an important secret to share. "C'mere," the old man said. "C'mere and talk with me." He waved his hand lightly. The big man followed, as if on a string. "Why the hell should I talk to you?" he said.

In American culture, power is most often expressed as force, as power over.

The drunk now had his back to me. If his elbow moved even a millimeter, I'd drop him in his socks. The old man continued to beam at the laborer. "What'cha been drinkin'?" he asked.

"I been drinkin' sake," the laborer bellowed. "And it's none of your business!" Flecks of spittle spattered the old man.

"Oh, that's wonderful," the old man said, "absolutely wonderful! I love sake, too. Every night, my wife and I warm up a little bottle of sake and take it out into the garden and we sit on an old wooden bench. We watch the sun go down, and we look to see how our persimmon tree is doing. My great-grandfather planted that tree, and we worry about whether it will recover from the ice storms we had last winter. We like to watch our tree when we take our sake—even when it rains!" He looked up at the laborer, his eyes shining with pleasure.

The drunk's face began to soften. His fists slowly unclenched. "Yeah," he said, "I love persimmons too . . . " His voice trailed off.

"Yes," said the old man, smiling. "And I'm sure you have a wonderful wife."

"No," replied the laborer. "My wife died." Very gently, swaying with the motion of the train, the big man began to sob. "I don't got no *wife*, I don't got no *home*, I don't got no *job*. I'm so *ashamed* of myself." Tears rolled down his cheeks; a spasm of despair rippled through his body.

Then it was my turn, recalls the student. Standing there in my well-scrubbed youthful innocence, my righteousness, I suddenly felt dirtier than he was. The train arrived at my stop. As the doors opened, I heard the old man cluck sympathetically. "My, my," he said. "That is a difficult predicament. Sit down here and tell me about it." I turned my head for one last look. The laborer was sprawled on the seat, his head in the old man's lap. The old man was softly stroking the filthy, matted hair. I had just seen aikido tried in combat

The story—adapted from *How Can I Help?* by Ram Dass and Paul Gorman—is about manifesting power. As human beings we will manifest power; there is no escaping that, no denying that. The only question is where that power is grounded, what is its source.

James Hillman, in his book *Kinds of Power*, reminds us that cultural determinants teach us what power is all about. In Italy and Japan power is largely defined as influence. In England power is still defined to a large extent by one's position in a class system: your accent and your manners determine your place. In some primitive cultures, power is secured by your relationship with spirits or ghosts. In American culture, power is most often expressed as force, as power *over*. Whether we are speaking of personal relationships, or corporate life, or foreign policy, we are interested in winning, in being on top. That cultural definition of power has had obvious and largely negative consequences: the overblown military budget; the frequency of rape and domestic violence; the right of citizens to pack deadly weapons. Our historical and literary traditions—the statues in our parks, the stories in our schoolbooks—tell us that the hero is one who wins against great odds by effort of will. "Power," says Hillman, "is persuasive force, muscular struggle, decisive command, productive result. . . . Power is imaged by the winner, even the slayer."

We see the abuse of power at every hand, in high places and in low. Bob Packwood fell from high political office, not because he liked women and was simply unskilled in approaching them, but because in spite of his considerable ability in oratory and in political maneuvering, he was a terribly insecure man who was tragically unaware of his own ego needs and how they drove him. He was a man who would write in his diary, "I tried blow-drying my hair in a natural way—that made me feel very confident." Bob, get a life! How pathetic! As with all people who really don't like themselves, his center of power was external to himself. Power was something "out there" that had to be grabbed at and manipulated. His sexual exploits were not about sex, but about "scoring"; not about wanting women, but about desperately wanting self-esteem.

And then there is the O. J. Simpson case. Talk about multiple levels of abuse of power! Think about it. The abuse began when blacks were rounded up and brought to this country on slave ships 200 years ago. From slavery, to Jim Crow, to the ghettos of despair in our cities today, symbolized in that trial by the L.A. Police Department. On any given day, a third of our young black men are in prison, in halfway houses, or on parole. One poll showed that only 2 percent of blacks believed Simpson should have been convicted of first-degree murder, whereas 60 percent of whites believed he should have. What this trial did was to absolutely lay to rest the belief that racism is no longer a live issue in this country, that it's over and done with. Simpson's acquittal was a vote against a system by a people whose experience has shown them the system cannot be trusted. The prosecution didn't have much of a chance, no matter what evidence they introduced: the system was on trial. Whites were on trial. Those deep wounds opened 200 years ago are with us still.

You see, sin begets sin. That's the way it is. The race issue shifted the emphasis from that of domestic violence. There was no doubt that Nicole Simpson was a battered wife. Each day, hundreds of women are battered and even killed by their husbands, lovers, boyfriends. The stronger one has the power. And power means force and control in our culture.

Then there is the issue of money and its relationship to justice. How could anyone in this country—whether black or white—come away from this trial without acknowledging the power of money in the courtroom? Without his power team, could Simpson have escaped conviction? What about all the people on death row in this country—are they there at least in part because they could not afford a Johnnie Cochran to defend them? What about our legal system? Is it effective in reaching just verdicts, or is it simply about smart lawyering and winning? So many abuses of power on so many levels were revealed by this trial. I hope that we will not turn away in cynicism, but that we will grow wiser than we are. That we will address the brutalities of racism that daily visit the lives of all blacks. That we will stop believing women are the property of men. That we will create a system of justice in which both black and white, poor and rich, will have a fair shot.

Given how power is seen in this culture, and given the frequent abuses of power, it is not surprising that the word itself is in some disrepute. You may hear people say, "I don't want power," or "It is wrong to seek power." Let's consider these statements.

In the first place, we all have power and we all seek power. To deny this is itself likely to lead to abuse of power, for such denial makes us unable to see how we hurt others. We become like a big German shepherd puppy that bounds into the living room, happily destroying every fragile thing in its range. I see this denial of power in particular in women, including myself. I think many of us have bought the cultural definition of power, and if power is force, then we want no part of it. Perhaps we should work on a new paradigm. What if we saw power as the ability to make change? It may be a change as large as the protest movement that brought the Vietnam War to an end—or it may be teaching an adult to read. It may even be something as simple as smiling at someone who has had a very bad day and saying, "You know, in my book, you're a great guy." Last Sunday, 321 of you signed a petition urging national political leaders to heal the gross economic divisions in this country. I believe these names will be noted, and I know that when enough voices join together to say these things, our leaders will listen. This is power put to good use.

We all have power and we all seek power. To deny this is itself likely to lead to abuse of power.

Perhaps we could begin to see power not as power over, but as merely using ourselves well in the world. Power doesn't have to imply competition or control; it can mean healing, transforming, leading, serving. To not use our power, in fact, is an abdication of the worst sort. It is looking the Holy One in the face and saying, "So you've given me these gifts? So what?" I believe we are obliged to honor our innate powers by developing them and by blessing the world with them. I believe this same principle applies to our institutional life as well.

This church is preparing to hire an architect to do preliminary drawings for the restructuring of our block. This is a project of some moment. I ran into a city architect at an arts festival recently and told him what we were up to, and he said this was one of the half-dozen most exciting urban church projects all over the country. I couldn't stop him from talking about it. He kept me a full hour. We still have a lot of work to do as a congregation in determining what we want on our block—we're not breaking ground anytime soon—but it is clear that we want to use the space not just for ourselves, but to serve the greater community. We will decide among many possibilities, including housing, social service agencies, performance space, day care, an after-school arts program. Owning this block in downtown Portland means we can exercise power—not power over, but power to give, power to witness, power to make positive change in our community. If we do this project right, we can be a model for other urban churches around the country. We have institutional power. And therefore we have responsibility. We should move ahead boldly and do what it is we are called to do.

For me, the most compelling image of real power is that of birthing, of giving life. As soon as I received the news of my pregnancy, I was given over to joy and to the new life within. I had to rest, to eat properly, for I was protecting this child, but these limits I gladly placed upon myself. As the time for the birth approached, I was awkward and ungainly; I had to get up frequently in the night for trips to the bathroom; I was easily fatigued. But my joy only grew stronger as I anticipated the birth. My labor started precisely on my due date, and I realized with a pounding heart that I was no longer in control of my body at all—it was completely given over to this little stranger. This relationship was not about equality, not about reciprocity. It was about submitting myself to the rhythms and needs of another. Power in this context is not about force or control or domination. It is about being an instrument of life, of losing one's self completely in service to the Holy. I understood for the first time what it is to love something more than I loved myself.

Perhaps our strength is at least partly found in our vulnerability, for it is often our very weakness that opens us to grace and healing, and our need that allows us to love and be loved. "Blessed are the meek, for they shall inherit the earth." What can that mean? Blessed are the humble, blessed are those who long for forgiveness, blessed are those who fear, blessed are those who care for the very young or the very old or the ill or the poor. *Blessed are the meek, for they shall inherit the earth.*

If power is to remain alive and vital, it must answer to its source and only to its source. It must return again and again to the spring from which it comes. This morning I admonish you: go bathe in living water. Your way will open before you, and you will begin to be aware of power you never before knew you had. When this power comes upon you, do not respond with pride, nor with domination, but with humility. Ask that you might be used to bless the world. And you, in turn, will be mightily blessed by the world, beyond all and any expectation.

SO BE IT. AMEN.

Prayer

O Spirit of Life, we acknowledge today—each one of us—that we are powerful. Help us never again, individually or collectively, to deny our power, for we know it is a gift we are called upon to use. May we never use power to aggrandize ourselves, but rather make ourselves a conduit for that living water that would call forth your blessing upon a parched and thirsty land. AMEN.

Benediction

Go now, both men and women, in the fullness of your power. Both can be strong and potent, both can birth new life.

American Icons: Marilyn Monroe and Elvis Presley

JANUARY 28, 1996

I saw that in our sensuality
God is.
For God is never out of
the soul.

—Dame Julian of Norwich

MARILYN AND ELVIS: two figures in American popular culture who are known simply by their first names. Marilyn died in her thirties, Elvis in his early forties, and so they remain forever young, forever etched in our minds as we knew them. As soon as Marilyn died, Hollywood tried to find a "replacement blonde," but others all fell short of her innocent sensuality. Elvis imitators abound, but they are just that—imitators, ludicrous at worst, and at best bringing poignance to memory. These two figures have become cultural icons—adored, placed on the altars of our cultural yearnings, sacrificed for our particular cultural sins. What can their short and tragic lives teach us about our values, our failures, our hopes?

To say that both Marilyn and Elvis had humble beginnings is an understatement; but gods often come into the world this way. This is an adaptation of Robert Gibson's narrative about Elvis's birth, from his 1985 book *Elvis: A King Forever.*

Elvis Aaron Presley lay in his mother's arms in the bedroom of a two-room wooden shack in East Tupelo, Mississippi. His brother Jesse lay in a cardboard box in the kitchen, stillborn. Mother and baby were both sleeping, exhausted by the ordeal of childbirth. The door to the kitchen opened and a tall, big-boned young man walked in, carrying a pail of water he had fetched from a hand-pump out back. He poured some of the fresh water into a bowl for the doctor to wash his hands. The two men talked, the small-town doctor and the part-time sharecropper. They talked of the birth, the health of mother and child, the future, and the fee. The father, Vernon, confessed he could not pay the $15 fee. He offered to work it off. The doctor nodded as he clicked shut his battered bag. He might not get paid in cash, but he would get paid. Vernon would mend his fence, paint his house, chop some wood. The doctor paused at the door. He looked at Vernon, who was slumped forward gazing into the fire. Gesturing toward the kitchen table and the cardboard box, he said, "I'll make the arrangements."

Both the mother and the father, Gladys and Vernon, came from poor families. They had married when she was 21 and he was 17. Early on, Vernon injured his back in a road accident, condemning the family to ongoing poverty; but the settlement did give them enough money to build the shack, 30 feet long, sliced in two by a chimney that provided heat for the bedroom and a stove for the kitchen. Needing money, Vernon and two friends later forged a check for which they received about $200, and Elvis's father was sent to prison for over a year. Gladys survived by taking in washing, sewing, cleaning houses, picking cotton. She was unable to have other children and so poured all her love and affection onto Elvis. She would scarcely let him out of her sight, walking him to school every morning until he was 15. When Elvis hit the big-time, the first thing he bought was a Cadillac for his mother—even though she didn't know how to drive.

What about Marilyn? She was born Norma Jean—she was illegitimate, as people said in those days. Her father had deserted her mother when he learned a child was on the way. Years later, when she was a successful movie star, she tried to get to know him, but he refused to have anything to do with her. Her mother, whose name was also Gladys, had a mental breakdown when Norma Jean was only five years old and went into an institution. Norma Jean's legal guardian was a woman she called "Aunt Grace," her mother's best friend, and at first Norma Jean lived with her. But then Grace remarried, the house became too small, and Norma Jean was placed in a Los Angeles orphans' home. She was nine. Later, Marilyn remembered, in these words: "[Aunt Grace] did promise me that as soon as she could, she would take me out of that place. She used to come and visit me often, but when a little girl feels lost and lonely and that nobody wants her, it's something she never can forget as long as she lives."

Norma Jean was in and out of foster homes. One of these was a boardinghouse where she was sexually abused, and when she tried to tell her story to her foster mother, the woman slapped her and shouted at her, "I don't believe you! Don't you dare say such things about that nice man!" Soon after that, she began to stammer. Movie directors found to their surprise that Marilyn sometimes stuttered when she felt uncertain or when she was criticized. As an adolescent, she lived with Grace's aunt, a woman she called "Aunt Ana," who became her protector. But that relationship, too, was short-lived—Aunt Ana was deemed too old to be her legal guardian, and so the only solution other than another foster home or the orphanage was an arranged marriage. Aunt Grace chose the son of a neighbor family, and he and Norma Jean went out for several months before they were married in 1942, a few weeks after Norma Jean's 16th birthday. The marriage was brief: photographers discovered Norma Jean's magical relationship with a camera, her modeling career took off, and young Jim Doughtery found that he had taken on more than he could handle.

Marilyn and Elvis: inauspicious beginnings. How is it that they captured the American imagination? What is it about them that embodied our core values? They had some things in common.

Both lived out the Horatio Alger myth, the American belief that even the poorest of the poor have opportunity here—that if you have merit, you can make good. Their working-class background, their poverty, the moral and spiritual failure of their people—none of this matters unless you allow it to matter. You can create your life anew.

Both embodied a kind of innocence that, again, is peculiar to American culture, the kind that Henry James explored in *Daisy Miller*. Both had a kind of wide-eyed response to the worldly sophistication of the milieu into which they were thrust. Neither had more than a high school degree. Elvis never stopped eating peanut-butter sandwiches (deep fried!), and Marilyn never lost the social awkwardness of Norma Jean. Ironically, the very innocence and naiveté that were so endearing left them open to misuse and abuse by the people who packaged and sold them in the entertainment industry. In becoming public figures we could worship, they failed to care for the fragile selves inside the image. The personae failed to respect the persons. And without that center of strength from which we all must go for sustenance, they were lost.

But it wasn't the innocence alone that was compelling—it was innocence combined with the sensuality so exhilarating to Americans in the '50s. After all, these were the days of June Allyson, the days of the Beach Boys. In popular culture, sexuality was expressed in the dark brooding of a James Dean or a Marlon Brando.

> *Ironically, the very innocence and naiveté that were so endearing left them open to misuse and abuse.*

But with Marilyn and Elvis, sex was "out there," and fun. There was no shame to it. Those of us in suburban homes, the boys in crew cuts, knew there was something much juicier to life than our parents were telling us about. The worship of Marilyn and Elvis came from a place much more visceral than we could understand or explain—it came from joy, from the life force, the *élan vital* that had been awakened within us.

Along with the sensuality, both Elvis and Marilyn had a childlike quality. Both were tender—"love me tender"—both easily hurt, anxious to please. Both had a yearning quality. Both were vulnerable and let that vulnerability be seen clearly in their faces—both had lips that quivered, eyes that were lowered. Yes, that's sexy, but it also characterizes the very young, the one unsure of things, who fears being hurt. We could see in Elvis and Marilyn these longings and fears within ourselves—our need to be loved, to be accepted, all the vulnerable places within, the pain of the abuse or the slap or the neglect, the material or spiritual poverty of our childhoods—all we have tried to keep hidden from others and even from ourselves. It was all there in the soft eyes and trembling voice: *love me tender*. In the vitality and promise of the body, connection is offered.

The promise of the body. Let's say some more about that. In this

133

culture we keep the body in the shadow. Our theological and philosophical heritage is that of the split between matter and spirit. Spirit, we have been taught, is all that is lofty and noble and airborne, all that is immortal; matter has to do with the earth, with flesh, with woman and all that is mortal, with death. The body, after all, is an avenue of pleasure, and our economic system demands that we eschew pleasure: pleasure is a distraction, is it not, from our work? From consuming? From being a good citizen, since being a good citizen in this culture is about working and consuming?

One of my sons says over and over that his goal is to work as little as possible. I have no doubt that he will find something creative and productive to do with his life—but he and many other Gen-Xers are asking themselves if it makes any sense at all to work themselves to death. It's a question worth considering. The promise of the body is pleasure. Not bought pleasures, but simple pleasures: good food cooked with care and tasted in leisure; a lovely flower in a vase; the feel of silk on flesh; a sinking down into a long, restful sleep. The body promises pleasure and connection. The young know that, and we have to work very hard to make them forget. Elvis and Marilyn remind us that we've put the body in the shadow, and they tease us back into consciousness.

They became cultural icons, onto whom were projected our own dreams and desires.

But what happened to these two? Why was it that neither ever knew love? Why did their stories end so tragically, both the victims of a certain kind of suicide—of alcohol and drug abuse? Why did they fail to find in their own lives what they invite in us? I think there are two major reasons. First of all, they were packaged and sold by people who wanted to make money; they were turned into products. Then they became cultural icons, onto whom were projected our own dreams and desires. Instead of loving our own bodies—which were not acceptable, since our bodies were so ordinary—we chose to worship theirs. We didn't want Elvis, the kid from the other side of the tracks whose daddy went to jail—we wanted the King, just the King. We didn't want Norma Jean, the orphan who stammered—we wanted the sex goddess.

And they, of course, bought into our projections. They needed the public as much as the public needed them. Marilyn said, "I knew

I belonged to the public and to the world, not because I was talented or even beautiful, but because I had never belonged to anything or anyone else." It is ironical that the sex goddess of the century probably never really enjoyed sex. Sex was what men did to her, by all accounts. "She was the compliant child-woman [who offers] sex without the power of the adult woman," says Gloria Steinem. "She allows men to feel both conquering and protective; to be both dominating and admirable at the same time." Marilyn found herself isolated from both men and women. Men made love to the symbol and not the woman, to the construct, not to the person. There was no room in the bed for Norma Jean. And women, of course, were threatened by her presence. Not owning our own power, in those days we women were still primarily competitors for males.

The single word most often used on film to describe Marilyn is that she had a "luminous" quality. *Luminous*—that which gives light. Where did this glow come from, a quality that drew both men and women and made all eyes turn to her whenever she entered the room? It couldn't have been beauty alone—there are many beautiful women, but there was only one Marilyn. I think about the word "numinous," so close to luminous—"numinous," meaning divine, mystical. I think of the halo around the heads of saints, around the head of the Holy Mother herself. I think Marilyn had the same kind of light. I think she never knew her own sacredness. And I think we could never know it either, because how could what is so sexy be so sacred?

Elvis, too, was destroyed by the projections and by the product he became. His was a combination of innocence and shyness, insecurity and paranoia. He allowed others, in particular Colonel Parker, to orchestrate his life, and it was a life no human creature could endure. The poet William Carlos Williams said, "The pure products of America go crazy"; and Elvis was such a product. He thought that money, sex, drugs, and yes-men could wash away doubt and fear. Of course they never can. But it didn't start that way.

His early influences were white country music, black gospel, and black blues. African Americans do not in their worship or in their music make the unhealthy split between body and spirit that is a given in white culture, and their music, both gospel and blues, was infused with an easy kind of sexuality. That is the quality Elvis brought to white music that has changed its character forever.

Elvis was also influenced by the revival preachers he heard in Tupelo. He said in one interview, "The preachers cut up all over the place, jumping on the piano, moving every which way. The crowd responded to them. I guess I learned from them." The overt sexuality of Elvis—Elvis the Pelvis, he was called—was frightening to good white church folk, and to parents and to TV producers. When Elvis was invited to be on the Ed Sullivan show, the TV camera showed his body from the waist up. I myself remember the excitement when Elvis came to Shreveport, Louisiana. I was about 14 and lived in a small town about 50 miles away. All my friends were planning to go to the show, but my father was dead-set against it. "That sexy thing!" he said. "I'll give you $15 if you don't go." I took the money and have regretted it ever since.

He thought that money, sex, drugs, and yes-men could wash away doubt and fear.

But it wasn't just the open, fun-loving expression of sexuality that drew people to Elvis. Elvis knew about need—theirs and his—and his own vulnerability drew him to theirs. It is reported that once in a concert he gave a scarf from around his neck, as he often did, to a young girl in the audience—a girl scarcely 12 or so. Then a hand reached out from somewhere and snatched the scarf from her. Elvis saw the grief on her face, and he stopped his band in midstream. From his neck, he took a favorite gold necklace inset with a precious stone and placed it around hers. "There yuh go, honey, that's just for you. Elvis Presley gave you that, and ain't no one can ever take that from you."

Marilyn and Elvis gave us what we wanted, and we worshiped them for it. They personified our longings, made us conscious of flesh, delighted us with their seeming joy, invited us to come close through their vulnerability. But they carried too much for too many, and the weight of it killed them. How could they dare to grow old and reveal their mortality? No, that would never do. Icons must remain icons, illusions must remain illusions. It's easier on us that way. No, they had to die. Otherwise we would have had to carry the weight of our own lives.

That is, of course, just what we are called to do. Love your own body. Trust the flesh. Trust pleasure and go where it will take you. Know that strength and vulnerability can coexist. Allow connection.

And understand that everyone wants a little tenderness—that in every life, there is more pain and terror and disappointment than one would ever guess. "Love me tender." Listen well. It's everybody's song.

SO BE IT. AMEN.

Prayer

O Holy One, we give thanks for joy and flesh and pleasure. Help us to love our creaturely selves, to carry the weight of our own lives. Give us the strength to live with less illusion and more hope. May we reach out in tenderness to all we come upon, most especially those from the wrong side of town. For love is really all there is. Bless us and keep us in that knowing. AMEN.

Benediction

From the poet Mary Oliver: "You do not have to be good . . . you only have to let the soft animal of your body love what it loves." Go in peace.

Meeting the Day with Courage

Living Like a Warrior

MAY 5, 1996

Inside, his heart is filled with peace;
Outside, he keeps his sword sharpened.
                    —Samurai warrior tradition

I HEARD AN INTERESTING EDITORIAL on PBS yesterday. It was by a man living in Sarajevo. He said he had just had his car towed from the main street, the street known as "sniper's alley." The street had acquired this name because so many civilians had been killed by sniper fire while walking down the street or stopping at red lights. It was more dangerous there than at the front. And now something simple and everyday and ordinary had happened—his car had been towed because of a parking violation. Back to normal. Yet he had to ask himself—and this is the fascinating part of the editorial—could he get used to a life this boring, after the excitement of war?

James Hillman is thinking in a similar vein when he asks the question, "Do we, as a species, need war?" He recalls a scene from the film *Patton*, in which the American general walks the field after a battle. Patton sees the ruined land, the burned tanks, the dead soldiers. He takes a dying officer in his arms, kisses him, looks over the scene, and says: "I love it. God help me, I do love it so. I love it more than my life."

What is this love, this love that is more than life itself—a love that calls to something strangely transcendent? What is this warrior role that soldiers remember with a joy found no other place, where they found a comradeship and willingness to sacrifice without equal? "It is

141

well that war is so terrible," said Robert E. Lee, "else we would grow too fond of it." Perhaps it is only in the midst of death, in the midst of this intense fear of not living, that we feel so alive.

War has existed as long as we have walked upon the earth. And there has been a special place for the warrior. The warrior was called out from the people, blessed by the shaman or by the priest; then he was ritually cleansed when he returned from battle, so that he could enter the tribe once again.

Somewhere along the way, that kind of warriorhood died. Perhaps it was during the Civil War, when brother warred against brother, and ranks of men were shot down at close range. Perhaps it was during World War I, when thousands of men were mown down with machine guns by men they couldn't even see. Or perhaps in World War II, when bombs brighter than the sun destroyed hundreds of thousands of civilians. Today there is no blessing, no ritual cleansing. You get your papers and 24 hours later, you step out of the plane and you're back home. Is it any wonder that thousands of Vietnam vets have committed suicide?

The warrior cuts through it all and stands there, poised, disciplined, unafraid of his power—or yours.

Let's talk about men for a moment, because traditionally males have been our warriors. They do sacrifice, they do act boldly, they put their lives on the line. But the honor is hard to find now. We send the poorest and the youngest off to die, too often for dubious reasons. Too often they are sent not to defend the weak and the innocent, but rather to defend the business interests of their country. Where do men go, then, with this warrior impulse? Many adopt the role of the shadow warrior. They become rebels—join gangs or militia movements. More commonly, they make the workplace a battleground, full of strategizing, conquering, controlling. Or they refuse the warrior role altogether and become passive, become invisible—the "soft males" spoken of by Robert Bly and other writers. Shorn of their masculinity, their ability to act decisively in the world, they shrink from the strength of women.

I see men struggling with their masculine identity. What does it mean to be a man nowadays? Because they have seen the shadow warrior at work—destructive energies unleavened by tenderness and

142

love—some reject that way of life. They don't want bullying or shouting or endless jockeying for position. But do they need to give up their boldness, their bravery, their strength? I was talking to a man about this masculine identity thing a while back, and I said that maybe it wasn't fair, but if we were walking in a dark alley and we were attacked, I'd like to think the man I was with could protect me. He said, "Well, I'd like to think that at least I wouldn't be the first to run."

The question I bring to you today is, How do we deconstruct war and deconstruct the warrior—for both men and women, since all human beings have masculine and feminine aspects of being? It appears that we need the god of war, who is also the god of awakenings, says Hillman. How can we be aware, awake, fearful, and ready? How can we be poised for action? How can we live life boldly, balanced and ready to sacrifice for the greater good? These are the ways of the warrior. How can we live like a warrior?

The warrior is in touch with his own woundedness.

Let me read to you from *Don Juan*, by Carlos Castaneda:

One day Don Juan asked me: "Do you think you and I are equals?" I was a university student and an intellectual and he was an old Indian, but I condescended and said: "Of course we are equals." He said: "I don't think we are. I am a hunter and a warrior and you are a pimp. I am ready to sum up my life at any moment. Your feeble world of indecision and sadness is not equal to mine." Well, I was very insulted and would have left, but we were in the middle of the wilderness. So I sat down and got trapped in my own ego involvement. I was going to wait until he decided to go home. After many hours I saw that Don Juan would stay there forever if he had to. Why not? For a man with no pending business, that is his power. I finally realized that this man was not like my father who would make twenty New Year's resolutions and cancel them all out. Don Juan's decisions were irrevocable as far as he was concerned. They could be canceled out only by other decisions. So I went over and touched him and he got up and we went home. The impact of that act was tremendous. It convinced me that the way of the warrior is an exuberant and powerful way to live.

Will, gesture, decision, action. That is the way of the warrior.

A warrior is present. A warrior shows up. Fully. Think about how seldom that happens in this culture. To show up, fully. To be really there, in all you are, and willing to be present as you are. What a gift, when it comes to us! It is so clean, so pleasing, so fearless, so deserving of respect! The warrior is balanced and focused. The warrior is able to listen, to be there, without needing your approval, and open to receive every part of you that you can bring to the encounter. Forget the chatting, forget the game-playing, forget the massaging of egos. The warrior cuts through it all and stands there, poised, disciplined, unafraid of his power—or yours. The warrior knows who he or she is and doesn't put on a face for you or anyone else. The warrior defends his boundaries and respects yours. You feel safe in the warrior's presence.

A warrior has enough self-respect that she will risk failing.

Simone Weil's mother disapproved of her activism with the French Resistance during World War II. Simone Weil simply said to her, "Mother, if I had two lives to live, I'd be glad to give you one. But I don't." And that was that. The warrior knows about death, knows how short and fragile life is, and knows that knowledge becomes the ground of authentic courage. Yes, I know that I can die, that I will die, and so life is ever so much sweeter, and I will not hang back in fear, but I will taste life fully. Around such a one opens a ground of freedom, a breath of sweetness, an invitation to fullness.

The warrior is aware of his anger. Every one of us is angry, because in this world we all experience loss and betrayal—when someone leaves or dies, when ideals are dashed to the ground, when the world's manifold injustices light upon us or upon one we love, when people are hungry or hurt or disrespected. If you are not angry, then you are not alive. If you are a man who denies your anger, you may become the soft male I spoke of earlier. If you are a woman, you may live wrapped in a cocoon of depression, waiting for your anger to transform you and give you wings to fly. But now, what does the warrior do with anger? She turns it around and redeems it. She blesses the world with it. Gandhi taught us about that, and Martin Luther King, Jr., who said: "Get angry, but don't get violent." Which is more difficult—to fight in the streets, or to go back to the segregated lunch counter day after day and get threatened and beaten and dragged off to jail? The warrior battles not with persons, but with evil. Again, the words of King: "Suffering is infinitely more powerful than the law of the jungle."

The warrior is in touch with his own woundedness. Have you ever noticed that people who do not know they are wounded are always bleeding on everybody else? When you know you are wounded, you can care for yourself, you can retreat from the fray and bind your wounds and rest. But if you don't know you're hurting, if you are too frightened to admit how hurt you are, then you become a dangerous animal. Never go after a trapped animal, you'll get hurt every time. I have learned to be wary of them, these hurt souls. They don't want to heal themselves, they would prefer that everyone else hurt too. They're vengeful, and they'll scratch your eyes out. But a warrior never fights for revenge; a warrior fights to defend the right, to protect the good.

The hardest battle we face is with outselves, with what we fear we may be or what we hope we will become.

A warrior is willing to take a stand, willing to act. Perhaps this is the essence of it—a warrior has enough self-respect that she will risk failing. Life is full of conflict and misapprehension. Anyone who acts will make mistakes, but the warrior is willing to be accountable—to say yes, I did that, and hey, I was wrong. Sorry. Which brings me to say that the warrior must be perpetually repenting, daring to be wrong, daring to be ignorant and foolish. And therefore having to forgive himself and be forgiven again and again. This life is full of paradox, and truth turns back upon itself; inside turns out, and back is front. There are two ways to go, and both cause pain. Be true to one principle, and end up false to another. The warrior acts nevertheless, and accepts the consequences of his action.

A warrior is fierce. Now that's a wonderful yang quality. Ferocity! The ferocity comes because something we love is at stake. We defend it with all our heart and soul. Listen to the fierceness in the voice of African American poet Audre Lorde as she writes about her breast cancer.

Well, women with breast cancer are warriors also. I have been at war, and still am. So has every woman who has had one or both breasts amputated because of cancer. For me, my scars are an hon-

145

orable reminder that I may be a casualty in the cosmic war against radiation, animal fat, air pollution, McDonald's hamburgers, and Red Dye No. 2, but the fight is still going on, and I am still a part of it. I refuse to have my scars hidden or trivialized behind lamb's-wool or silicone gel. I refuse to be reduced in my own eyes or in the eyes of others from warrior to mere victim, simply because it might render me a fraction more acceptable or less dangerous to the still complacent. . . . I refuse to hide my body simply because it might make a woman-phobic world more comfortable.

Audre Lorde is so fierce here, and so loving! Her words tell us that a woman must be more than "an externally defined sex object." That we must stop poisoning ourselves. That her breasts are beautiful, and she misses them, but she will love herself as she is, with her scars. Yes, she was a warrior, a great warrior.

Because a warrior honors and respects himself, he or she honors and respects others. He is modest, having no need to boast or to display his prowess. She has integrity—and by that, I mean that she is consistent with her words and actions. You can count on her; what she says is true, and she lives out of that truth every day—even when no one else is looking. He is gentle, and he can afford to be, because his gentleness rests in strength. He has nothing to prove, no one to conquer but himself.

Do we need war, as Hillman says? We need much that war brings to us and makes of us. We need to be disciplined and present. We need to be in touch with our anger, our ferocity. We need to know our own woundedness, and we need to acknowledge that we are marked for death, that we might live fully in the moment. We need to act, even when there is no clear way to go. Most of all—and I think this is what gives the warrior the strength to go on—we long to be in service to something bigger than ourselves, a transcendent purpose outside the self. A person can endure heat and cold and fatigue and poverty and pain if there is a reason, and if that reason is grounded in love and hope. The true warrior's life is organized around commitment to something he believes in and wants to serve.

So why aren't there more warriors around? Instead, why are there so many mere soldiers, following lock-step in line? Why do we deny our strength, our ferocity? Why do we not step out boldly? I'm remembering a scene from *Dr. Zhivago*, a movie I saw trillions of years ago. The Russian Revolution was beginning, and as I recall, there were mounted troops, the White Army (the Czar's troops, I take it), and the foot soldiers of the Red Army, both on the same side at first, but then the Reds turn on the Whites. Most of the Whites flee, but one White officer waves his saber in the air and tries to force the Reds back in place, and of course, he gets pulled off his horse and cut down. The friend I was sitting next to bent over and whispered to me, "I think I would have gotten down off my horse and mingled."

I think that's my biggest temptation—to get off my horse and mingle. Just fit in—don't stand out. People will notice and react. People might not like what I say or what I do. When you act boldly, you become a target, and there are always those who are ready to pull you down off your horse.

And then there's the desire for comfort. For escape, for ease. Oh, just eat another Snickers bar and forget about death. Forget about living well. Forget about the moment and all its realness. Forget about the face in the mirror. Forget about the dream last night, and drift off into illusion with whatever is your ticket out.

The hardest battle we face is with ourselves, with what we fear we may be or what we hope we will become. The bravest act of all is to be with ourselves as we are, to acknowledge all we are not, and to forgive ourselves and to love ourselves. As a person hating and pretending and judging and escaping—and dying, yes dying, that's the big one. When we are able to be with ourselves as we are, then we will surprise ourselves and our warrior nature will begin to unfold. We will have nothing to lose. If someone says, "You are arrogant and foolish," you can just say, "And that's not the least of it, you haven't seen anything yet!"

And the peace of the warrior comes to you. Because, you see, you have nothing to lose. Nothing is at stake. You are free to give yourself away. To serve the king, the anointed one. And oh what a freedom it is! Every day, you fall to your knees in thanksgiving.

SO BE IT. AMEN.

Prayer

We come today confessing our reluctance to act boldly, our refusal of our own strength. Forgive us and set us straight. May we stand upright, may our anger be turned to the work of justice, may we be fierce in our loving, may we protect the weak and innocent and not count the cost. May we, O God, in a world that needs warriors, agree to be present and to be counted. AMEN.

Benediction

Go now, and be true warriors all: be fierce, be bold, be gentle. Go in peace.

Slaying the Dragons

JANUARY 7, 1996

I call heaven and earth to witness today that I have set
before you life and death, blessings and curses.
Choose life so that you and your descendants may live.
— from the Torah (Deuteronomy 30)

WE ALL HAVE DRAGONS in our lives. Some are playful and friendly, like Pete's dragon, the lead character of a charming children's movie. One of my fondest memories is that of holding my two boys, all three of us with tears streaming down our faces, as Julie Andrews sings from the lighthouse to her long-lost sailor, "I'll be your light across the water." Pete's dragon saves the day, and the family is reunited. Then of course there is Puff the Magic Dragon—the Puff of Peter, Paul, and Mary—a dragon who delighted children on the one hand and those who puffed the forbidden weed on the other. These likable dragons are perhaps descended from the Orient, where dragons are a symbol of royal power and are benevolent.

In Western culture, quite a different picture emerges historically. In Christianity, the dragon is the embodiment of evil, closely identified with Satan and with the snake. *Draco*, the Latin source of the word "dragon," means "giant snake."

For hundreds of years, people actually believed in dragons. During the medieval period, they were considered an ever-present danger. A knight was not of the first rank until he had slain his first dragon. And so knights often came home from their quests with tales to tell.

In *A Connecticut Yankee in King Arthur's Court*, Mark Twain has this to say of them: "As a matter of fact, knights-errant were not persons to be believed—that is measured by modern standards of veracity; yet measured by the standards of their own time, and scaled accordingly, you got the truth: you discounted a statement 97 per cent; the rest was fact."

Well into the 17th century, learned men wrote learned accounts of the habits and appearances of dragons. In Europe, preserved "baby dragons" were fairly common in collections of curiosities. The Italian mathematician and physician Cardanus saw five dried "baby dragons" in Paris in 1557 and described them as follows: "Two footed creatures with wings so small that, in my opinion, they could hardly fly with them. Their heads were small and shaped like the heads of snakes, they were of pleasant color without feathers or hair and the largest of them was as large as a wren." In 1640 a book called *The History of Serpents and Dragons* was published by a man named Aldrovandi; it contained pictures that became models of the standard dragon as we know it today.

We seem to need monsters in our lives

Given the ludicrous nature of a literal belief in dragons, we might ask ourselves why the belief persisted for so long, and why the dragon took such a firm hold in our psyches. And not just in our culture, but in the Orient as well, in Africa, and in North and South America. We seem to need monsters in our lives—and the dragon is the greatest monster of them all. What does the dragon call forth from us, and why do we keep this creature so close to heart?

Well, for one thing, the dragon represents the presence of evil. We sense that there is such a thing, and too often we experience it. Unitarian Universalists don't much like to talk about evil, because too many of us have been guilt-tripped by religious authorities from our past: we've been told that the body is evil, pleasure is evil, other church doctrines are evil. Then there is the propensity of liberals to think of evil as just "bad upbringing" or "ignorance." But hang around long enough in this old world, read enough history and enough newspapers, see enough hostages taken—and we begin to suspect that evil does exist. In addition, we begin to understand that we ourselves have the potential to do evil. But because that understanding shakes us to our very bones, we human beings—in all times and in all lands—are prone to project it onto someone else. Onto people who are different in some way or another—in their skin color, their ethnic background, their religious beliefs. We demonize them so they can carry the weight of our soul's understanding. We make a monster, a dragon that needs slaying. And that of course calls for a hero. It is the externalizing of the dragon and the externalizing of the hero that is the problem. We need to understand that the dragons are chiefly within us, and that we must act as our own heroes.

Consider the dragon slayers of our cultural tradition: Beowulf, St. George, Siegfried, the Archangel Michael. These heroes are enlarged and enriched by the dragons they face. It is through battle that heroes find themselves coming fully to life, their qualities of courage and compassion being thrown into relief in the *gestalt* of combat.

The typical hero story includes a community at risk and a virgin chained to a rock. I don't know why a mother of four couldn't be chained to a rock just as well, but that somehow doesn't have the same appeal. (Who writes these stories, anyway?) The point here is that the hero is not just on a spiritual quest to ennoble himself—he is the representative of a community at risk. His deeds are done to preserve community. The virgin tied to the rock is, of course, unblemished purity and goodness.

In slaying the dragon, the hero not only gives himself sacrificially for the good of the community, but symbolically speaking, he unites the parts of his own psyche by facing the dark side, the shadow. The result is wholeness in the people and peace in the countryside: no more dragons roam, destroying innocence and goodness. People are free to work in their fields, to travel from one village to the next, to let their children play unencumbered by fear.

Now there's nothing wrong with having heroes—we all need them. And indeed there are people whose spiritual questing and self-sacrifice benefit the rest of us, those who give themselves for the greater good, those who epitomize honor and courage. And yet we need to remember that the aura around them, the larger-than-life quality, comes largely from our laying our own aspirations for goodness and bravery upon them. We so often let our heroes carry our nobility for us, thereby taking ourselves off the spiritual hook, so to speak. We look at others with admiring eyes, never understanding that we are able to see in them only the values that exist in our own selves, waiting to be nourished and developed, waiting to be given as good gifts to the community.

In *Murder in the Cathedral,* T. S. Eliot wrote

Of the men and women who shut the door and sit by the fire;
Who fear the blessing of God, the loneliness of the night of
    God, the surrender required, the deprivation inflicted;
Who fear the injustice of men less than the justice of God;
Who fear the hand at the window, the fire in the thatch, the fist
    in the tavern, the push into the canal,
Less than we fear the love of God.

We are as frightened of our capacity for goodness and beauty and nobility as we are frightened of our capacity for violence. It's easier to admire Mother Teresa than to love the poor ourselves. What will we be led to sacrifice? Are we afraid we'll actually become like Mother Teresa and wear robes and say rosaries twice a day and touch the broken bodies of the sick and dying? If we become too much like her, we might even stop believing in birth control! Such thinking is nonsense! We won't become more like Mother Teresa—we'll become more like ourselves. We won't have to say, "I could never be a Mother Teresa—I'll just admire her." We would be able to sense where compassion touches us, speaks to our own unique lives, and follow that leading. What would it cost to be your own hero? Do you fear that the cost would be too high?

What would it cost to be your own hero?

Two things go wrong, says Jungian Robert Johnson, if we project our shadow—our unowned parts—onto another. He says, "First, we do damage to another by burdening him with our darkness—or light, for it is as heavy a burden to make someone play hero for us." (That includes your minister, I might add. I don't want your goodness projected onto me—own it yourself. Otherwise, I'll surely let you down.) Second, says Johnson, "we sterilize ourselves . . . we miss the ecstatic dimension of our own lives. . . . If you can touch your shadow and do something out of your ordinary pattern," he advises, a great deal of energy will flow from it.

Lewis Carroll, in *Through the Looking-Glass,* describes a species of dragon:

"Beware the Jabberwock, my son!
    The jaws that bite, the claws that catch!
Beware the Jubjub bird, and shun
    The frumious Bandersnatch!"

He took his vorpal sword in hand;
    Long time the manxome foe he sought—
So rested he by the Tumtum tree,
    And stood awhile in thought.

And, as in uffish thought he stood,
    The Jabberwock, with eyes of flame,
Came whiffling through the tulgey wood,
    And burbled as it came!

One, two! One, two! And through and through
    The vorpal blade went snicker-snack!
He left it dead, and with its head
    He went galumphing back.

So where does this leave each of us, going now into a new year? Is there a Jabberwock out there? What are the dragons you need to slay? Like the heroes of old, you must go on the quest, in order to bring your goodness, your gifts, into bold relief.

Now, there are big dragons and baby dragons. The baby dragons will grow bigger if nourished by the fire-breathing, scorching hot, raging, tearing mama dragons. Those baby dragons are things like envy and idleness, overeating or overworking, overcharging on your charge cards, neglecting your friends, failing to keep the house in good repair—the usual things that turn up on lists of new year's resolutions. But these, I repeat, are just the baby dragons. The big dragons are two: one is called No-Meaning, and the other is called No-Love. They birth and nourish all the others. If you can slay them, you've got the whole nest.

These dragons are fearsome, for their wounds are never superficial: they go for your very soul. They growl and rage when they are aroused, and at night through their foul breath they whisper disturbing thoughts to you in your sleep. The papa dragon, the one called No-Meaning, tells you that life is just one long series of pains and losses and nothing really has any significance. He tells you that your gifts lack originality, and the work of your hands is not appreciated. He says also that upon your death, you will simply cease to exist, and that will be that—life is "a tale told by an idiot, full of sound and fury, signifying nothing."

And then the mama dragon, whose name is No-Love—her claws are even more fearsome, her breath more blinding, for she tells you that you are not worth loving. You've never been loved, and you never will be. You are alone, and that is what you deserve. In fact, there is something inherently wrong with you, and it can never be fixed.

In my own life, the dragon named No-Meaning is pretty much a goner. The jugular has been severed, and he's going fast. I have been blessed with challenging and creative work, a strong and capable staff, a healthy and wise congregation—all in a city that is beautiful and nurturing to my spirit. But meaning for me is not only attached to this specific work. I'm convinced in my heart of hearts that my every gesture and every word have meaning beyond what I could ever intend, that my call will continue to unfold, and that I am in service to something much larger than myself.

Whatever you disrespect in yourself, stop doing it, for strength to fight the dragon can only come from within, from a pure heart.

It's the other dragon, the one called No-Love, that tears at my flesh, trying to get at my heart. Oh, I know where that dragon sprang from—I've looked at the issues until I'm sick of looking, and now I'm sharpening my sword. I'm afraid, of course. Dragons are scary creatures. But I have already engaged No-Love in several skirmishes and have suffered only flesh wounds, as they say. I'm alive and well. And I have companions who are there beside me, who will not desert me in the battle. I understand that killing this dragon does not involve finding a knight to do it for me. I will wield the sword myself. I am strong enough. This is my quest, and I am committed to it.

And what about you? What is the dragon you will do battle with in the new year? Is it loss, or drink, or broken relationship? Is it failure? Is it illness? Is it bad habits and unfaithful friends? Forget will power, forget resolution. They will fail you, you can count on it. Instead, prepare yourself as a warrior. Practice your spiritual discipline. Treat your body like a friend: care for it, and make it strong. Whatever you disrespect in yourself, stop doing it, for strength to fight the dragon can only come from within, from a pure heart.

And as you go to defeat your dragon, remember that you defeat it for us all, for your community. You see, we need your courage to make us brave. We need the expression of your gifts to help us articulate our own. We need your loving presence so that we can walk about in our own skins without fear. Don't postpone this engagement. Sharpen your sword. We'll stand with you.

SO BE IT. AMEN.

Prayer

O Holy One, you have put the quest before us—each of us knows what he or she has to do. We pray for the courage to begin, we pray for tenacity when the dragon's breath is hot upon our neck, we pray for reinforcements when we need help in finishing the fight. We are thankful that when our own strength lags, we have a community of faith to sustain us. May it ever be so. AMEN.

Benediction

In this new year, may your blades go snicker-snack!

Just As I Am

FEBRUARY 12, 1995

No one ever told us we had to study our lives.
—Adrienne Rich

"JUST AS I AM, without one plea, but that thy blood was shed for me . . ." This is a hymn I am familiar with because I sang it Sunday after Sunday for years in the Southern Baptist Church. Each verse ended, "I come, I come." I come to Jesus. It was often sung at the end of the service, the time for decision-making. I would stand there singing, scared to death, for it was during the singing of this hymn that people walked down the aisle and gave themselves to "full-time Christian service."

Since women couldn't become ministers, that meant that if I got called, my call would be to the foreign mission field. I might have to go to China or Africa, and I would probably die of some strange disease whose name I couldn't even pronounce. Or I might be led to do something like write Sunday School literature—literature that explained to Baptist teenagers how Mary, who was a virgin, had the Baby Jesus. Or even worse, maybe I would be led to marry a minister and serve cookies and lead a life devoted to chatting. So when the choir sang "Just as I am, without one plea," I was praying, secretly, fervently, that I would not get a call.

Back then, I thought a call was something that came out of nowhere and forced a person to do what he or she least wanted to do. Now I see it differently: a call comes directly out of who we are and where we've been, and it is more likely to manifest itself in an ongoing inclination than in a heavenly stranglehold during a worship service.

Not that the Lord is averse to being heavy-handed at times when those he calls are reluctant. I love the Bible stories about the great men and women who were called and—in one way or another—responded, "Who, me? You've got to be kidding!"

Like Moses. After being presented with the burning bush and God's commandment to deliver the Israelites out of bondage, Moses first of all says, "Who am I, that I should go to the Pharaoh?"

God answers, "Just tell him I sent you."

"But—excuse me—who exactly *are* you?" Moses asks.

And God says to Moses, "I AM THAT I AM." I can just imagine Moses thinking to himself, "Oh great, that helps a lot: 'I am who I am'!"

Then Moses tries a new tack: "They won't believe me," he says. So God gives him a magic stick that turns into a snake. Even then Moses tries to slip out by suggesting that God consider his brother Aaron, who after all was more eloquent.

God says, "I *know* Aaron can speak well. He's going to be your PR man." So at last Moses reluctantly agrees.

Then there is Sarah, the long-barren wife of Abraham. God tells her she is to bear a child, and she laughs at him, because she knows she is way beyond child-bearing age, and Abraham is no spring chicken either. Yet Isaac is born. God's promise comes true.

We all remember Jonah, the procrastinator. "Sure, sure, I'll go down to Nineveh, Lord, and deliver your prophecy—but *later*. First a few side trips—" And he ends up in the foul, dark belly of the whale and has to be vomited up to do his work. Well, some of us have to learn the hard way.

Even Mary, the mother of Jesus, wasn't too pleased to see the angel in her bedroom in Nazareth. "Hail, O favored one, the Lord is with you!" the angel said. But Mary "was greatly troubled at the saying," the scripture reports. "How shall this be, since I have no husband?" she asks. A good question! At least she had a fiancé. That's a start.

Who knows why these particular people were called to holy service? They were, after all, ordinary people with ordinary fears and concerns, people who lacked confidence in themselves and who lacked vision at times. I suspect that they often had doubts about success. But they were ultimately available to be used for God's purposes. "Thy handmaiden awaits," said Mary. That's the key: *Thy handmaiden awaits.*

I used to think that great men and women had achieved greatness because they were special people with extraordinary intellect, many talents, and superior emotional and physical health. That's hardly ever the case, actually.

Think of some of the outstanding figures in our own movement: Joseph Priestley, the great scientist and father of English and American Unitarianism, had a tendency to stammer in public speaking.

A call comes directly out of who we are and where we've been, and it is more likely to manifest itself in an ongoing inclination than in a heavenly stranglehold

Hosea Ballou, the Universalist leader, was virtually self-educated. He so lacked confidence in public speaking that the first time he was to preach, no words at all came forth. The second time was not much better. Yet he is said to have been the most influential religious figure in 19th-century America.

And William Ellery Channing. Channing hardly weighed more than 90 pounds fully dressed and was in poor health virtually all his life. His large, luminous eyes and pale cast made him appear angelic and almost ready for his heavenly home. He hated controversy—yet he was in the forefront of the abolitionist movement.

In our modern period, the person I think of is Martin Luther King, Jr., not a Unitarian Universalist, of course, but a Baptist. This young man was catapulted into the leadership of the civil rights movement, not because he was bright and articulate and charismatic—which he was—but chiefly because he was a man given over to purposes larger than himself. Blacks chose him, history chose him, God chose him, and he accepted his call, even though he knew early on the price he was to pay.

Well, what about you and me? Do only religious leaders have calls? Or is everyone "called" in one way or another? Personally, I think everyone is. *The call is the point at which a person's inclinations, talents, and deepest desires intersect with the demands of time, place, and circumstance, to serve the greater good.* Sometimes I have people come into my office, plop down on the sofa, sigh, and say, "I need to make a change—what should I do?" My own sons are asking that same question. I like the answer given by Teresa of Avila: "Do what most kindles love in you." *Do what most kindles love.*

For each one of us, that call is different and special, and for each of us, it is a challenge to bring forth the best, the fullest flowering, of which we are capable. But we have our excuses: it's easier not to respond so fully to life, but to drift on through, to do the ordinary things that are expected, to take the easy way, and not to accept the larger challenges that pull at us. Like Moses, we say, "Someone else is more able." Like Sarah, we disbelieve and laugh at our deepest longings, saying, "It's too late for that—I'm too old." (Or too *whatever.*) Like Jonah, we postpone, saying, "Next year I'll do it—not right now." Like Mary, we are frightened, and we pull back from the pain of birthing the sacred in ourselves.

These responses are natural and understandable, because to live fully and richly out of one's deepest self is difficult. For one thing, it brings trouble in the world: you don't "fit in" so well. Besides, dependency is very enticing. Somewhere in each of us is a child who wants nothing more than to be at mother's breast. Really growing up, reaching out for spiritual maturity, is exacting. It requires effort and discipline and courage. Then why bother?

I'm not sure I know the answer to that question. Maybe just because it's there for us to do—the flowering, I mean. Let us consider an analogy. When I grow tomatoes, I want the plants to grow large and strong and the blooms to come and the blooms to turn into little green buttons and the little green buttons to grow into heavy, red, ripe tomatoes. Sometimes lack of water or nutrients will stunt the plants' growth. Sometimes a storm comes and tears off blossoms or breaks stems. But those tomato plants reach out for the sun and rain and give it all they've got. I feel satisfied when I pick the tomatoes, and I feel satisfied when I pull the dead brown stalks out of the ground at the end of the season.

I used to have a recurring fantasy about an afterlife—a kind of hell, if you will. I see a woman standing in the distance, her back to me. I move closer and closer to her. Then she turns suddenly, and I see myself as I might have been if I had said "yes" to myself, to the divine potential in me. I see the face I might have had, and the eyes, and I fill with the agony of regret.

"Just as I am, without one plea." *Just as I am.* Uniquely myself, with all my frailties, and yet given over to something much larger than I—the self-same Mystery that sustains and strengthens me along the way. To be given over! That's my prayer today and every day, and that is my only prayer.

SO BE IT. AMEN.

Prayer

Sometimes it's hard to find the way, O God. Often we head off in the wrong direction, or stumble, or get lost and find ourselves in a dense woods without a compass. Help us to understand that we must only stop and listen patiently, and we will find our way. Guide each one of us on our journey, and bring us to a place of peace and joy and satisfaction. AMEN.

Benediction

May we—each one of us—walk in the knowledge of our own true worth, and may we give freely out of the abundance of our lives.

On Loving and Learning

APRIL 4, 1993

Love opens the doors into everything, as far as I can see,
including and perhaps most of all, the door into one's
own secret, and often terrible and frightening, real self.
—May Sarton, *Mrs. Stevens Hears the Mermaids*

IT NEVER OCCURRED TO ME that I might fail as a teacher. The structured security of the classroom had always been pleasant to me, and before I had finished elementary school, I knew I would become a teacher.

I did become a teacher, a high school English teacher, and took my first job in New Orleans, teaching at a school for gifted children. I loved it, as I knew I would. But in my seventh year of work, my life changed dramatically: I married a young surgeon and moved with him to Liverpool, England, where he was to do a residency. I scuttled around and got a job—the only unfilled position for an English teacher in all Liverpool. I soon found out why.

It was a class that had lost teacher after teacher, for they were considered an impossible group. You see, in England, at least at that time, children were "streamed," or put into groups according to ability at a very early age. This class was the eighth stream out of eight, so they had been labeled as the poorest of students. They were sixth-graders—30 of them, in a school for boys. Never mind that I had studied secondary education and not elementary—in England, the headmaster said, if you have a teaching certificate, you are supposed to be able to teach at any level. So in I went, like a lamb to the slaughter.

The first day went well. I didn't know enough to be afraid. I started by answering their questions about the United States.

"What does a dollar look like, Miss?"

"Hey, Miss, does the policemen over there really carry guns?"

"Do ye know any hillbillies, Miss?"

"Are there lots of gangsters, Miss?"

Their main source of information about the United States was American television, so in their minds America was just one vast shoot-out. They thought I talked just like the characters in "The Beverly Hillbillies," and they were always asking me to repeat words or phases they didn't understand. They mocked me: "Boys," I would begin. And one would take it up: "What's 'at, Miss? Boy-eeez!" Then another would try to imitate, "Boy-eeez! BOY-EEEZ!" until the whole class was almost hysterical with laughter, pounding their desks and rolling their eyes. Of course they spoke a very heavy Liverpudlian dialect that I couldn't understand—so basically we could hardly communicate, and I was supposed to be teaching them English. One of them finally told me outright in class one day that I had no business teaching them English. "After all, it's our language," he said.

I needed a familiar retreat, but there was no sanctuary. Nothing went the way it should, and my assumptions and expectations were being overturned at every hand. I assumed, for example, that all my 11-year-olds would be able to read. But about a quarter of them could not. I tried out the language exercises in the text and found that the students could not master the instructions. Most could not write a complete sentence. We put away the text, and I determined to devise my own curriculum. I went home that night in tears, the first of many times, and asked my husband, "What does an 11-year-old boy like?"

"Camping," he answered, thinking back years to his boyhood. "Camping and snakes and building fires. Let's see," he paused. "Cleaning rifles. Jungle animals. And cars and airplanes." Of course, being an 11-year-old in the middle of Liverpool, England, was somewhat different from growing up in a small town in Kentucky 30 years before, but nevertheless, my husband gave me some inkling of direction. I was determined not to fail.

I studied the other teachers, trying to learn how they handled the boys. One was Mike Williams, who taught history to the lower streams. Mike, who had come to the classroom via the British Navy, was a gruffish man. He was very woolly, having let his hair grow long and his full beard flourish untrimmed. He taught by issuing rapid-fire commands and then by punishing laggards.

One morning Mike spotted one of his homeroom members wearing a white shirt with a dirty collar. As the unwary boy walked past Mike, he was suddenly lifted about a foot off the floor by his lapels, his spindly figure dangling helplessly in the air. Mike lectured him for about 30 seconds then released him abruptly. "Yes, Sir," was all I heard the boy say.

Mike was the most popular teacher in the school, at least in the lower streams. He ran his classes as if the students were sailors engaged in an emergency drill on shipboard. He demanded order and neatness above all. On his ship everyone must at least try to produce quality. After school and sometimes in the evenings at his home, he played war games with any boys who dared to challenge him. It was always the English against the French, their traditional enemy. Over the years Mike and the boys had made and collected hundreds upon hundreds of miniature soldiers, some on horseback, some with swords aloft, some hoisting flags, some firing cannons, some marching in colorful ranks. Mike always led the English troops, and the English always won. Since Mike made up the rules as the game went along, he did have considerable advantage.

The boys loved him, and I think the reason was that he cared enough about them to demand that they conduct themselves honorably.

The boys loved him, and I think the reason was that he cared enough about them to demand that they conduct themselves honorably. Not much was expected of these boys usually, and so self-respect was hard for them to come by.

As for me, each day it was the same. I would walk into the classroom determined to be confident, dead-set on being cheerful. Inside, I felt like stone. Armed with carefully worked out lesson plans and rigid resolve, I soon crumbled in the face of the students' demands. They didn't want what I knew about grammar and literature. They wanted me, first, to be strong, and second, to care enough about them to provide a discipline. They kept asking me, in one way or another, to give myself. No one can really tell another how to teach. Teaching is an engagement of personalities, not a passing on of information, and for such an engagement, one prepares heart as much as head. I felt I should love them, that they needed me in a way no former students had. But I was afraid of them, and I hated them.

I would start by calling the roll. "Abrahamson?"

"Here, Miss."

"Brown?"

"Here, Miss."

"Bustrow?"

Bustrow was a hell-raiser. He was known to all the school for his misdeeds. Once he stole £150 from his grandmother and passed the money out to his school friends. Bustrow had a chunky little body and a chunky little red face. He invariably had food—gravy or chocolate or custard—smeared round his mouth, and his hair stuck up in uneven patches. Whenever he laughed, I wanted to hit him. I did hit him. I made him write lines, made him stay after school, shamed him, and threw him out of class countless times. I bribed him, coddled him, teased him, talked motherly to him. Still, every day, Bustrow turned my classroom upside down. He started fights, he stole pencils, he threw spitballs, he told lies. He was my bad boy.

Teaching is an engagement of personalities, not a passing on of information, and for such an engagement, one prepares heart as much as head.

After roll-call, I began the lesson.

"Today I thought we would talk about jungle animals." I tried to say it as though I were fascinated by the topic, but I guess my boys knew what was going on inside me. I wanted to be away from them. If only I could get away. "I could quit," I thought. But then how would I ever be able to face a class again? How would I ever be able to face myself again?

"What is the largest jungle animal?" I asked. "Who knows?"

"The elephant, Miss."

"Yes, that's right. Think about that. He is so large that he is in no danger from any other animal. All the other animals are preyed upon by larger beasts. Only the elephant is not in danger."

"Tigers attack elephants, Miss," Peter says.

"Are you sure about that?" I ask, very much in doubt.

"Yes, it's true, Miss. They do. They get up in a tree and when the elephant passes below, they jump down on his back and bite his neck. A big tiger can kill an elephant like that."

I back down because he acts so sure of himself, and what he says seems logical enough. I try to picture the scene in my own mind: the elephant lumbering through the jungle, and the hungry tiger leaping on his back. Maybe Peter's right . . .

A furious argument breaks out in the class over whether or not tigers can kill elephants. I think the boys are putting me on, but I can't be sure. I retreat further, and the din grows louder and louder. I can't hear it, though. It's as if I'm just viewing this melee and am not a part of it at all.

"Mrs. Sewell. Mrs. Sewell!"

I looked up and was startled to see the science teacher from across the hall. "Excuse me, Mrs. Sewell," he said, and turned to my class. Abruptly, the noise and scuffling stopped. The boys sat quietly and turned their eyes to the front. "You boys are making so much noise that my class cannot carry on with their lessons. I will not have it. Am I understood?" My boys settled into a sullen silence for the remaining ten minutes of the period, reading or writing out their homework. I stood staring out the window. The day was cold and gray. When the bell rang and the last boy had rushed away, I sat down at my battered, dusty desk, put my head on my folded arms in front of me, and cried until no more tears would come.

As I was about to close the door on the disarray and leave for the weekend, I saw Joseph coming up the steps.

"What are you doing here, Joseph?" I asked the boy.

"I missed the first bus, Miss. Do ye need me to 'elp ye dust the erasers?"

"Yes, Joseph, I wish you would help me. Come on in." I turned to go back into the room. "I was feeling . . . too tired to tidy up the room by myself."

Joseph was my special pet. The headmaster had told me not to expect much of him, saying that he was perhaps the dullest boy in the school. He sat quietly in the last desk in the second-to-last row of the class. His written work was indecipherable. He misspelled words so badly and ran words together so often and punctuated so randomly that no one could read what he had written. His speech was slow. He hardly ever said anything in class, and when he did, the other boys laughed at him. But he always listened and tried to do as I asked. He liked me, I knew, for whenever I spoke to him or touched his blond head, he smiled up at me. His large gray eyes were guileless and open, and he never seemed hurt by the laughter or discouraged because of his mistakes. I don't know what gave him the will to keep on working with so little success day after day. Perhaps it was his mother. There was someone who cared about him at home, for he was rarely absent, his face was invariably scrubbed, and his clothes were pressed.

I saw his mother once at a school soccer match. She was thin, and she was wearing one of those shapeless woolen coats that British working-class women wear. Her hair was covered with a cheap flowered scarf, tied under her chin. We were standing in about an inch of mud, watching our varsity squad lick the winded staff team, when I spotted Joseph standing nearby. "'At's 'er, Mum," I heard him say, and a woman stepped closer to speak. She told me "'ow much Joe enjoyed 'is English class." I wanted to tell her that I loved Joseph, because I did love him, but I only remarked that he was improving with his work right along. And it was true. He was perhaps my one success. By the end of that semester, he was able to write short, simple sentences of his own.

There was someone who cared about him at home.

After what seemed an endless length of time, school was almost out. On the last day, my boys begged me to let them act out a play they had written; it was about two rival groups known to all Liverpool youngsters, the skinheads and the greasers. Bustrow showed more enthusiasm than anyone else, and the plot was chiefly his: a group of greasers are inside a confectioner's shop, enjoying some sweets. They are approached by a gang of skinheads looking for trouble. After a few threatening words and gestures, the two gangs have at each other until a policeman comes along and breaks them up. Bustrow and company asked to go to the auditorium to act out their play, where they would disturb no one, they assured me. "What can I lose?" I thought to myself. This was the first project Bustrow had shown any interest in, and I was reluctant to quash his enthusiasm.

I lined the boys up and walked them down to the auditorium. We had just begun putting some chairs together for a makeshift set when I heard the sounds of many marching feet. I peeked out of the curtain to see the auditorium filling with students. Noting the headmaster standing to one side, I asked him what program was about to begin. He explained that his secretary had told him I was presenting a play today (I had cleared the use of the auditorium through her), and since many of the teachers had to be in meetings, their students were being sent to the auditorium. Wasn't it fortunate that my class had prepared an entertainment, he said.

"We haven't really rehearsed that much . . . ," I started, but he cut me off with a smile.

"Go right ahead with what you've planned, Mrs. Sewell. We'll all be interested to see it."

I turned and walked back to my boys. "Oh God, how did I get myself into this?" I thought. Hurriedly, I gave the young actors a few whispered instructions then stood back to watch from the wings. About 500 boys, several teachers, and the headmaster were waiting expectantly as Joseph opened the curtain.

The boys did everything wrong: they mumbled their lines, they turned their backs to the audience, and they shuffled their feet. Then they began to push and shove one another and finally to fight, as the script called for. They fought with great gusto and seemed to forget they were in a play. They ended up in a big heap in the middle of the stage. The whole play took about five minutes, of which three and a half minutes were taken by the fight. I wasn't sure what to do next, so I let them repeat the scene. They went through it again and again, some eight or ten times in all. Each time the fight became longer and more enthusiastic and more realistic. Finally, after an agony of time passed, I was released by the bell. No prizefighter being smashed to bits by his opponent could have been happier than I to hear the ringing of the final bell to end that semester.

I decided to stay barefoot and pregnant for a long time after that experience. I had two babies sixteen months apart and spent the bulk of my time for the next ten years raising them. Teaching once again became part of my life, though it was teaching adults in a university setting. For years I thought of the teaching in Liverpool as an absolute failure. But you know, I don't believe that now. You see, I could have been one more teacher who left them, but I didn't. I didn't desert them. I'm proud of myself for that. When I think of Joseph, he's still the little boy I left in Liverpool, not the 32-year-old man he must be by now. I wonder about his life, who he's become, if he's happy. It's strange. For years, long after I returned to the States, I sometimes thought I saw my little Liverpool boys. I would see one moving in a crowd or riding by in a car or standing in a crowded elevator before the door closed. Then I would look again and realize I was mistaken. I missed them very much, I think. I think I loved them, and I didn't even know I could.

SO BE IT. AMEN.

Prayer

Let us think upon the children we know, the ones who have been entrusted to us by birth or adoption or by teaching or perhaps just by living in our neighborhood. As we teach, whether in the classroom or in the home, may we understand that the strongest lessons come from our hearts, come from who we are in relationship with a child. May each child who knows us hear from our whole being, "You are worthy. You deserve to be loved." AMEN.

Benediction

Bless the children in your lives, and bless the child in each one of you.

Wise Teachers, Changing Lives

JUNE 2, 1996

*We teachers can only help the work going on, as servants
wait upon a master.*

—Maria Montessori

I WAS TALKING to my younger son Madison the other day about
his future, his goals. You know the kind of talk I mean. He has his
undergraduate degree and is trying to decide what to do next. He said
to me, "You know, Mom, I'm just going to apply to a lot of different
schools in different subjects and see who will give me money to go to
school. I'm going to stay in school as long as I can. That is my goal."

I can understand that. Like mother like son. I have spent half my
years as a full-time student. Along the way I've had many teachers
who affected me in some way or other. Several changed the course of
my life.

My first-grade teacher was Miss Cady, a tiny woman with white
hair in a bun on her head. Miss Cady took children into the coat closet
and paddled them when they were naughty. In the third and fourth
grades I went to Holy Name, where I was taught by nuns, swooping
black ravens with white circling their faces. They gave me pastels to
draw with and listened to me recite my catechism. "Who is God?"
"What is the Trinity?"

Then there was my fifth-grade teacher, Mrs. Crump. She liked
the stories I wrote, and she noted on my final report card, "I hope to
see some of your stories in print one day." Funny, how some teachers

set you to dreaming bigger dreams than you could ever dream alone.

In the sixth grade I was planning to sing in the school choir for our Christmas program. But during rehearsal, Miss Linton, a cadaver-like teacher, stopped in front of me and bent down to listen. She then said to the music teacher, "You're not going to let *her* sing, are you?" and I was removed from the choir a day or two before the program. A neighbor had just made my choir robe for me. That really hurt. I can tell you that at this church, we will never tell a child, "You can't sing in the choir." Some teachers tell you you can't, and sometimes you believe them.

High school was something of a black hole for me. I was too tall, too smart, too prudish, and besides had those horrible 1950s glasses, a poodle haircut, and very bad skin. I loved school—it was my refuge. And reading was a way into a larger world than this little northern Louisiana town allowed. There were stories that made me laugh and weep; there were places where people believed in other gods with strange names; there were cities like Paris, where as Mark Twain said, "Everybody, even the children speak French." So—no football player would ever ask me out. But that was all right. I had hope. I knew this other world was out there, and I would be a part of it one day. My teachers liked me because I loved ideas, loved to learn. That's a crucial thing, for a child to be liked. No wonder I loved school so much.

I sought out the very finest teachers, not only those who were the most knowledgeable and skilled, but those who respected themselves.

By this time I was a Southern Baptist and going to Sunday School and Training Union and Youth Choir and Youth Group. I practically lived at the church, as did all my peers. I think of our youth here at this church, and I want for them the same kind of safe place to come and learn how to be responsible, caring adults. As a teen, my church teachers were there for me. Miss St. Claire, tall and stately, who married a rotund widower when she was in her '40s and had a baby in the nick of time. She was our choir teacher. Miss Altalene, a saintly woman who took care of her parents and so never married. She taught us scripture and waited on us when we went to White's Dry Goods. Mrs. McKinley, who tried to convince me that Jesus at the wedding feast turned the water into grape juice and not wine. I didn't buy that one! Again, I felt cared about. I had a place. It was largely my teachers, at school and even more particularly at church, who provided the center of warmth and safety that invited me to grow. Roots hold me close, wings set me free. These are my roots, these are my wings. I know it, and I am thankful.

I attended five different colleges and had many teachers who nurtured me along. I had a few confrontations along the way, like with the teacher who dismissed class so that we could watch Kentucky play a basketball game, and the teacher who gave the same final exam every year, and the teacher in seminary who dismissed the comments of his women students. I spoke, I tried to change things. These teachers did not like me.

He was his own man, and clearly in service to something larger than himself.

As I grew older and wiser, I sought out the very finest teachers, not only those who were the most knowledgeable and skilled, but those who respected themselves, for those are the teachers who are free to give to another. The ones who do not like themselves are busy shoring up their flagging egos. Unable to see their own beauty, it is impossible for them to see beauty and goodness in another. They'll get you every time.

One of the finest teachers I was ever privileged to study with was Wendell Berry, the Kentucky poet, essayist, and fiction writer. Wendell is a farmer, and his understandings about the environment and the centrality of community come from his connection with the earth. I first encountered Wendell back in the 1970s when I was a young wife and mother in Lexington, Kentucky. My boys were little, two and three, and I was trying to be a good Southern woman, married to a surgeon. That meant that I didn't work outside the home, and I didn't rock the boat. I gave dinner parties and smiled a lot. In short, I was going crazy. I decided to take a class at the University of Kentucky—a writing class. I wanted to cash my writing skills in on a few ego chips, since my head had turned to solid granite, and I badly needed to feel adept, to stop swimming upstream, to be valued for merely following my natural inclinations.

I was in for a surprise. I knew little about this teacher Wendell Berry—he was just beginning to be widely known. But as soon as our first class met, I knew he was a force to be contended with. On the surface of things, he was not imposing—tall and lanky, dressed in flannels, speaking with a distinctly Eastern Kentucky accent. And yet he had a remarkable kind of presence. He was his own man, and clearly in service to something larger than himself. Even then, Wendell had the feel of an Old Testament prophet—he spoke the truth, from the center of his being. Others sensed this presence too, and for some it was frightening—the class rapidly dwindled to half its original number.

For my opening gambit, I reviewed one of his books, *The Memory of Old Jack*, for the local newspaper—"Ha, take that!" I thought. The first paper I turned in was a long, judgmental essay on examinations. The subtext, I now realize, was, "You think *you* can evaluate *me?*" When I got my paper back, there was no grade, but rather a blanket rejection of my carefully constructed, perfectly punctuated sentences. Wendell said, in effect, "You don't know what you're talking about. Where is your authority to make these statements?" I couldn't believe what was happening. I just stood there clutching my paper and cried, a lot. Wendell was uncomfortable, and all I could say was, "I don't know what to do, I don't know what to do." The beginning of wisdom. This experience was not what I would call an ego boost. But then Wendell fancied himself a writing teacher and not the school psychologist.

All that semester Wendell kept sending my papers back. I knew he was right, but I wasn't ready to articulate the change, to do what he was pushing me to do—to give something of myself. It was easier to present that detached, ordered intellectualizing that was the formula for success in the usual school paper. I starting visiting with him in his office, and every time I went, some tenderness in me felt exposed. I would talk about myself and often cry, and he listened with interest, always. I got the feeling that he thought I was worth something. I kept writing.

My other teachers had all told me how good I was. Wendell was the only one who told me how bad I was. And he is the only one who taught me anything about writing. You tell the truth about what you know. That's all. And that's the most difficult thing in the world.

Finally the last day of class came. It was December, and there was snow on the ground. I had been up all night, literally, in a last-ditch effort to write something that was honest. I finished typing at 8 a.m. with Kash, my elder son, sitting on my lap. Then the babysitter failed to show. What to do? Something inside told me I had to be in class that day, so I dressed the two boys in their warm jackets and put them in the back seat of the fire-engine red Volvo. I took them to the hospital, parked in the emergency spot, and went up to the fourth floor, to surgery. I gave the boys to the nurses, said, "Dr. Sewell needs to take care of his sons this morning," and left. Now I don't want you to think I did things like this all the time—in fact, I never do things like this: I am generally nauseatingly responsible. But I knew I had to be in class on that particular day.

We sat around a table, in a circle. I always sat just to Wendell's left. He went around the circle, asking each in turn if anyone wanted to read. Everybody refused, including me. I hadn't even had time to proofread what I had written, and I had no

I had touched these individuals, I knew, by simply revealing who I was.

confidence that it was any good. I only knew that I had tried my best to tell the truth about myself.

On the second go-round, I tentatively agreed to read, and the floor was mine by default. I read about my failure as a teacher in Liverpool, about my depression, about friends who tried to help but couldn't, about a husband who loved me from a distance, about my pregnancy, about giving birth. As I remember, I cried during the whole reading of this 20-page paper, and I did not once take my eyes from the paper. When I finished, I threw the paper across the table at Wendell and said, "Here, that's what you wanted."

Then I looked up uneasily to see how the other members of the class were reacting. To my surprise, I found that many of them were crying too. There was not the usual period of analysis and criticism; rather, after a few quiet moments, people said good-bye to one another, and almost everyone had a warm word or a hug for me. I had touched these individuals, I knew, by simply revealing who I was. They were drawn to me, not because I was confident, strong, or intelligent—but because I was honest, for the first time. I was strong, vulnerable, joyful, desperate, hopeful, mean, generous, naive, determined, angry, and loving. I was all these great contradictions and more—and I was acceptable.

I turned to go and looked at Wendell. Did I see tears in his eyes too? I think so. He handed me the manuscript and said, "Don't let yourself think of this as finished." And of course it will never be, for I write more of this story every time I put words to paper. Just tell the truth about what you know. It was a moment of grace that opened in me a way for loving. That year was the first year I saw spring come. "Oh, is this how it has been all along?" I asked myself, in wonder. I was 33 years old, and I had let myself see spring at last.

Says Isaiah, "He who teaches you shall no longer be hidden out of sight, but with your own eyes you shall see him always. If you stray from the road to right or left you shall hear with your own ears a voice behind you saying, 'This is the way; follow it'" (Isaiah 30:20–22). I learned from Wendell what I can never forget: not technique or correctness, but to trust my own voice. I learned courage and faith. And I began to learn to love myself, opening the way for me to love others. As Diane Ackerman wrote, in a poem called "Entreaty": "Sir, if you love me, teach me to thrive without you, to be my own genesis."

Many months later, when I tried to thank him, to give him credit for my rebirth, Wendell would hear nothing of it. He said, "I just encouraged you to use words well." As a matter of fact, he would accept nothing less than all I had, all I could put on the altar. To educate means to draw out. That is what a great teacher does: beckon forth the sacred from within you, light the fire of love, make a way for you to give your gifts.

Our greatest teachers inevitably teach through who they are, teach from their being. Their integrity calls for the same in you; their passion, the same; their tenderness and love, the same. You become not what they want you to be, because they have no such vision of that. You must have your own vision, and they say yes to you, yes, over and over again, yes, yes, yes, until you hear it. They will not have half-measures, the shoddy, the good enough. They know your soul is a treasure, and they insist that you share it.

I have often heard that when your heart is ready, your teacher will appear, and I believe the truth of that. It has been that way over and over again in my own life. I had to be a little desperate to find Wendell. Just watch and wait. Struggle internally. Feel a little hopeless. Allow yourself to not know: *I don't know what to do, I don't know what to do.* And then open your eyes. In due time, your teacher will appear, to lead you out to where you can live.

SO BE IT. AMEN.

Prayer

We are thankful for those men and women who have chosen to teach—who open our eyes, who invite us to hear, who touch the core of our selves and bless us with their being. They have given us life, and it is now for us to give life to others. Bless us as we teach and as we learn. AMEN.

Benediction

Go now, and gladly teach and gladly learn.

Seasons of Renewal

Giving Up What Hurts Us

FEBRUARY 18, 1996

I do not understand my own behavior; I do not act as I mean to, but I do the things I hate. Though the will to do what is good is in me, the power to do it is not; the good thing I want to do, I never do; the evil thing which I do not want—that is what I do.

—Paul the Apostle

LAST WEDNESDAY was Valentine's Day—a day to say "I love you" to those we care about. Do you remember when you exchanged Valentines in grade school? We wondered even then how much to say to whom. We didn't want to be rejected when we passed out hearts. And even now as grown-ups, we look in the mailbox, hoping for the red envelope. We all long to be loved.

Gerald May, psychotherapist and spiritual director, says in his book *Addiction and Grace* that desire is rooted in a longing for God: "After 20 years of listening to the yearnings of people's hearts, I am convinced that all human beings have an inborn desire for God. We may experience it in different ways, as a longing for wholeness, completion, or fulfillment. Regardless of how we describe it, it is a longing for love. It is a hunger to be loved, and to move closer to the source of love."

May continues: "The longing at the center of our hearts repeatedly disappears from our awareness, and its energy is usurped by forces that are not at all loving. . . . We give ourselves over to things that, in our deep honesty, we really do not want." May is talking about addiction. Moving towards something that hurts instead of heals. Not being able to pull away.

Years ago I saw a pair of newspaper photographs that moved me deeply. The story behind the pictures spoke to me of the desperation that comes when longing has no appropriate object. One picture was of a man sitting on a partially submerged park bench with a dripping wet puppy in his hands. The companion picture showed him flinging the six-week-old puppy into the water. According to the caption, each time after the puppy was thrown into the water, he would swim back to the man, only to be flung out again, until he eventually drowned.

Addiction is living like that puppy, going back again and again to the source of harm, because you don't know where else to go. The hands that reach out seem to offer comfort of some kind, seem to relieve the pain, the stress, the yearning—and you can't help swimming somewhere, because you know you're drowning. But coming back is deadly, to you and to others.

It is possible to be addicted to almost anything. Common addictions are to alcohol and drugs, to sex, to food, to work—but a person can be addicted to golf, to e-mail, to exercise, to shopping. Whatever you are addicted to becomes your God, and therefore, says May, "Addiction makes idolaters of us all, because it forces us to worship these objects of attachment. . . . It erodes our free will and eats away at our dignity."

In her book *Addiction to Perfection*, Marion Woodman talks about the "divine muffin": we take the profane and treat it as sacred. She says,

> [The] projection of the Perfect was once on God. When God died, that perfection was often projected onto the husband. And now the terrible truth is that in many lives that projection has been taken off the husband and put onto a muffin. . . . At the same time, however, some voice of sanity . . . mocks the whole idea of [mystical participation] with a holy muffin. The muffin is not sacred, and the power it is releasing is not holy power even when flavored with blueberries. . . . The muffin cannot replace the divine wafer, nor can alcohol replace the divine spirit, nor can starving replace a religious fast.

Which brings us around to Lent. Next Wednesday is Ash Wednesday, the beginning of Lent, a time in the Christian calendar when adherents are invited to fast, or to give up something, in remembrance of the sacrifice of Jesus and in preparation for the celebration of Easter. Lent is not circled on the calendars of many Unitarian Universalists I know; it is not considered a major religious holiday. I do remember it from my early days, though. As a little Catholic girl I would go to church, kneel with the others, and have my forehead marked with ashes. Each of us was asked to give up something for Lent, some food we particularly liked. As I remember, I tried to finesse this request by giving up something like watermelon, which was out of season.

Today as we move into this Lenten season, we're exploring another kind of giving up: giving up what is hurting you.

This is no casual invitation, no easy request. Not for you, and not for me.

We need to move not with judgment, but with compassion, for ourselves and for others. We are part of a culture that is addictive.

Once the story goes that a woman brought her son to Gandhi. She said to him, "Teacher, please tell my son to give up sugar. It is bad for him. If you tell him to give it up, I know he will obey." Gandhi said, "Bring your son back in one week, and I will tell him." And so the woman did so, and Gandhi told the boy to give up sugar. Then the woman pulled Gandhi aside. "Why, teacher, did you require me to go and then return a week later? You could have told my son last week." "Because," said Gandhi, "last week, I hadn't given up sugar."

I would like to tell you this morning that I have given up sugar—that is to say, my addiction—but I have not. I will tell you that I have come to know my addiction more intimately in recent months, and that I am not satisfied living the way I am living. Change will not be easy, but more and more I know it to be necessary. My addiction is to work. My addiction is rooted, as are all addictions, in need. My need to be on top of things, to cover all the bases. To be the best minister I can be. To be perfect. To please everyone. Oh, that's a woman's thing! And underneath that need—the deeper need—is the need for relationship: for friendship and for intimacy. This is not a need you can fill. We can love one another as minister and congregants, but you cannot be my friends nor my intimates. I must have a life outside the church. And that is what I will open myself to in the coming weeks and months. You see, this church, with its rapid growth and increasing demands, is a setup for my particular addiction. I love my work here, and I take great joy in it. Yet so much of what I do is so intense, so emotionally demanding, that I must make a separate time to rest, to exercise, and to play. So my commitment to you is that I will get some help from a consultant and redefine my role so that my life will be more balanced. And I will seek out sources of nurture and care for myself.

I know that as the minister I need to model a healthy, balanced life for staff and for congregants alike, and I'm not doing that right now. Part of the problem is institutional. Please know that we have a church of 1,300 members and only two ministers. According to the books, we should have at least four. Plus we are in a period of transition, needing to move on with our plans to make more space. My role in that effort is superimposed upon my other tasks. So some things that should be done are not going to get done, and that's going to have to be OK. The larger truth is that I want to be present for you when I am with you, and in order to do that, I have to nurture myself more completely than I have been doing.

I believe we can only be set free through grace. I don't think self-help books will do it, or psychotherapy, or will power.

I have said that this change in me will not be easy, nor will the changes you need to make in your own lives. For you see, we're talking about more than individual vulnerabilities. We need to move not with judgment, but with compassion, for ourselves and for others. We are part of a culture that is addictive, for there is no longer any common mythology to contain our deepest longings. The muffin cannot take the place of God. We find that, like all people, we are born into a time and place not of our choosing, and even if we have the most loving and well-balanced parents in the world, we live in a culture that is not life-giving. Eros is challenged on every hand by the cult of greed and injustice. Our economic system and the political system that supports it set us over against, in competition with, using up others and being used up, exploiting our mother the earth in the grossest of ways. It is very difficult to be a part of such a system and to feel integrated and whole. Rather, we have a sense of guilt and loss and fragmentation. The children of this country are acting out the cultural death wish, as suicides and juvenile killings climb. They have not yet learned to deny and displace their pain as we have done. Our anxiety and our loneliness are not some kind of individual flaw—nor should this suffering be pinned entirely on our families of origin, as the "recovery movement" is wont to do. If our parents couldn't love us well enough, we need to ask ourselves why that was so. We are called upon not only to heal our personal lives, but to resist the larger social and political structures that reinforce unhealthy living and relating. Don't buy goods you don't need. Don't do jobs that are demeaning to you or to others. Don't let political candidates who are pro-greed win the day.

I think of my parents, how they lived and how they died. Yesterday I saw the film *Leaving Las Vegas,* in which the main character Ben decides to drink himself to death. It is a wonderful film, but it was difficult for me to watch because Ben reminded me of my father. Like Ben, my father was charming and good-looking—but he died of alcohol dementia. He didn't know me at all in those final years. I do remember the last coherent words he said to me. I was trying to tell him what my life had become, who I was. Maybe my goodness could make up for his badness. "I'm a minister, Daddy," I said. He looked at me with his watery, blue eyes, uncomprehending. "I'm a minister, a minister," I repeated, more loudly. Still he didn't understand. Finally, even more loudly, I said, "Daddy, I'm a preacher!" "Give 'em hell!" he said.

And my mother. She had been a professional dancer as a young woman. But she gave up any notion of a career when she married my father. That's the way it was done then. As my father tells the story, she put on a dress one morning to go to work. She planned to leave me with a babysitter. When she told my father, he put his hand in the neck of her dress and ripped it down the front. She was to stay at home with me. Lucky me. He lost my mother, who was in and out of mental institutions. As a man, he could not speak of his pain, and so he drank. My mother, earthy and romantic, never looked at another man. As she lay dying, she asked for word of my father, who could not speak of her except when he was drinking, when he would weep and remember. She died, then a few years later he died. That was just before I came here to be your minister. I remember when I got the call that he was dead. Both of them gone. I cried so deeply—not so much for myself, but for my mother and my father and the pain they had endured, these two good people who loved each other, but couldn't find a place of peace.

And like each of you, I have become what I have become because of what birthed me, and the choices I have made out of that wonderful and terrible mix that families are. As a minister, I want to help create liberating structures, containers for pain and joy, so that people can come here to church and experience healing—and then go out and heal those broken places in the larger world. I want to create with you a church community where people are accepted as they are, where the addiction can be released because the love and sense of purpose are there to fill the emptiness and the longing.

And yet the church community can only go so far. It can give you safety and comfort. It can point the way to wholeness. But you, each one of you, must ultimately enter your own darkness with your own demons. How will you face them, the compulsions that control you and make you do that which you would not do?

I believe we can only be set free through grace. I don't think self-help books will do it, or psychotherapy, or will power. I don't believe you can do this hard thing on your own. Nor can I. I believe we must first acknowledge our own brokenness and need. Only then can grace flow into our lives. I know this is difficult for Unitarian Universalists to hear. I remember in one church where I served, we sang "Amazing Grace" one Sunday, and when we finished, one woman made no bones about it: she resented singing the line "that saved a wretch like me." She was not a wretch, and she wanted us to know that. Then someone else stood up. He was a man who had AIDS and who suffered from mental illness. He allowed that down at the Salvation Army they liked to sing "Amazing Grace," because you see, they knew they were wretches.

And the Kingdom of God will be made known to such as these. We have to really be open to grace, as scary as that is. We can't through our usual consumer mode rid ourselves of addiction. We can't use prayer as a kind of leverage to get what we want, as though God is some kind of vending machine in the sky. Rather, we enter into a covenant with the Holy: we come in our weakness and in our need. We vow to do our part. Then we leave the rest to God.

We have to "try to make friends with the spaciousness," says Gerald May. There will most likely be the fierce pain of withdrawal, and the temptation to substitute one addiction for another. But stay with the spaciousness, the void. And out of that void will emerge our authentic longing, and then the blessing that awaits us.

Let me be clear. Our desire must not be focused on ridding ourselves of the addiction. That is a by-product. Our proper desire is to be at one with the Mystery, the ground of our being. We cannot make it happen. But we can be sure that we are being pursued. Do you remember when you were little and out playing in the evening and your mother called you to dinner? She would call and call, and if you did not respond she would call again. "Come on home," she would say. "It's time to come home." There will be constant invitation. Direction will emerge. You are beloved. Dare to take the Holy as a partner, and you will find the way home.

SO BE IT. AMEN.

Prayer

We come today in all humility, confessing that we have tried to cure ourselves, and we have been unable to do so. We still have that sharp and angry tongue, or we still drink too much, or we still try to find love in all the wrong places. Love us, even when we don't love ourselves. Surprise us with grace when we find ourselves in a thicket of fear and confusion. Lead us to lives of honor and dignity. Lead us home. AMEN.

Benediction

May the love of God be in you and abide with you both now and forever more. Go in peace.

The Hard Work of Resurrection

APRIL 7, 1996

The Rabbi of Kotzk surprised a number of learned men who happened to be visiting him. He asked them, "Where is the dwelling of God?"

They laughed at him: "What a thing to ask! Is not the whole world full of His glory?"

Then he answered his own question: "God dwells wherever we let Him in."

—Hasidic master Rebi Menahem Mendel of Kotzk, reported by Martin Buber

NOBODY EVER TOLD US that life would be so hard—that it would be so hard to live life well. And perhaps that's as it should be. We wouldn't want to tell small children, "You think that skinned knee is bad—just wait 'til you become a grown-up. Then you'll really suffer." No, we know they will find pain and disappointment all too soon, and we wish it were not so—for them, or for us. And so we help them each step along the way to adulthood, dressing the skinned knee, explaining why their best friend had to move away, comforting them after the first broken heart.

And we ourselves, time after time, are confronted with the unraveling of the cloth of our expectations.

A woman discovers a love letter in her husband's dresser drawer—and she didn't write it. Yes, he's having an affair, but how could that be? He has been her best friend for 20 years, and they share everything. Her world seems shattered. If he can betray her, no place, no person is safe. A kind of innocence is forever lost.

A man works for a company for 17 years and suddenly he is laid off, a victim of downsizing. He has given the best years of his life to the company. Forget eight-hour days, he has worked until the job was done, sometimes even neglecting his family. He is 57 years old and devastated. Now what?

Change comes, and it is wrenching—it twists us into shapes and forms we don't recognize. Where is that smile, that tilt of the chin, that said to the world, "It's nice to be alive"? Change often brings chaos. We are thrown into a place we've never been, and we don't know where to go for help or how to ask. We are pushed up against the wall of our limits, our mortality, our imperfections. Our assumptions about the future are blown away. We no longer have the luxury of denial—of imagining that we are in control of our life and it is really going pretty well, thank you.

It is at these times when we must invite resurrection. But first we must descend into the silence of God, into the emptiness of the tomb. We must give up what we hoped for, what we always dreamed of, to come to some place of security deeper than we have known. We have the opportunity to face ourselves in a way that is transforming. "But," you may say, "I don't want transformation! I like things the way they are." My friends, I'm sorry, but you don't get to say how you want things in this world. You don't get to say that we shouldn't have illness and death and broken relationships and heartache. Well, you can say it, but you're going to waste a lot of time and energy if you do. This world really is about loss, the Buddhists say—it's about endings of all kinds. And in the Christian myth, it's about tombs and darkness and the loss of the only one you ever loved. *And* it's about rolling back the stone and facing that loss and finding that the tomb is empty. In other words, life is about death and loss, but it's also about resurrection and hope.

The African American writer James Baldwin wrote in his book *Nobody Knows My Name*:

> Any real change implies the break up of the world as one has always known it, the loss of all that gave one identity, the end of safety. And at such a moment, unable to see and not daring to imagine

what the future will now bring forth, one clings to what one knew, or thought one knew, to what one possessed or dreamed that one possessed. Yet it is only when [a person] is able, without bitterness or self pity, to surrender a dream he has long cherished, or a privilege he has long possessed, that he is set free—that he has set himself free—for higher dreams, for greater privileges.

Let's think about these words: to surrender a dream is to set yourself free "for higher dreams, for greater privileges." No, surely I know what is best for me! Surely my plans, my dreams, these are sound and good. Have you ever thought that your dreams might be too small? Have you ever thought that the very nature of your dreams might be transformed by a God who loves you more than you love yourself, who treasures your mind, your body, your spirit, a God who finds you infinitely precious?

I want to tell you some stories, stories about people who have been transformed, who have gone from the darkness of loss, the darkness of the tomb, into a resurrected life.

The first story is about a couple you all know—Jimmy and Rosalynn Carter. It's easy for us to think that people of some wealth and power escape life's pain. But they do not. In November of 1980 the Carters left the White House, after Jimmy had endured a crushing defeat by Ronald Reagan. When they moved back to Plains, Georgia, the family peanut business was $1,000,000 in debt and their youngest child had gone off to school. They were lonely. They were at home together all day every day, and as much as they cared for each other, they found this much closeness difficult. They began to walk through the woods and fields for miles, and to seek ways to serve in their home community. They began to heal.

Then something strange happened. As Rosalynn reported it, "One night I woke up and Jimmy was sitting straight up in bed. He always sleeps so soundly that I thought he must be sick. "What's the matter?" I asked. "I know what we can do at the library," he said. "We can develop a place to help people who want to resolve disputes. There is no place like that now." He talked on enthusiastically about other areas where negotiations might help. And you know the end of the story. Jimmy Carter is all over the world, from Ethiopia to Nicaragua, mediating disputes. And whereas some have questioned this role, there is no doubt that at times he has been successful where others have not, for he has no political agenda. His agenda is peace, mutual respect. The Carters have also been leaders in the Habitat for Humanity program in which our church is involved, and because of their efforts, many poor families live in greater dignity and comfort.

The next story is that of a theologian, Melanie May, who tells her own story in her book *A Body Knows: A Theopoetics of Death and Resurrection*. As an academic and a Harvard graduate, she was always a high achiever. She gave herself to her work with a fierce intensity, and she was rewarded. But somewhere along the way, she forgot about her body and her roots. She forgot about Grandma May. Grandma May was a gardener who knew the sun and the soil. Melanie remembers her among the cornstalks and bean poles and tomato plants, in her broad-brimmed hat, with her hoe. Grandma May used to say, "A body knows." This is profound theological knowledge that academia had covered over.

We must descend into the silence of God, into the emptiness of the tomb.

Then life came along and changed Melanie's plans. She was on vacation in New Mexico when she felt a sore spot on her right breast in the shower one morning. She rehearsed all the reasons why this could not be breast cancer. For one thing, she was too young: only 35. But her body knew: it was cancer, and her world fell apart. She says that everything she had thought was important was "instantly trivial." She knew in a way that she could never forget that she was mortal, that she was dying. Whether she would die now or at age 90, that knowing changed her life forever.

She had some work to do—spiritual work. Mainly her work centered on learning to love herself. It's not that she was not loved by others, she says—she was well loved by parents, by friends, by teachers, by lovers. But she didn't *know* she was loved, couldn't somehow take in that knowledge. Perhaps it was because when she grew up, she didn't fit society's definition of what is lovable. As a young teen, she was already nearly six feet tall, with acute acne and braces. Her religious tradition was one of shame and unworthiness. Later she was to read the words of African American poet Audre Lorde, and to know their truth: "Know we are worthy of touch before we can reach out for each other." But she grew up thinking that she must love others unselfishly, when she didn't even know how to love herself.

The breast cancer opened Melanie's eyes to love. Love was poured out lavishly upon her, and she saw signs of love wherever she looked: flowers, casseroles, her lawn mowed, cards, calls, dinner invitations, offers of rides to the doctor. She could no longer deny her lovability. She learned there was only one thing she was called upon to do: to let herself be loved. She had to "heal the wound of unworthiness." Her books could not teach her to love herself, but her body did—her very woundedness and the simple touch of others, body to body, flesh to flesh. She writes: "When I speak of presence I speak, first and foremost, of presence in my body. I live, and think, in my body, no longer alienated or abstracted as I have been most of my life." The body knows.

"'I practice resurrection,'" Melanie says, using the words of Wendell Berry. I like that. "Practice" has a dual sense. First, make of resurrection a practice, in the manner of a spiritual practice. Make resurrection a regular daily experience, for every day brings to us the little losses, the little deaths, that foreshadow the larger cycles of our existence. Even our breathing: breathing out we die to the old, breathing in we become alive with the new. And then, practice resurrection in the sense of practicing a skill, until we get really good at it. Be willing to go into the void over and over again, for the void is not a place to fear, but rather a place of gestation, of fecundity.

Resurrection is hard work, because it's done after the innocence is gone.

Maybe, though, words are too easy. They slip off the tongue so glibly. The body knows how hard resurrection is. Never mind philosophy or theology. How do we respond in our bodies when the unthinkable occurs? When our beautiful, brilliant son becomes mentally ill and we know he will never, never be well? When the order of things is turned upside down, when we are supposed to die first, but instead our child dies? Or when the unthinkable thing happens to a whole race of people, as it did in the Holocaust? Though Easter is a Christian holiday, paradoxically, I believe it is the Jews who have the most to teach us about resurrection.

The darkness made manifest during those years of the Holocaust was, is, incomprehensible. The Jews who survived were deeply and permanently transformed, and indeed none of us who consider the depth of the evil set loose in the human soul during that time will ever be the same. Where does that much hate come from? Six million Jews died, one and a half million of them children. Nine out of every ten rabbis perished. In less than ten years, all Europe was decimated of its Jews. It was a time when evil reigned, and God seemed silent. Martin Buber, a theologian who was himself a refugee from Nazi Germany, calls this moment in history "the eclipse of God." He writes, "The Bible knows of God's hiding His face, of times when the contact between heaven and earth seems to be interrupted. God seems to withdraw Himself utterly from the earth and no longer to participate in its existence. The space of history is then full of noise, but empty of the divine breath."

In these times, where do we find the will to pray? Can we trust a God who does this kind of disappearing act? Is there a God acting for the good throughout history, as scripture tells us? If so, where was this god during Auschwitz? Buber continues, "One can still 'believe' in the God who allowed these things to happen, but can one still speak to Him? Can one . . . enter into a relationship with Him? [Can we say with the Psalmist,] 'Give thanks unto the Lord, for He is good; for his mercy endureth forever'?"

In *The Spirit of Renewal: Crisis and Response in Jewish Life,* Jewish theologian Edward Feld poses these questions then reaches for "an alternative vision to madness and nothingness." He believes we have thought of God too much as a person, when God is in fact a spirit. It is idolatrous, he says, to see God as a person in control of events. There was a holy presence even in Auschwitz. Whoever survived was helped by another, was saved by help and the memory of that help. Every survivor tells that same story, says Feld. "The woman who, in Auschwitz, brought her friend a half-rotten raspberry for her birthday gave that person her life."

Feld continues: "We can no longer believe in a divine intervention that will come from the outside, but we must learn that we can let holiness enter, that we can make a space for the divine, that which is most deeply nourishing, that which sparks the soul of each of us. When we listen to the silent calling of God, impelling us to reach out and shatter the hard reality constructed by evil, to affirm the humanity of our neighbor—that is divine intervention."

The holiness we seek is central to the world and blooms amidst even the greatest evil. Do you seek God? Then notice the impulses toward the sacred in yourself, and make holy moments. Touch your wife's face, look her in the eye, and risk telling her how much you love her. Be present with a ragged street person, really present, even for just a few moments. Call up somebody who's having a hard time and say, "How are you?" and be open to hearing the answer. Stop and listen to the singing of birds. Hear the promise, and believe.

We do not have an all-powerful God who pulls the strings so that good wins out. And the forces of hate and fear are great. And so it is up to us: we are, as Feld says, "the preservers of the holy." And we do that in the ordinary and in the everyday. There are countless opportunities. We have only to ask, "How can I serve the Holy One?" and the answer will come. Don't expect God to save you; you are to save God. Oh, what a disappointment! Oh, what a terrible reversal!

Resurrection is hard work, because it's done after the innocence is gone. It's done after our fantasy is stripped down to the bone. It's done after the wound has left us shattered and sober with reflection. We know we'll never be the same.

When we are left in that abyss, we learn that we practice resurrection, and we do it in community. It is we who protect and lift up the good, who make a dwelling place for the Holy. It's done through our bodies, as we see, as we touch, as we speak. In the words of Denise Levertov, we "hold to our icy hearts a shivering God." And love blooms once again.

SO BE IT. AMEN.

Prayer

O Living God, this is Easter Sunday, and some of us are still in the tomb of despair. Let us be open to new life this day. May we roll the stone away from our hearts so that we may be touched by love, receptive to the newness of life, awakened to joy. Teach us to make holy moments, tender moments. Teach us to bring your healing love to others. AMEN.

Benediction

Go now, and practice resurrection.

Hope Is the Thing with Feathers

APRIL 16, 1995

Hope is the thing with feathers
That perches in the soul,
And sings the tune without the words,
And never stops at all.

—Emily Dickinson, "Hope"

A YOUNG MAN comes through the line after the worship service and takes my hand. I see in his eyes that he has not slept well. Maybe he has not slept at all. He says to me, "Is it a sin to be depressed?"

My son Madison calls me last week. He is due to graduate from Yale in a few more weeks, but he thinks maybe he won't because he's behind in a required math class. Way behind. Hopelessly behind. Maybe he'll just drop out of school, he says. It's only a piece of paper. Besides, why should anybody study math when people are starving? In his voice I hear confusion, desperation. What have these four years of school been about? He doesn't know.

A woman comes into my office and tells me her husband has left her. She can't believe this has happened. She can't imagine life without him. She doesn't know what to say. She just wants to tell me. She starts to weep, and she weeps and weeps and weeps. She says, "I'm sorry, I didn't mean to cry."

These three people are potentially people of hope, though they may not have seen themselves that way at the moment. I say they are people of hope because they are like the Israelites wandering in the wilderness. They have left home. They no longer know what their moorings are, what will give comfort or meaning or peace. The future is uncertain, and they live in darkness. Out of such circumstances is hope born. I mean *real* hope. Not the hope of the innocent. Not the hope of the naive, the thoughtless hope of one who has never had the boot of life squarely planted on his neck.

No, real hope is born of darkness. It needs a womb-space for gestation. It needs patience while it grows. And it will not come without the paradox of pain, the sickness of the morning when one has appetite for nothing, the strange cravings and renouncings that pregnancy brings. Anxiety will be the companion of one birthing hope, for who can predict what the child—this new life—will be like? The agony of labor will go on much longer than you thought you could stand. "When will this end?" you will cry out.

When we speak our truth and witness by the way we live, things change.

"No, depression is not a sin," I say to the young man. Then I grab his arm and pull him back to me. I catch his eyes with my own. "But not dealing with depression is a sin," I say.

I wake up with my son's telephone call on my mind. Before exercise, before prayer, before breakfast, I write to him.

Dear Little Bear—

Please remember that all thinking people are appalled by the world we have made. You are asking the right questions. Why should you study math while people are starving? You may decide to help make a world where there are fewer hungry people. You may also decide that beauty and order are important for our survival, too, and that math teaches us these values. In the meantime, you do need your degree from Yale. No, you may not drop out. I love you very, very much, but even if I could take on the pain of growing up for you, I wouldn't: you'll learn more by navigating these rough waters yourself. I *will* promise to be with you.

Love, Mom

To the woman whose husband has just left her, I say, "Go ahead and cry. I have a whole box of Kleenex for you," and I hand her the box. I watch while she uses an incredible number of tissues. I'm glad:

these tears are soothing her soul and giving her rest. Finally I say, "One day you will love again." Her eyes deny me. "I know you don't believe me," I say. "But one day you will love again. Take my word for it."

Hope, real hope, is born out of darkness, out of despair.

Let's talk for a moment about the difference between hope and illusion—for they are very different. Living with illusion means living in a dream-world, in a world of denial. There it is, the truth I mean, staring you in the face, and you refuse, absolutely refuse, to see it. With illusion, no hope is possible, because illusion is an escape from darkness, and as I said, gestation takes place in darkness. Let us suppose a woman is married to an abusive spouse. When he slaps her, she tells herself that she provoked him. She tells herself that he really loves her, he didn't mean to do it. She tells herself the same things the first time and the tenth time and the twentieth time. She says he is a good man, and if she can just be a better wife, he will change. He doesn't, of course. Illusion works against hope.

But now, what would hope look like? Let's start over. Let us suppose a woman has an abusive spouse. He strikes her in anger. She is surprised. It happens again, and again. Finally she says to herself, "I love this man, and he's hurting me. He's hurting me physically, and he's also battering my spirit." That understanding takes her deep into darkness, deep into a hard truth: someone she loves is hurting her. She tells her husband, "You may not continue to hit me. Either you get help with this problem, or I'm leaving." And she means it, because she knows she does not deserve this treatment. Hope is born—the possibility of new life.

Why is it that one woman stays in the abusive relationship, stays with the illusion and the hopelessness, while another woman acknowledges the darkness and allows the seed of hope to grow? Why is it that some people fall into despair and stay despairing, while others fall into despair and find it fertile ground? I'm not entirely sure I can answer that question, but I was intrigued by a recent film, *The Shawshank Redemption*, which made me think about the issue.

In that film hope is literally "the thing with feathers" for an elderly lifer named Brooks (the bird, incidentally, is an ancient symbol for the spirit). Brooks has been in prison 50 years, and when he is finally released, he also releases his pet bird. But he is desolate at losing his pet, for the bird had embodied his hope and kept him going every day. He wanders to a park and feeds pigeons, hoping to see his beloved bird among them. Failing to find some meaning outside prison walls, he finally hangs himself. He was in jail so long, he has no idea how to be free. There are all kinds of prisons, my friends, and once you accept the one you're in, no change is possible. The spirit dies, and with it the possibility of hope.

In this movie, the main character Andy, on the other hand, never abandons hope. He keeps on moving toward his goals with almost unbelievable persistence. When he is refused money to build a prison library, he begins a letter-writing campaign to the state legislature. He writes weekly; after a long time, he receives a small check, scarcely enough. He steps up his effort, writing twice a week. After six years he receives the money and donated books and records to build the prison library. He knows he has to create experiences that feed his soul and those of his cellmates. At one point, he flagrantly disobeys orders and plays Mozart over the prison PA system. The prisoners stop in their tracks and stand in awe as they listen to the music flooding their compound with passion and longing. Andy receives hope through the "dailies": working on projects to better himself and his cellmates. He receives hope through reading and art, through love for his friend Red, and through the persistent belief that he is not made for this place, that the abuse and degradation will not take his spirit.

But why did Andy believe, against all logic, that he would one day be free? "Hope is the thing with feathers": it is a thing of the spirit, simply there, singing against all odds, saying "yes" when "no" seems so obvious, so certain. It is more than human, this little song that perches so quietly, so defiantly in the soul.

Some people might say the feeling of hope is merely biochemical. Well, it's clear that if your chemistry is out of whack, then hope can get out of whack too. But hope is bigger than biochemistry. It's more than a survival instinct. I think of it as a kind of whispering from the Spirit, a quiet nudging, that keeps at me, that won't let me go, no matter what. I can't define it, but I know it lingers around me, even when I think it's gone for good. It hides out, just waiting for an opening. That opening might come in one of many ways.

Spring gives me hope. I can't believe that the wisteria vine curling along the top of my porch can possibly be alive. Every winter I look at it and say to myself, "This thing is dead. It couldn't possibly sprout anything." Then these sensuous purple blooms announce themselves once more, and I am amazed.

Children give me hope. They don't know enough to be cynical. They are not afraid to love. They know that muddy shoes are the price to pay for splashing in puddles, and they don't care.

You, my congregants, give me an immense amount of hope. I want you to know that. We have had a lot of numerical growth here, and I'm glad for that. But the real thrill for me is the spiritual growth I'm seeing in your lives. One of you—a businessman type—says to me, "I've been giving rides for the 'care and concerns' committee, and now I want to visit someone who is dying. What do I say? Can you help me?" Another says she has prayed for the first time in 18 years. One of our lay ministers is in almost daily contact with a young woman who is mentally ill and going through a bad spell right now. Then there is a woman who has been grouchy, grouchy, grouchy—for as long as I have been in this church, until this year; now she's softening and smiling, and I know part of that change is the love she's experiencing from us here in church.

Hope rests in the nature of God.

I could go on and on. I see lives being transformed. Let's start with the ministers. My life is being transformed. And I see it with so many of you. That, my friends, is so very hopeful. I see people doing the work they were meant to do, people reaching out to others who need them, people playing and celebrating. As I have said from the beginning, I think this church is called to greatness, and I'm seeing that call unfold. When I say "greatness," do not mistake my words: I don't mean dominance; I mean witness and service. And my hope is that in transforming ourselves, we will also be a transforming influence on our community and our denomination, and thereby on our nation and our world.

Hope comes to me through history too, both cultural history and personal history. I was talking with Ron Johnson, the minister of First Baptist, and he told me a shocking bit of local church history. He said that in 1872, at a church conference here in Portland, the main topic was a debate on the subject, "Do the Chinese have souls?" The churches were trying to decide whether or not to extend missionary efforts to the Chinese, upon whose backs much of the Northwest was built. If they didn't have souls, of course they didn't have to have their souls saved. Racism is by no means done with, but things are not the same—not for the Chinese, not for blacks, not for women, not for homosexuals. When we speak our truth and witness by the way we live, things change. That's hopeful.

In my own personal life, I am always being "surprised by joy," as C. S. Lewis put it. I'm less and less hooked by desire, by wanting, these days, because I'm discovering that the Spirit has bigger and better plans for me than I could ever dream up for myself. So my life has come to rest in a quiet hope, a sustaining hope, and an expectation that opportunities for work and love will show up, as they have right along, surprising and challenging and delighting me. All I have to do is "tune in" so I won't miss the signal.

I do know dark times. I think it's hardly possible for sensitive people not to. But I know that the darkness is not all there is, that the darkness is the place of conception, the beginning of rebirth. That pattern is so apparent and repetitive that I no longer doubt it. The coming of hope does not depend on my own virtue, thank goodness, which comes into question each and every day. Rather, hope rests in the nature of God, and I trust in that.

In her short story "Revelation," Flannery O'Connor presents Mrs. Turpin as an upright Christian lady who has devoted her whole life to uprightness and correctness. At the end of her life, "She sees a vast swinging bridge extending upward from the earth through a field of living fire. Upon it a vast horde of souls were rumbling toward heaven. . . . She could see by their shocked and altered faces that even their virtues were being burned away." *Even their virtues were being burned away.* Hope comes to us not by our own goodness, but by grace.

The darkness of Good Friday by grace becomes the new life of Easter Sunday. That's the message. Forget the theology, the ideology. The question is not whether Jesus really rose from the dead. The Baptists think one way, and most of us think another. That's not the point. The point is that you yourself enter into the dying and rising. You don't just talk about it, you enter into it. And you'll have all the hope you need. It's a promise. That's what the story is about.

SO BE IT. AMEN.

Prayer

We come today confessing that the times of darkness are hard for us, and our faith seems to disappear. During those times, hold us close, send some comforting presence to warm our cold and frightened hearts. Give us the understanding that the darkness is not all, and give us the courage to go through the pain of birth to newness of life. AMEN.

Benediction

May new life be yours on this Easter day.

Sources of Thanksgiving

NOVEMBER 21, 1993

Praise the lives you did not choose.
They will heal you.
—Marge Piercy, "The Sabbath of Mutual Respect"

WRITING IN THE *New York Times,* Susan Schnur tells the following story.

Once, many years ago, sleeping on the sofa bed in the living room of my boyfriend's parents' house in Teaneck, New Jersey, I witnessed a performance of gratitude the likes of which I have never seen elsewhere.

It was in the middle of the night—I was up with my own back pain—when the light flashed on in the upstairs hall and Jon's father came padding down into the room. Oblivious of me, he went into the kitchen, cut himself a slab of rye bread with a butcher knife, and then stood with it in the dining room under the street shadows.

"Chleb!" he said finally, thrusting the bread into the air. "Broit" —he held the bread against his pajama pocket. "Pain"—he shook it. "Lechem"—kissed it. "Bread"—took a bite.

This he did over and over, saying the word in more languages than I could imagine existed—thrusting, hugging, shaking, kissing, biting, exclaiming—until he stood in the room empty fisted. Then he burped roomily and went back up the stairs to bed.

I think of that night a lot, especially when I am up myself at 3 a.m. It seems almost premonitory.

I think: what did I know about this man?

That he loved his wife, yes. His children. That he checked on his kids too often in their rooms; changed the oil in his car every thousand miles; kept unnecessary dry goods in his basement. His family used to laugh at him.

He seemed sometimes, on an ordinary morning, almost stunned by the fierceness of his happiness. He was, it now seems clear to me, exhausted by his blessings, in a sense, afraid of them.

He was a Holocaust survivor, Jonny's dad. The contrast woke him in the night.

Ironically, sometimes the greatest source of thanksgiving is the pain we have survived. The memory of the longing, the loss, circles back to us, and we find that we have moved on, the grieving is mostly done, and the hard knot inside has given way to softness and receptivity. From somewhere in the depths comes gratitude for the release, for the newness of life, for the sense of possibility.

We all need to begin again, and life blessedly offers us new beginnings over and over again. The brokenness is restored, yet the form of the gift is ever new. What we once had is gone, but unexpected blessings overtake us, tap us on the shoulder, and invite us to walk down roads we never knew. Wendell Berry, the farmer and writer—and incidentally my first writing teacher—puts in this way in one of his poems:

> At start of spring I open a trench
> in the ground. I put into it
> the winter's accumulation of paper,
> pages I do not want to read
> again, useless words, fragments,
> errors. And I put into it
> the contents of the outhouse:
> light of the sun, growth of the ground,
> finished with one of their journeys.
> To the sky, to the wind, then
> and to the faithful trees, I confess
> my sins: that I have not been happy
> enough, considering my good luck;
> have listened to too much noise;
> have been inattentive to wonders;

have lusted after praise.
And then upon the gathered refuse
of mind and body, I close the trench,
folding it shut against the dark,
the deathless earth. Beneath that seal
the old escapes into the new.

Thanksgiving is a state of mind, and it cannot be forced, no matter what the season seems to demand. We probably all remember a teacher's or parent's admonition: "You need to change your attitude!" I always thought that was a strange command, as though you could change your emotional and intellectual perspective the same way you change your underwear. So I will not urge thanksgiving upon you, but instead invite you simply to prepare yourself—to allow thanksgiving to arise in you by grace, when it will.

There will be times in all our lives when we feel especially needy. Periods of transition are particularly hard—when we lose a relationship or a job, and we feel part of our identity being ripped away. It is difficult to be in that void in which there is no love and no satisfying work. Or sometimes we reach those transitions of age, in which we must change direction and purpose. The kids grow up and move away—now what? Or the kids grow up and don't move away—then what? Or we find ourselves dealing with serious illness or debility. We age and find our physical faculties failing us. Thankfulness seems hard to come by. It is especially important at these times that we try to find ways to give of ourselves, even when we are least inclined to do so. A friend of mine told me she had had a disastrous year at work. She said she decided to volunteer at a center for the homeless, preparing dinner once a week. That evening became the focal point of her week. "It got me through the year," she said. Giving releases you from the vise of self-concern and opens your heart to thankfulness.

A minister friend of mine was chafing under the necessity of writing a Thanksgiving sermon when he was feeling anything but thankful. He is a fervent environmentalist, and he found himself sitting one November day beside an inlet to the ocean that was full of rusted metal and waste paper and broken bottles. He began getting more and more depressed, and less and less thankful. Then he realized that in order to get to thankfulness, he had to acknowledge his negative feelings: his grief, his anger, his fear. It's that way with each of us. We have to own what we're really feeling, even when it's hard, even when we would prefer to feel something else.

If we are able to be present in the moment, we will find ourselves responding authentically, in depth, to the truth of that moment. We will not stay stuck in the pain or fear when we enter it—in fact, that is the only path to freedom from it. I believe that in each one of us is a deep well of thanksgiving. Is something pulling at you and subverting the feelings of abundance that are surely alive within you? Dare to ask that question and to face what you find. Dare to be where you are, and free yourself to move to another place.

Allow thanksgiving to arise in you by grace, when it will.

At this point I want to distinguish between self-pity and grief. Grief is the profound recognition and acceptance of loss. Grief is something you can move through because the sadness is acknowledged at the most profound level. It places you at one with other human beings, in high places and in low, for it is a universal experience and is understood as such. Your tears come to be shed for us all, for we all lose what we love.

Self-pity, on the other hand, is a pseudo-grief. It looks something like grief, because there are tears and sadness—but in fact it separates you from other people, because you believe that you somehow have been singled out for pain. You say, "What did I do to deserve this?" and you find no answer. You conclude that life is unfair, and most of all it is unfair to you. At dusk you walk down a street in your neighborhood, and you look at the lights in the windows. You envy the inhabitants. You imagine that all is well within—that these homes are full of loving spouses and happy, resourceful children. You are the only one who is different. You, who suffer so much, for no reason at all. That, my friends, is self-pity—a bog of despair that will only pull you in deeper and deeper.

The same minister friend I spoke of earlier told me about an 89-year-old woman in his congregation who was diagnosed with a terminal illness. When the minister went to call on her, she asked him, "Why me?" The answer was so obvious and the denial so great that the minister was rendered speechless.

This story is in stark contrast to another, a story written by a son in which he remembers his elderly mother with great love and affection. He said that his mother was dying, and he was standing at her bedside weeping. She looked up at him and simply said, "If not now, then later." She knew that she must die soon, she accepted that fact, and she lent comfort to her son with her acceptance.

Perhaps it is best to expect little in this world, but to hope for much. For so often it is our expectations that make us so disgruntled and unwilling to accept what *is.* The more you know that life is sure to be a surprise, that you are really owed nothing at all, the more you can rejoice in what you have. Again, that requires living in the moment and noticing what that moment is offering.

To live in the moment, without regrets or expectations, to be fully present to the "now" of our lives, is to live in faith. A Native American poem says it well:

> I saw the tree in winter
> Reaching toward the sky
> With bare branches tangled
> Like so many paths and yet
> Each path had a purpose,
> Leading back to the roots of the tree.

Living with a sense of purpose beyond what we can know or control, giving thanks with our whole being, by the way we stand or speak or touch or swallow our food: that kind of thanksgiving might be called *primal,* for it is as primitive and original as our very bones. It will keep us rooted and whole, no matter what our particular circumstances may be. And out of that rootedness will flow an abundance the like of which we have not seen.

When we live in primal thanksgiving, it becomes possible for us to identify with the joy of others instead of longing for what others seem to have, for we know that the source of the blessing is infinite, that in fact at the very heart of life is a blessedness that holds us and keeps us. When we begin to see ourselves at one with others and not separate at all, we receive as they receive, we give thanks as they give thanks. The dinner table, you see, is large enough for us all.

Thanksgiving has very little to do with our actual circumstances and almost everything to do with our spiritual stance: the eyes we see with, the ears we hear with. As I say this, I think of my mother. In the last few weeks of her life, she said to me, "You know, I've had a wonderful life." I was taken aback. These words were from a woman whose struggles with mental illness and alcoholism cost her her marriage to the only man she ever loved. She lost her three children as well. Now she had breast cancer and was dying too young. So how could she say, "I've had a wonderful life"? You see, she had an extraordinary capacity to love people, and they loved her back. She loved her brother and his wife and her nephews and nieces. She worked for a group of priests as a housekeeper and cook in order to maintain herself, and she cared deeply for them. The people in the apartment house where she lived were real neighbors. A few years before she died, she was reconciled with her three children, something that she, a devout Catholic, prayed for every day of her life. When I went through her things, I found scrapbooks of bad poetry and warm memories—memories of her dancing career before she married, memories of her friends, memories of her courtship, memories of her babies before they were taken from her. So much loss. And yet so much love was there, and it never left her. I remember her bright brown eyes and rich, earthy laugh. She had, as she said, a wonderful life.

The more you know that you are really owed nothing at all, the more you can rejoice in what you have.

We are wanderers through this life—pilgrims of sorts, though thinking of ourselves this way is more than a little disconcerting. We don't like to see ourselves as fumbling through this world, mostly not in control of all that is dearest to us. So we try to keep the pictures straight on the wall, the cupboard full of comforting food, the socks rolled right in the dresser drawer. But in fact we do wander, and we are pilgrims.

The real question is, What kind of pilgrims shall we be? Shall we journey in terror and trembling? Shall we walk in anger and self-righteousness? Shall we go bound up in our own self-pity for all the things that didn't go right? Or rather, shall we see the beauty of the falling leaves as their colors twist to the ground, the comfort in the hand that reaches out to us, the hope in the rising of the new moon?

We are all pilgrims. But we can choose to walk in scarcity or in abundance, in fear or in faith. May we allow ourselves the loveliness that is ours; may we not turn away from the fullness of the moment, the harvest of time. There is enough, there is enough. May you know it is so.

SO BE IT. AMEN.

Prayer

Sometimes we feel our want like a knife, and thankfulness becomes difficult. Our need turns in upon us and leaves room for little else. Bless us, and in that blessing make a way for us to open and receive the bounty that is there. Fill our reluctant hearts with thanksgiving—for the beauty of the autumn days, for the miracle of being alive, and most of all for those who love us and walk beside us and give us the courage to take the next step. AMEN.

Benediction

May your hearts be filled with thanksgiving; may your lives be filled with hope.

Living in Abundance

Grace fills empty spaces, but it can only enter where there is a void to receive it, and it is grace itself which makes this void.
— Simone Weil, *Gravity and Grace*

FROM THE TIME my two sons were old enough to understand language, I made a practice of a certain nightly ritual when I put them to bed. First I would read them a story, then I would tuck them in with one of their stuffed animals—Wilbur the pig, named for the pig in *Charlotte's Web,* or maybe the stuffed moose, who was just called, well, Moose—and then I would ask them to tell me what they were thankful for. I can hear the litany now: "I'm thankful for Mommy and Daddy and Granddaddy and Nonnie and Aunt Martha Ann and Uncle Tom and Carmie and Susan and Aunt Donna and Uncle Gary and Al and Benjamin," and on and on and on. Sometimes, after a long day at work, I found myself wishing they would find fewer people to be thankful for—but that was only a momentary thought, for I knew that so long as they could remain thankful, they could not be cruel or mean-spirited or depressed.

Thankfulness takes us out of ourselves and makes us open, expansively, to the world. Thankfulness massages our body armor and softens our hardness. Thankfulness brings up the joy we didn't even know was lurking there and fills us with feelings of abundance, of bounty, no matter what our actual circumstances might be. And so I wanted my sons to cultivate the habit of thanksgiving, not just one day a year, but every day of their lives. I wanted them to live in a kind of primal thanksgiving, if you will, so their every thought and action would flow from that attitude.

Have you ever been surprised by a sudden surge of thanksgiving in your own life? Sometimes it's something little that sets you off, like a gorgeous flower that startles you with its beauty on a gray day; or maybe you'll see a puppy playing in the park, trying in vain to catch a butterfly; or you'll see the face of a very old woman that stuns you with its beauty. Maybe there was an occasion when you were down and out—for whatever reason—and bam! Here comes a tidal wave of thanksgiving that picks you up, turns you around, and puts you down in a new place. I remember one Christmas when that happened to me. It was a difficult Christmas. I was newly divorced and a single mother working as a social worker for $10,500 a year, full-time. On this particular evening, I had promised my two boys we would buy a Christmas tree. But when we found the one they liked, a modest enough tree, it was still too expensive. An elderly gentleman, a stranger, heard me discussing the problem with the boys and came over to chat a few minutes. Then we moved on, looking for a tree that would fit our budget. Finally I decided to buy the tree I couldn't afford, but when I went up to pay, the manager of the lot said, "Your tree is already paid for." "What do you mean?" I asked. "That old man, the one you were talking to, he left money for your tree." "Well, what's his name?" I asked, thinking to thank him. But the manager said, "I don't know. He didn't leave a name. Just said he wanted to pay for your tree." Thankfulness filled my heart, and my eyes filled with tears. Here was someone who didn't know me, didn't know my kids, didn't want anything from me—he just wanted to give something of what he had to make someone else, a stranger, happy.

Thankfulness takes us out of ourselves and makes us open, expansively, to the world.

We have a theological term for these unexpected, undeserved gifts from the universe: it's called grace. You may be feeling set apart in your pain, isolated, alienated from others; then suddenly you're gifted with grace, and you feel strangely and wonderfully connected with all that is.

You know, those Pilgrims of the first Thanksgiving could have found a lot to be discouraged about. First of all, they had left their native country because they could not worship freely there. That itself tells you a lot about them—can you imagine being that concerned about freedom to worship? We take so much for granted sometimes. They left everything—possessions, family, friends, familiar surroundings—to go to a new and uncharted land, literally a wilderness. Landing at Plymouth in December of 1620 was of course a bad move. The Pilgrims faced winter without enough food, and they were sheltered from the elements only by such rude dwellings as they could put up immediately. They didn't know whether the Indians were friendly or not, or what their intentions were towards the settlers. The first act of the settlers upon reaching land was to kneel and pray. Records of this first settlement are full of references to occasions when "solemn thanks and praise" were offered. Only 55 of the 102 Pilgrims lived through the first winter, but when spring came, all 55 committed themselves to life in the New World, and so they watched the *Mayflower* sail back to England without passengers. Squanto, an Indian who had been taken to England at one time by some fishermen and had learned to speak English, helped them learn to plant New World crops of corn and squash, helped them learn where to catch fish and how to hunt. Squanto also served as negotiator and interpreter, helping them conclude a treaty that kept the peace for 50 years.

The following autumn, the colony had an ample harvest, insuring that there would be food for the winter months. Governor Bradford proclaimed a day of thanksgiving to God and, being an astute politician, extended an invitation to neighboring Indians to share in the harvest feast. The meal went on for three days and was punctuated by displays of the power of English muskets to impress the Indian guests. Preparing a feast for 90 Indians and 50 settlers must have been quite a job—especially if it was left entirely to the four Englishwomen and two teenage girls who had survived the winter. You see, thirteen Pilgrim women had been buried that first terrible winter. The feast was not much like the one we expect today. There was no milk, butter, or cheese, and no bread, for no cows were aboard the *Mayflower,* and stores of flour from the ship were long gone. Undoubtedly they had venison, and most likely they had partridges, ducks, geese, and turkeys. They had plain boiled pumpkin and corn in various forms, from pudding to corn cakes. Cranberries may have been boiled and perhaps sweetened with a little wild honey. Oysters, clams, and fish rounded out the feast. The Pilgrims laid aside their expectations, their memories of past holiday feasts, and gave thanks for what they had before them, for what was available in their new land.

What does it mean for us to live in the moment, without regrets or expectations—that is, to live in the wilderness of our own lives—hoping, yes, dreaming, yes, but without expecting or demanding something of the future? What does it mean to live out of this sense of abundance, this feeling of plenty? That's hard, especially when nothing in our personal lives seems to be going well. Sometimes we feel the way my son did one evening at bedtime when I asked him what he was thankful for, and he said, "I'm not thankful today. I'm angry. And I don't want to say what I'm thankful for. I'm tired of that." And so I let him be, because sometimes we need to be angry before we can be thankful, and that's OK, that's human.

Sometimes we just need to yell and scream and shake a fist in God's face. But over and above and through all that, there can exist the kind of primal thanksgiving I've mentioned, an attitude of living that says to God, to others, and to one's self: "Hey, I'm here. I'm available. What surprises, what manifestations of grace, will today bring?" To live like this is to be awake, to be utterly open, to wait palms up for the touch of the Spirit. It is strange and bewildering to me that some people feel miserly and grasping and in want, even though to outside observers they have so much to be thankful for.

I had a friend like that once. She was beautiful, highly intelligent, talented—and she had wonderful parents who loved her dearly. But she was always complaining, always had a kind of whine in her voice. With all she had, she never had enough. What she complained most about was not having a man in her life, and so when she found a handsome architect and fell in love, I naively thought she would be happy. But you know, she wasn't. There was something in her that made her unable to experience the bounty; instead, she always focused on what was wrong in her life. She lived in an attitude of scarcity rather than an attitude of abundance. She could never be filled.

Living in abundance is living by faith. It requires a groundedness in something larger than ourselves. The words of Wendell Berry say it well. Let me recall the last few lines of "The Memory of Old Jack":

"He saw that he would be distinguished not by what he was or anything that he might become but by what he served. Beyond him was the peace and rest and joy that he desired. Beyond the limits of a person's strength or intelligence or desire or hope or faith, there is more. The cup runs over." It is that *more* that allows the sense of abundance to exist, no matter what the actual circumstances. To live with a sense of purpose beyond what we can know or control, to give thanks with our whole being—by the way we stand, or eat, or speak to a stranger —such thanksgiving will keep us rooted and whole. Such thanksgiving has little to do with our situation, but everything to do with the eyes with which we see. Easy to say, you might be thinking. But how do I learn to see this way? As Annie Dillard puts it in *Pilgrim at Tinker Creek*, "I cannot cause light; the most I can do is try to put myself in the path of its beam. It is possible, in deep space, to sail on solar wind. Light, be it particle or wave, has force: you rig a giant sail and go. The secret of seeing is to sail on solar wind. Hone and spread your spirit till you yourself are a sail, whetted, translucent, broadside to the merest puff."

Under such a sail, your sense of scarcity leaves you, and you are moved beyond what you thought possible to give of yourself, out of an abundance you never knew was there, out of the *more* in which we live and move and have our being.

SO BE IT. AMEN.

Prayer

O Spirit of Life, be with each person here in this sanctuary today. Each of us has reason to pull back, to be afraid; but at a deeper level, each of us longs to live in the abundance only you can give. Help us to set our sails that the winds of grace might catch in them and fill us with the love that passes all understanding. AMEN.

Benediction

Go now, and live in such abundance that your lives spill over with joy and thanksgiving.

The Coming of the Child

DECEMBER 19, 1993

Each night a child is born is a holy night.
—Sophia Lyon Fahs, "Each Night a Child Is Born"

I LOVED BEING PREGNANT. As a woman in waiting, I felt beautiful and ripe. I remember smiling so much that my mouth hurt. I remember blessedly feeling that just *being* was enough—I didn't have to perform or achieve: I just had to grow this baby inside me. I just had to be an instrument of the Holy. I felt holy myself; I felt shot through with God-ness. In a way, every baby is conceived of God, is fathered by the Sacred. Yes, a kind of Immaculate Conception, pure goodness joined with flesh.

For the first time in my adult life, I felt absolutely given over. When the baby began moving in my womb, I knew he was his own little person—yet his existence was yoked with my own. Later, in the final stages of pregnancy, my whole being seemed to be in service to this child: I was awkward, I couldn't get around easily, nor could I find a comfortable way to sleep. But these things didn't matter: when you're in the midst of a miracle, you tend not to notice the small stuff. I went into labor on the day the baby was due, and in an even larger sense, knew that I had no control over events: I was there merely to cooperate. In about 16 hours, the baby came. He didn't like leaving his warm, protected space, and so he cried for at least an hour. And as he cried, I lay there celebrating and giving thanks.

If it were up to me, I'd go on having babies forever. But that is not to be. There come times for other birthings. The Holy is always bursting forth in startling ways in all our lives, and it is for us to prepare for the birth, to expect the unexpected, to be the instrument, to make room for the Holy.

Think for a moment about the birth of Jesus. An angel makes an unannounced visit to Mary, a young woman of Nazareth. He says, "Hail, O favored one, the Lord is with thee: blessed art thou among women." And the scripture reports, "Mary was troubled at his saying." You might imagine that she is thinking something like, "Who is this feathered creature, and what does he want?" He continues: "Fear not, Mary: for thou hast found favor with God." He tells her she is to conceive a child she will name Jesus, who will be known as the Son of God. Whereupon Mary—who seems to have her feet on the ground—asks a very practical question: "How can this be, since I have not known a man?" The angel says that God will take care of the details. And Mary says, "Behold, the handmaid of the Lord; be it unto me according to thy word." She says, in effect, "I don't understand. But I'm available." *Behold, the handmaid of the Lord.*

The Spirit invites, persuades, but we have to be the ones who make room for the birth. Think about the other characters in the story. Think about Joseph. His girlfriend Mary turns up pregnant, and he knows he's not the father. Should he marry her, or should he put her away from him? An angel appears in a dream and tells Joseph not to be afraid. He chooses to take his part in this great love story. He chooses Mary. And so he is the one who protects her and cares for her during the difficult journey to Bethlehem, when she is so swollen and awkward and easily fatigued.

Then there is the innkeeper. He is perhaps a good man, a fair man. But he doesn't recognize the specialness of this couple who come to his door. He just can't make room. Besides, she's about to give birth, and that whole woman's thing, he doesn't want to deal with. Furthermore, it might upset his paying guests. So he turns away from the Holy, back to the mundane. He just can't make room.

In contrast to the innkeeper, the shepherds are not busy. They are, as the scripture says, "abiding in the field, keeping watch over their flock by night"—just hanging out with the sheep, making sure none of them wanders off and gets lost. Once again, this time in the quiet Judean countryside, an angel appears in a great swath of light.

The shepherds are astonished, afraid. But they pay attention. And once again, the angel says the words that were said to Mary and to Joseph, "Be not afraid." The shepherds needed that reassurance. The coming of the Holy shakes us to our roots, turns us around, points us in a different direction. Be not afraid. Come and see the child. Come and receive the Holy. And so the shepherds drop everything and go. "They came with haste," the scripture says. And when they saw the child, they went throughout the countryside telling others of this wondrous event.

The wise men, too, put everything aside to follow the star that would direct them to the baby, to this new birthing of the Holy. They dressed in their finest robes and took their most expensive gifts for the child. For after all, when the star appears, the star you've waited for all your life, you don't dally with lesser things. You focus. You move. You get on with it. The wise men were ready for this birth; they were prepared for the journey and gave the best they had to give.

When you're in the midst of a miracle, you tend not to notice the small stuff.

The problem with the birthing of the Holy is that often we are not ready. You see, it usually comes unannounced; it comes in places and at times that are not convenient; it comes dressed in the ordinary and the humble, and we're expecting the large and the grand. We expect to find it in the symphony orchestra, and we hear it from a street musician. We expect to find it at Saks Fifth Avenue, but we stumble across it at Hamburger Mary's. We think it will be in Paris, and it turns up in Iowa City.

So how do we prepare? We don't try to psych out the Holy, to predict it, to make it happen; we prepare our hearts to receive. But here we have another problem. In order to prepare, we must go down into the darkness. We must give up the control and the illusion of control. In such a darkness, we become childlike again, childlike in our ignorance of what will happen next, childlike in our vulnerability and our innocence. The cynic in us wants to pretend knowledge, to disregard possibility, to sneer at magic. But the child knows the world as a magical place full of possibility. That is where we must be willing to go—to the purest, most elemental form of who we are, the part of us that is the most honest, the most spontaneous, the most creative, the part that gives us access to our tenderest and fiercest feelings.

We should know also that such preparation inevitably includes loss: for every new thing we become, we give away something of what we were. We are always leaving, are we not? Yet there are times when letting go is particularly difficult. We are not prepared. This leave-taking comes all too soon. The familiar is a comfort, and the new—however Holy, however redemptive—is not welcome. We feel confused or sad or scared. Just as the child grows in the darkness of the womb, we must descend into our own darkness, a place of dormancy, of resting, that makes a fertile ground for the seed of the Holy. And we must trust in the promise of new birth.

The Spirit invites, persuades, but we have to be the ones who make room for the birth.

I remember a time in my own life when I needed to go on a journey, and I was afraid. I couldn't make enough as a social worker to support myself and my two young sons, so circumstances demanded a change. After much heartache and searching, I decided to go to a seminary, Starr King School in Berkeley. I was living in Kentucky at the time, and I had grown up in Louisiana. I had never even been to California. Berkeley seemed like the other end of the world to me. Let's face it— it *was* the other end of the world. I also made the decision to leave my preteen sons with my former husband, in Kentucky, where they would have a large extended family and plenty of financial resources. Leaving them was like cutting off a piece of my own flesh.

I particularly remember the last day I spent in my home in Lexington. It was a grand Victorian house, three stories high, made of stone. This house was my castle, where I felt safe. On the day I left, I was alone in the house. My heart was heavy with loss, and I didn't know how to say good-bye to the life I had led in that house. I sat at the kitchen table a long time, watching the afternoon light sift through the green gauze curtains. I decided to go all over the house, into all the rooms, and touch the things I loved, and say good-bye that way. I went into the boys' bedroom and touched the red wallpaper with the golden eagles. I touched their beds where I had sat so many nights to read them stories. I went into my own bedroom and touched the carved mantlepiece and the clock. I touched my bed, which had been empty for too long.

I went down the hall to the spare room I had once rented out to a carpenter. I stood on his balcony and looked out over the huge back-yard with the maple tree and my garden, where I grew every vegetable you can imagine. I went back down the spiral staircase, past the blue and gold stained glass window, to the living room and touched the elegant lace curtains and the fireplace, the most beautiful of the six in the house. I went into the dining room, which I had turned into a dance floor after my divorce, and I remembered the parties with my friends from the local Unitarian Universalist church. Especially the Rocky Horror Picture Show Party. I went back into the kitchen, my favorite room, and touched the cabinets and the stove and the table where I made bread and where my boys had eaten so many good meals over the years. It was like saying good-bye to parts of myself. I began weeping, and the weeping went on as if it would never stop.

The problem with the birthing of the Holy is that often we are not ready.

Then something strange happened: it was as though great white wings came down and enfolded me, and I felt clean and pure and soft and open, like a child. "Be not afraid." I knew that I could leave, and that it was right for me to leave.

On our various journeys, our own trips to Bethlehem, we must prepare, and yet we must be patient—we must wait for the fullness of time: the child will come when it will come. We may go through a time of confusion, ambivalence, despair. We may feel all alone, and we may cry out with the pain of this birthing. We want someone else to do this hard work for us, but even the best midwife cannot do more than be with us through our travail. During this time, we must remember that the pain is not all there is: the pain is in service to the birthing.

Darkness and light. I don't know why we have these endless cycles in our lives. I don't know why fear and promise appear at once. The season of Advent is the darkest part of the year. And it is our necessary preparation for birthing. It is where we must be willing to go, if we would have wings enfold us and bless us and prepare us for the new. In this season of darkness, do not forget the angel's voice: "Be not afraid. I bring you good tidings of great joy. Be not afraid."

SO BE IT. AMEN.

Prayer

Be with us in this Advent season, and let us not despair of the darkness. Give us the faith that the child will come, faith that the new is possible, faith that the unknown will become known. Comfort us through the hard times, enfold us with great white wings, and let us rest, and let us hope. AMEN.

Benediction

Go now, and make yourself ready for the coming of the child. Make yourself ready for blessing.

Gifts Beyond Price

DECEMBER 20, 1992

No heaven can come to us unless our hearts can find
rest in it today—
Take heaven.
No peace lies in the future which is not hidden in the
present instant—
Take peace.
The gloom of the world is but a shadow behind it, yet
in our reach is joy—
Take joy.

—Fra Giovanni

GIFT-GIVING can be problematic. I'm thinking of my first Christmas gift exchange with my husband-to-be, which was something of a disaster. If I had had a mind to, I suppose I could have learned something from it. For Frank, I found a small leather elephant in a little Christmas shop called "The Magi." The clerk told me that the more the elephant was touched and held, the softer and more beautiful he became. "How appropriate!" I thought, and went home to box him up beautifully.

Christmas morning came—we were visiting with my family that year—and the gifts were distributed. I watched hopefully out of the corner of my eye as Frank slowly opened his package from me. He drew the elephant out of its box as though it were something dangerous. He turned it over and over and looked at all sides and then, bewildered, looked at me and asked, "What is it? A bank?"

"No, it's an aesthetic object!" I answered. "It's to look at and touch."

"Oh," he said.

Then it was my turn to open my gift from him. The box was large and heavy, and it rattled. As I tore off the colored paper, I saw the words "Hibachi: Directions for Assembly Inside."

"What is it?" I said.

"It's a thing to cook on," he said. "I thought you could cook some steaks for me on it."

"Is this a barbeque pit?" I said, looking at the picture. "You got me a barbeque pit for Christmas?"

"Sort of," he said. "You don't like it?"

Frustrated and close to tears, I said, "I was hoping for something more *personal!*

Gift-giving can be problematic.

Clarke Wells, a Unitarian Universalist minister and writer, suggests that in order to gain perspective on the gifts we really want to give to others, we might draw up a list of the nicest gifts we have ever received. I liked his list, and I'd like to share it with you. Says Clarke,

> While I remember a Daniel Boone hat and a magician set with special affection, the nicest gifts I ever got are in quite another category: the bell-ringer at Rockefeller Chapel who let me strike one of the largest tuned bells in the world during his playing of *Ein Feste Burg;* my mother giving me a complete Shakespeare for my 14th birthday; coach Al Terry saying, "Little Wells, grab your bonnet," and permitting me to enter as a freshman into my first varsity football game; a beautiful lady on a ship when I was still an acned teenager who kissed my face all over and told me she thought I was handsome; Dr. Henry Nelson Weiman telling me he had thought for several hours about a question I had raised and responding with a written answer the next day in front of the whole class; night after night my father playing catch with me in the back yard until it got so dark we couldn't see the ball; a Unitarian minister in Kalamazoo who put his arm around me after my father died and kept it there for a long time; a friend who flew several hundred miles to visit me when I was sick; a buddy who went to see three movies with me on the same day.

The nicest gifts people have given me have been enabling, confirming gifts, bestowing understanding and self-esteem, help in time of trouble and delight for ordinary days.

The gifts Clarke Wells speaks of are redemptive in nature—in the original meaning of that term *redeem,* to "get back" or to "buy back." They are restorative gifts, gifts that move one again to wholeness.

And these are not gifts we can get for ourselves—they do not come to us out of our own volition. As Lewis Hyde says in his wonderful book *The Gift,* "We cannot buy such a gift; we cannot acquire it through an act of will. It is bestowed upon us."

Hyde points out that in gift cultures, such as in many primitive Indian groups, no one really owns property; whatever is given is passed on to someone else in a year or two. The circular motion of the gift parallels the cycles of nature, where loss and renewal occur again and again. Only that which is given up is found again. That which is saved or hoarded is truly lost.

Our society is a commodities culture, and though we have much more material wealth than these primitive societies, we live by an economy of scarcity in which one's value is *Gifts have the power* measured by how much he or she accumu-*to join, or to bond.* lates, not by how much is given. In a gift society, people live by an economy of abundance, because what is passed along remains abundant. "Satisfaction," says Lewis Hyde, "derives not merely from being filled, but from being filled with a current that will not cease."

Giving, then, can become a way of life, yet giving is but half the process. One must also be able to receive well in order for the magic of abundance to work. In fact, as Hyde points out, it is only when we have truly received, only when "the gift has worked in us . . . that we can give it away again. Passing the gift along is the act of gratitude that finishes the labor. The transformation [or redemption] is not accomplished until we have the power to give the gift on our own terms."

I personally find that giving and receiving are tied together in my own life. I have trouble receiving and therefore end up starving myself until giving also is difficult. There have been missed opportunities in my life, which I recognized after the fact, and regret.

Soon after we moved to Lexington, Kentucky, I went to a Christmas party, a dressy affair right across the street from our home in the inner city, where new money and old money and slums were side by side. I knew no one but the hostess—she was old money. Alone, I wandered around trying to look elegant and comfortable. Then a woman approached me and said, "My husband would like to talk with you. Would you be willing to talk with him? He's over there," and she gestured to an old man seated across the room. "Sure," I said, and to my surprise I found myself talking with John Jacob Niles, the famous songwriter and ballad collector. He had snow white hair and a beard of the same silver white, and the most alive eyes I had ever seen. He must have been near 90. He entertained me with stories of his life during World War II. I told him how much I admired his work, but that I'd never heard him sing. He said, "You just get together a group of your friends, and I'll come to your home and sing for you." He meant it, I knew, but I found his offer difficult to accept. "Why should someone this well known sing for me?" I thought. And I let the days pass and the weeks pass, one year, two years. One morning I opened the Lexington paper to see a large colored picture of John Jacob Niles. He was dead. My gift could no longer be redeemed.

"What is there in me that cannot receive?" I thought. "Why could I not accept the gift of his music and pass it on in whatever form my own life's music became? What other gifts do I miss all around me, every day, because I refuse on some level to see or hear?" Perhaps receiving comes like loving, from a "yielding at the center" (in the words of M. C. Richards). That yielding is not done without some trepidation.

The nature of gift-giving involves emotional ties between the individuals involved. "We do not deal in commodities when we wish to preserve ties of affection," says Hyde.

Because of this emotional quality, gifts have the power to join, or to bond. And therefore, some gifts must be refused. One summer I worked as a chaplain in a prison, where as part of our orientation, we were taught never to accept a favor or a gift from an inmate, not so much as a soft drink or a piece of candy or a cigarette. For to do so might have started the bonding that puts one in a compromised position with another, so that professional objectivity is lost.

Gifts imply relationship. We need to take care in our giving and receiving. Even conversation is an erotic exchange if it involves more than chitchat, and when we give speech, we become part of what we speak with, Hyde says. Folk wisdom advises silence before evil.

A further quality of a genuine gift is the way it comes to us—not by our own searching or act of will, as I have said, but freely, by grace. Artists and writers speak of their talents and inspirations as gifts, and they experience their work this way. In Fellini's film *And the Ship Sails On*, which is about a great opera star, the heroine says about her singing, "It doesn't come from me. I am just a vessel." Writers find that ideas and characters appear as gifts, and when one's work is going well, the words come from sources deeper than thought. Whole poems may appear. Works of art, books, music may be sold, but they remain as gifts when the artist has labored in gratitude for that which came gratuitously.

What happens when a gift of talent or inclination is misused, or not used at all? The result is a deadening of the spirit and of the erotic, or life-giving, powers of the individual. One of *We, too, are gifts* the tragedies of a commodities culture like our *beyond price.* own is that consumer goods—things—have so much market value, yet the gifts of our artists and thinkers are difficult to redeem. Almost no serious writer can live from writing alone—our writers survive by teaching and giving readings. And visual artists have a hard time of it too: art with popular appeal is often unimaginative, whereas the truly creative work may go begging. So individuals who after all must earn their daily bread, end up painting houses so they can spend some time painting canvases, giving their gifts.

Some of our greatest writers and thinkers have done their work in constant privation or stress. In her book *Silences*, Tillie Olsen records the unfinished works, the plans that never came to fruition because of want or other responsibilities pressing upon these writers.

Women have especially suffered this way, because of cultural demands that they be caretakers of others. Many have denied their natural gifts in lieu of giving in other ways. But men, too, have taken jobs that were not in keeping with their real talents or likings, because of the pressure on them to make money and support the family financially. The commerce of the spirit suffers, and would-be givers and receivers lose in our modern industrial world. Perhaps the deadness in the eyes of so many workers comes from this, the denial of their gifts.

Our talents are gifts, surely, and in the largest sense, our very lives are gifts. Who can doubt this at the birth of a child? Here comes this tiny new human being, with potentials and powers so far beyond our making. I don't need miracles beyond that. I don't need evidence of divinity beyond that.

Henry Nelson Weiman, Clarke Wells' teacher whom I referred to earlier and a leader in the school of process theology, refers to human growth as "God working in our midst." He says:

> The individual undergoes this growth [in the same way that] sunshine, air, and earth undergo transformation into a scarlet poppy. A [human being] can do more than the poppy. A [human] can seek out the conditions that are required for this growth and for its greater abundance. Above all, a person can yield in blessed abandon to the transforming power of it. But [one] undergoes it; [one] doesn't cause it.

There it is—that "yielding at the center" again. This is not a supernatural process for Weiman, but "ultrahuman"—that is, beyond the control of conscious volition.

Our greatest spiritual leaders have lived out of this awareness of life as a gift, a gift to be given away.

In Taiwan, they tell the story of Wu Feng, and they say the story is true. In the 18th century, the island of Taiwan was inhabited by aborigines who hunted and fished to survive. They worshiped an angry god who demanded a human sacrifice every year. Gradually the Chinese began to trade with these aborigines and win their trust. Wu Feng, a young Chinese man, became a translator and mediator between his people and this mountain tribe. He went to live with the aborigines and taught them many things: how to farm and how to read and write. He also taught them about the preciousness of human life, and they gave up the practice of human sacrifice. After 40 years went by, Wu Feng was considered a sage, the wisest of wise in the tribe.

At this point there was a terrible drought followed by a flood, followed by a drought again the next year. The aborigines believed their old god was angry, and they wanted to appease him with a human sacrifice. Wu Feng talked to them at length, explaining that nature had caused their troubles, not an angry god. But they would not hear of it: they demanded a human sacrifice.

Wu Feng said all right, he would send someone the next day to ride through the forest wearing a red gown and a red hood. He was the one they were to kill. The tribesmen waited in the bushes the next day, and sure enough such a figure came riding into the forest. They fell upon him from all sides, stabbing him to death. Then they pulled the hood from his face, only to discover they had killed their beloved friend, Wu Feng. They screamed and shouted to the sky. They beat upon the earth. This went on for three days. They never offered a human sacrifice again. Later a small chapel was built to the memory of Wu Feng, a chapel that can be seen today in the city of Chaiyi.

Wu Feng sacrificed himself to teach these people, who were not even his own. We might say, he died for their sins—not to appease an angry god, but to teach these blind people how to truly see.

"He came that we might have life, and that more abundantly." These are words from our own scripture, our own story. It is said the story is true. "And she brought forth her first-born son, and wrapped him in swaddling clothes, and laid him in a manger, because there was no room for them in the inn."

The gift of the baby at Christmas is a redemptive one. It is a gift beyond price, bestowed upon us from a source beyond our power.

The inherent message in this wondrous gift is that we, too, are gifts beyond price. And we can do no better than to give ourselves—no hoarding here, but life in abundance, freely offered, flowing from a stream that will never cease.

SO BE IT. AMEN.

Prayer

We come today with thankful hearts, remembering gifts of person and of plenty, gifts that have come to us by grace. Help us to be able to receive. And help us to see ourselves as worthy, that we might freely give, and complete the circle of our being. Hold us fast during the rush of this holiday season, that its real gifts may be ours. AMEN.

Benediction

May you have the faith to give yourself as a gift, not counting the cost, knowing that nothing which is given from the heart is ever lost. Go in peace and joy.

The Circle of Being

The Journey Is a Circle

SEPTEMBER 12, 1993

*The place God calls you to is the place where your deep
gladness and the world's deep hunger meet.*
—Frederick Buechner

ONCE IN A WHILE I run across a cartoon I love so much that I
want to keep it forever, so I tuck it away in my file. I'd like to
begin this morning by sharing one of those cartoons. It's by Jules Feif-
fer. He begins with a frontal drawing of a very fragile-looking man,
whose right half is not quite connected with his left half. As the cartoon proceeds, the two sides move further and further apart. The man
says, "People are always saying the same thing about me: 'Bernard,
you don't have a center.' They tell me, 'It's OK in your twenties to not
have a center . . . but now you're 45. You've got to find your center.'
Well, 10 years ago, I did find my center." (And now jagged lines appear in the space between the two halves.) "I did find my center. It had
sharp, white teeth and ate people! Let those who can handle it, have a
center. I'll stick to my edges."

Does this strike a familiar chord? We find it difficult to trust
what's inside—who knows what monsters might emerge? So we stay
busy, play our usual roles, dwell upon the past or fear the future, and
are careful to stay away from the center, away from the real. It's too
scary, it might have sharp, white teeth. Let me tell you something. It
does have sharp, white teeth. And it also has longing, and pleasure,

and beauty, and the deepest sources of love and compassion. It is the path to reality. It is the path to the divine.

One of the ways we folks in the Western world have of avoiding reality, and God, is to conceptualize the world as working almost exclusively on a linear plane. Each of us is supposed to develop, even spiritually, according to certain steps. In our work lives, we set goals and objectives and move towards them. We're even supposed to grieve in stages. It's all so logical, so clean. We get to have the illusion of control, but there's a trade-off: we never get real, and we rarely find God.

What if we conceptualize our lives differently? What if—instead of a march onward and upward—the journey is a circle? What if we leave the home of self only to return again and again to self, to the same person, and yet to a person paradoxically transformed? To see our lives this way, it helps immensely to understand deep within our bones that we really are going nowhere, that even as we are born and experience the loss of our first home, our mother's womb, and gain the world, we move again and again in cycles of loss and gain, until we give up this mortal flesh and move once again to the realm of the soul. There will come the time of the harvest. Our plans, our schemes, our dreams of conquest will vanish, whether we are a hungry beggar or a person of power and wealth. The journey is all we have, and the journey is a circle.

I have spoken of finding reality, or finding the divine. The Sufis speak of "opening the eye of the heart." For them, the heart is the seat of knowledge or wisdom, not of sentiment. The eye symbolizes an immediate and direct sense of vision. According to the Sufis, opening the eye of the heart will overcome the illusion of duality, including the most profound duality of all, that between subject and object, and will bring "arandat," or the peace and bliss that come by overcoming separation. We cannot do this alone, they believe, but only with the help of God. When we awaken to who we are, we become who we are. And—this is the tricky part—we actually come to know that we are what we always were. As the Zen Buddhists would say, "Before enlightenment, we chop wood and carry water. After enlightenment, we chop wood and carry water."

The central paradox of the journey home to self is that to really be at home, we must leave home. Perhaps we must travel north, which symbolizes a spiritual journey; or south, a journey of the flesh; west, to new frontiers of experience; or east, a journey to the past.

Let me tell you the story of Rabbi Eizik, son of Rabbi Yekel of Cracow. After many years of great poverty that had never shaken his faith in God, he dreamed someone told him to look for a treasure in Prague, under the bridge that leads to the king's palace. When the dream recurred a second and then a third time, Rabbi Eizik prepared for the journey. But when he arrived at Prague, he found the bridge was guarded day and night, and he dared not start digging. Nevertheless, he went to the bridge every morning and walked around it until evening. Finally, the captain of the guards, who had been watching him, asked in a kindly way whether he was looking for something or waiting for somebody. Rabbi Eizik told him of the dream that had brought him from a faraway country. The captain laughed: "And so because of a dream, you wore out your shoes to come here! Poor fellow. If I had had faith in dreams, I would have gone to Cracow to dig for treasure under the stove in the room of a Jew—Eizik, son of Yekel, that was the name! I can just imagine what that would be like—in Cracow, half the Jews are named Eizik and the other half are named Yekel!" And he laughed again. Rabbi Eizik bowed, traveled home, dug up the treasure from under his own stove, and with it built the House of Prayer that is called "Reb Eizik Reb Yekel's Shul." Hear this story, and let its truth stay in your heart: there is something you can find nowhere in the world, and yet there is a place where you can find it.

It helps to understand deep within our bones that we really are going nowhere.

The Prodigal Son is a familiar character who had to leave home to find it. You know the story. There are two sons. One says to his father, "Father, give me my inheritance." The father does so; the son then journeys into a far country, where he soon squanders the money in "riotous living." We can only guess what that included—probably the usual "wine, women, and song." Anyway, soon his money is gone, and he finds himself deserted by his erstwhile companions and hard at work at the only job he could find—feeding pigs. He is so hungry he wishes he could have the food the pigs are eating. He determines to return home and ask his father for forgiveness. I love the next part. The Bible says, "His father saw him and had compassion, and ran and embraced him and kissed him." The son asks for forgiveness, and the father says, "Bring quickly the best robe and put it on him; and put a ring on his hand, and shoes on his feet; and bring the fatted calf and kill it, and let us eat and make merry; for this my son was dead, and is alive again; he was lost, and is found." At this point, those of us who have young adult children *know* this is a parable and not a real-life story. A friend of mine said, "I tried that when I was young, and not only did my father not kill the fatted calf, he damn near killed the prodigal son!"

The really interesting thing here is the response of the older son, the one who had stayed faithfully at home and worked in his father's fields. He says to his father, "*I* never got a fatted calf, *I* never got even a goat, to eat with my friends." What a little prig! What a whiner! The younger son journeyed to explore his dark side; he learned about hunger and poverty and compassion—and he learned the depth of his father's love. The elder son, the "perfect" son, remained exacting and self-righteous and envious. Sometimes the journeys we take are not easy on ourselves and not easy on others, but to fail to take the journey that is calling to us is to fail at becoming who we are meant to become.

An essential part of the circle is reconciliation with the past. *Reconciliation:* to make consistent, to make compatible, to be content with. I have an aunt I visited with this summer. She is the very model of what a woman can be as she ages. Now 83, she still loves to exchange ideas and try new things. We went to the beach in Washington State. I was holding back, because I knew the water was cold. She immediately took off her socks and shoes, rolled up her pants, and waded in. "Aren't you coming?" she shouted back. What could I do? I had to take off my shoes and follow her. And yet as wonderful a woman as she is, she carries a burden inside. She brings it up every time we are together. "I can't forgive Papa," she says, referring to her father. "I try, I pray about it, but I just can't forgive him." He was a brutal, selfish man who beat his children and demeaned them constantly. Her hatred weighs upon her, pulls her down, pollutes the clean, clear space in her heart, prevents her mainly from loving herself as well as she could.

If we do not make peace with the past—with whoever may have hurt us—we will never make peace with ourselves. And that restlessness of the soul will use our energies, energies that could be used for working, for playing, for loving.

Some think that psychoanalysis is all about change. But it's not. It's about self-acceptance. Of course out of that self-acceptance will come change, as a matter of course. That's the irony of it. You have to love the child. You have to see the child in the adult. When my boys visited me this summer, one evening I did as I always do: I took out the family photo album, and we sat together and looked at it. I see myself as a six-year-old in my white communion dress, with my white gloves and white shoes and white prayer missal. I see my hands clasped tightly around the prayer book. I see my rigid little body. I imagine the thoughts of the child that was, that is, myself: "Am I a good girl? I want to be a good girl. Will I ever be good enough?" We slowly turn the pages.

I'm a grown-up now, and those are still my questions: "Am I good enough? Will you stay? Will you love me forever?"

There is a picture of my family, the last time it is intact. I am eight years old. I am sitting with the same rigid body, my knees close together, my hands clasping this time my little purse. My mother has on a wide-brimmed hat and is smiling broadly, and I am looking up at her. Again, I imagine my thoughts: "I want to be a good girl. If I am good enough, will you stay? Will you love me forever?"

I'm a grown-up now, and those are still my questions: "Am I good enough? Will you stay? Will you love me forever?" I'm learning to answer them as an adult.

"Yes, I'm good enough. Not good enough on my own—but with grace, amazing grace, good enough to be of service."

"Will you stay?" Nothing ever stays. All is in movement. All is dynamic. It is the nature of things. But when I am with you, in this moment, I am yours. I will never betray you.

"Will you love me forever?" Yes, I will love you so long as time and memory exist. I will love you because you have touched my life, and I have touched yours, and neither can ever be the same.

The child that was lost, that child has been found.

The journey is a circle. But when you circle round to the same place, you find that it's never the same. Recently I was talking with someone who was experiencing a painful bout of depression. "But

I've been happy for a year!" she said. "I thought that was all behind me, I thought I'd never be depressed again." Well, if she's prone to depression, it may always come back for a visit now and then. But each time she'll be stronger, because she will have lived through it one more time. Each time she'll be friendlier to it, and less abusive—less abusive to herself—and over time depression may lose its hold on her. Depression may decide to pass right on by, finding that she no longer succumbs to sorrow.

The circling round will often let you measure your growth. A few months ago I received a package in the mail. It was from an old friend, someone I had not seen in 12 or 15 years. I knew what was inside. It was my long-lost nightgown, a lovely flowered gown my former mother-in-law had bought for me at Neiman Marcus. I was an overnight guest at my friend's home and had left the gown there. But I had lost track of her and despaired of ever seeing her or the gown again. I still have the matching robe, and whenever I wore it, I would long for the missing gown. I tore open the package, and sure enough—there was the gown! It looked as though it had been hanging in my friend's garage for a few years, so I washed it carefully a couple of times. When it was all clean and dry, I put it on. That is to say, I tried to put it on. It would not fit what is now my "mature figure." I stood there in the bedroom, held it in my hands, and thought for a long time. Why was the gown so important to me? Why had I fantasized about it so often? How could I have imagined the gown would fit, that I could just step right back into it? It represented my old life, some of the safety and security I had enjoyed. I couldn't confine my body or my spirit in that way now.

Journeying home, we become who we are, what we always were but didn't know we were. We open the eye of the heart. We remove the barrier between subject and object, and so become one with others and with the earth. The journey is a circle, with each round of the circle bringing us closer to home.

A story about the great Hasidic leader Zusia appeared in the winter 1992 *Storytelling Magazine*. One day Zusia came to his followers, his eyes red with tears, his face pale with fear. When they asked him what was wrong, he said, "The other day I had a vision. In it I learned the question the angels will one day ask me about my life."

His followers were puzzled at his anxiety. "Zusia, you are pious.

You are scholarly and humble. You lead a model life. What question could be so terrifying that you would be frightened to answer it?"

Zusia turned his gaze to heaven. "I have learned that the angels will not ask me, 'Why weren't you a Moses, leading your people out of slavery?' And they will not ask me, 'Why weren't you a Joshua, leading your people into the promised land?'"

"What will they ask you?" asked his followers.

"They will say to me, 'Zusia, there was only one thing that no power of heaven and earth could have prevented you from becoming.' They will say, 'Zusia, why weren't you Zusia?'"

It is a telling question for each of us. Why aren't we who we are?

When the circle comes round right, we feel a sense of peace, of connectedness with all that is. It's like that feeling when the last puzzle piece falls neatly into place, and nothing more is missing. It's like that first breath of cool morning air. "All you have is your soul," sings Tracy Chapman. Take whatever journey you need to take to make your soul grow. She's right. Your soul is all you've got.

SO BE IT. AMEN.

Prayer

O Spirit of Life, we so quickly run away from ourselves. We run from the wholeness that beckons to us at every hand. We refuse to see our own beauty. We think we can escape through work or love or money or alcohol or whatever. But when we allow the eye of the heart to open, we know we belong to you. Let us walk in that knowledge daily. Give us the courage to leave our fears and misgivings behind. Let us believe we can be who we were meant to be. In the name of Life itself we pray. AMEN.

Benediction

May each one of you here today have the courage to follow the path you need to follow, and may we as a community lift one another up when we fall and mirror the beauty of the one in the other's eyes.

The Blessings of Aging

APRIL 25, 1993

Praise God for His mercies,
For His austere demands.
                    —May Sarton, "Gestalt at Sixty"

*I*SUPPOSE in order to talk about aging, we need to define what "old" is. I have generally defined an old person as someone about 20 or 30 years older than I am. Someone becoming 40 can feel old; on the other hand, people turning 70 can be so alive and vital that they never think of themselves as old in any sense of the word. A lot of being "old," then, is in your head.

Of course, American culture conspires against us after we reach middle age, for although we are a nation growing older and older, we are surrounded with images of the young and the beautiful, and we are told the good life has to do with particular pleasures that are the prerogative of the young. We learn to dread growing older, for we wonder what life will offer when we move into that realm.

When I was studying in seminary, I remember running into another student, a woman who engaged me in conversation, who seemed to know me though I couldn't place her. Finally I had to own up to the fact that I didn't know her. "I'm Irene," she said. "You know me." I said, "Irene, oh, sure. But you look different." That's when she told me she had had plastic surgery on her face. I had to find out more. All the seminary students I knew were poverty-stricken, living on savings and student loans. How could anyone spend money on plastic surgery? And why? I thought I might as well get to the heart of the matter. "Irene, does this have anything to do with your fear of death?"

"No," she said. "Death I can handle. I just hate ugly." She was never ugly, of course—just showing some signs of aging as she moved into her late 40s. I felt judgmental about her decision, but if I had bothered to look a little deeper into my own fears, I would have been more compassionate. I remember thinking that my body would never age—and indeed, it held up really very well. Then one day I was looking at some photos that had just been developed, and I asked myself, "Who is this woman with the double chin?" I looked closer. It was me. She was I. No matter how you say it, it didn't feel good. Yes, my flesh had begun to sag. Wrinkles appeared, and energy lagged. Yes, I really am going to age, just like everyone else. Yes, I really am going to die. So this sermon came out of my own wanting to know more about the final phase of life. Not that I'm there yet! I want to know more about the compensations of this part of life. I want to know more about how to do it well. So I've been reading about it and talking to older people about how they experience their lives.

About 40 of you met me for a brown-bag lunch on the subject, and your comments were helpful. You spoke of new freedoms that come with age. You no longer feel the need to "produce," so you are taking up new interests that you never had time for before. One person has gone back to playing the trumpet; another is writing poetry. You told me that you can now indulge yourself—do just what you want—without feeling guilty. You have the freedom to be fully yourself, to not worry about what other people think, even to be outrageous, if you like. Because you have come to a deep sense of self-acceptance, you can express yourself more clearly and strongly. You are free from competition, from the drivenness that characterized your earlier life.

And you also spoke of a growing awareness. Some of you said you experience works of art or music in greater depth and intensity than ever before. You have time for quiet, for contemplation, solitude, and so you begin to sort out what is really important from what is of lesser consequence. Perhaps as you see the body giving way, you are pushed to consider things of the spirit. Time is precious, and you may feel deeply thankful for the hours, the days you are given. You want to use them well. You may begin to lose yourself in a kind of giving that seems a part of a larger pattern.

But these blessings of aging are not assured, are not guaranteed, just because you are growing older. We all know some people who just become grouchy and demanding as they grow older. M. F. K. Fisher, known for her writing about the pleasures of food, writes,

> I have formed a strong theory that there is no such thing as "turning into" a Nasty Old Man or an Old Witch. I believe that such people . . . were born nasty and witch-like, and that by the time they were about five years old they had hidden their rotten bitchiness and lived fairly decent lives until they no longer had to conform to rules of social behavior, and could revert to their original horrid natures.

These blessings don't just happen naturally; to some extent, they must be earned. We need to consider the last phase of life as a developmental phase, just as all the others have been. There are tasks to undertake, if we want to age well and to die well. So, what are these tasks of aging, the tasks that if completed, will lead us to harmony and peace in the last phase of living? I have identified four.

The first of these is to finish your issues—your issues with the people who were supposed to love you, the people who were never supposed to hurt or abandon you. Not that we ever totally finish our issues, of course. But if you arrive at the cusp of old age and are still stuck in anger or grief, take some time to put it behind you. Having years of living behind you helps, I think, because you are able to see the long picture. You don't take things so personally. You see that people are mainly acting out of their own needs and limitations, not because they set out to hurt you. And you can then marshal some compassion. You understand that perhaps you expected more than husband or mother or friend could deliver. You remember that you, too, have hurt others—not because you wanted it to be that way, but because of your own longings and limitations. And so you stretch spiritually. And you forgive.

I am reminded of my grandparents, with whom I grew up. Of course, in those days we didn't talk about family systems theory, and how we need to be reconciled with our family of origin. We just sort of muddled through as best we could. My grandparents lived to celebrate their 67th wedding anniversary. Big Papa was dominant and controlling, and Granny was passive and sweet, and so they seemed to fit together most of the time. But she knew how to get to him. I especially remember their domino games, when they were in their 80s. The card table is set up on the front porch. They are drinking iced tea. Big Papa is cheating on the points, as he always does when he is behind. Granny never calls his hand; instead she starts talking about her former suitors. "I wonder whatever became of Edward," she says. "My, oh my, how that boy did love me."

"Will you be quiet, Mama, and let me think," he says. He plays. No points this time. Granny is humming softly, "In the sweet by and by, we shall meet on that beautiful shore . . . ," and she plays the double six, for fifteen points.

These blessings don't just happen naturally; to some extent, they must be earned.

"Everybody said I should have paid him some attention, but I was stuck on you," Granny says. "He told me I was the prettiest girl he had ever seen. Well, that's what they all said—that I was the prettiest girl in five counties." Big Papa's frown grows deeper. He concentrates on the game, and swats hard at a fly that's buzzing round his head. "Ha!" he says. He makes ten points and records fifteen.

Granny continues about Edward. "They say he made a lot of money. In the lumber business. He always had his head about him, that's one thing for sure." She scans the table. "Domino!" she says, as she plays her final piece.

Papa knocks his dominoes down. "This is the last time I'm playing with you, Mama. Lord-o'mercy, if you can't keep your mouth shut, how can I think what I'm doing?" He stalks inside, slamming the screen door behind him. Granny puts away the dominoes, still humming "Sweet By and By." She knows he'll be back tomorrow for another game. She'll let him win, and he'll be all right.

Granny and Big Papa died six months apart, for neither could live without the other. They had become one. And yet he had not been able to forget about Edward, and she held on to her one weapon in this game of hearts.

The second task I suggest is that you use your memory well. Memory is what you make it, you see. There is no such thing as the truth about the past: there is only what you select from the past and how you make meaning from it. Tell your story, for the story is the crafting of raw experience into meaning. Your story is where your real theology emerges. It is no accident that the child says, "Tell me a story," for this is the child's way of saying, "What does it all mean? What can I trust in? What can you give me to carry me into the future?"

Loren Eiseley, the naturalist and essayist, tells of a tree, a cottonwood sapling, that he and his father planted when Eiseley was a young boy. He remembered his water bucket and his toy spade. The tree, as he said, took root in his mind, and he took shelter under its branches, though he himself was passed from hand to hand, and the people who were supposed to grow old under the tree died or moved away. Sixty years later something drove him to return. He flew 2,000 miles and walked another mile to the site. But when he arrived, the tree was not there. Eiseley writes,

> the tree, the tree that no longer was, that had perished in its first season, bloomed on in my individual mind, unblemished as my father's words. "We'll plant a tree here, son, and we're not going to move any more. And when you're an old, old man you can sit under it and think how we planted it here, you and me together."

The tree that grew in his imagination had become a living symbol of his father and the love he carried for his father. Even in its impermanence, it had connected him with the permanent. Choose your memories well; tell your stories, for they will tell you who you are, and they will give courage and direction to those who will follow.

The third task I would suggest is to stay young in spirit, no matter how old you are chronologically. Youth is so much a matter of spirit and not years. I had a striking experience when I went back home to North Louisiana for my father's funeral about a year ago. I was just leaving the Baptist Church, where I had talked with the minister about funeral arrangements, when I ran into Miss St. Claire, who was my youth music director when I was in high school. I hadn't seen her since I was a teenager. She looked just the same: a large, handsome woman with white hair gathered into a bun on the back of her neck—but she was no longer a "miss": she had outlived one husband and was about to outlive the second one, a small man who was leaning on her unsteadily. "Miss St. Claire!" I said.

She squinted and stared and finally said, "Why, Marilyn!" And she squinted and stared some more and said, "You look so much— younger." As a matter of fact, I was about 30 years older—but I thought for a minute, and I knew what she meant. "I'm so much happier now," I said.

I hope I'm able to continue growing younger. I look at certain older people for direction. I see they have stayed engaged with the world, with interesting people, with ideas, with work as they define it. I see the life in their eyes, for the eyes are the key to knowing who is young and who is old. I think of Harry Scholefield, the minister emeritus of the San Francisco church, whose eyes have all the innocence and wonder of a child's. In our own congregation, I think of Barbara Feeley, the well-known landscape architect who just turned 90, whose eyes gleam with excitement as she talks about her next project. Barbara Feeley will never be old.

There is no such thing as the truth about the past: there is only what you select from the past and how you make meaning from it.

French writer Maurice Goudeket in his book *The Delights of Growing Old* puts it this way:

> Every morning my breakfast coffee has a fresh taste, and this comes as much from me as it does from the pot. There is the paper too, which will put me in touch with the entire world; and any paper, properly read, has an almost incredible amount of astonishing, moving, ludicrous items in it. . . . Eventually I emerge into the street, and of all wonders, the street is the most wonderful. . . . There are faces, a sea of faces, with everything that they conceal and everything that they give away. At the same moment I feel both united to them and entirely separate. I walk on, on and on, faster and more happily; my senses grow sharper, my thoughts soar up and away, and all the time there is the humming of the great swarm of memories. . . . My day has only just begun; I have hardly even begun to reckon up my intangible treasure.

These are the words of a man who will be forever young, for he experiences the world with intensity and delight. An interesting biographical note: he married the French novelist and essayist Colette when he was 36 and she was 52, and when she died 30 years later, he was married again to a young widow. At the age of 71, he became the father of a son, his first child.

The fourth task I would put before you is to accept the reality of death. The very first person who spoke at the brown-bag lunch said, "I just want to say that I never think about death. I stay active. In fact, I don't think I will ever die." At that point, I put my hand on his shoulder and said, "As your minister, I need to tell you something . . ."

Why should we consider death, accept it, and finally embrace it? Because we will never know the fullness of life, the poignancy of experience, until we do. We will never ask ourselves the important questions, questions like, "What do I want to do with the gift of time?" "What do I want to give myself to?" "What do I want to be remembered for when I die?"

Cesar Chavez died just last Friday. He was a small man, only 5 feet, 6 inches, not an imposing figure. As the child of migrant farm workers, he attended 65 elementary schools. He never even graduated from high school. But more than any other single person, he is responsible for improved conditions among migrant workers. Many of you took part in his protest by boycotting grapes. Indeed, for a time, the whole world watched while this tiny, frail man fought the power structures that would exploit human beings. In one protest effort, he went on a 36-day fast, which severely damaged his health. He knew the reality of death, and he knew why he was living. There is a very real and present connection between the two.

The flesh will not hold. But in its very failing, it teaches us to look beyond itself for meaning.

Sometimes elderly people ask a question that disturbs me, like one asked by a 93-year-old man named Herb, a former congregant of mine. Herb, a man still in fine health, asked me to come and visit him in the retirement home where he lived. He gave me a cup of tea then told me of his concern. "I'm not happy," he said. "I just don't feel useful any more." It is a Western concern, I think—the echo of a specifically American question, a Calvinist question: "Am I worth anything if I can't do anything, if I can only be?" It made me sad to hear him say this. With tears in my eyes, I said to him, "Herb, don't you understand how important it is for me, for everyone at the church, to have you seated in your special seat every Sunday morning?" (He always sat in the last seat on the end of the second row.) "It gives me courage to see you there. It gives me hope." It was enough for Herb to be a witness. It's enough. As one of the participants in the brown-bag lunch so eloquently said, "You think there's enough love in this world? So long as you have love in your heart, you are needed."

Truth is, we do age. The years pass ever more swiftly, and with their passing, we come to know that no matter how we try to postpone our decline, eventually we will bag and sag, we will puff and pant. The flesh will not hold. But in its very failing, it teaches us to look beyond itself for meaning. Truth is, there's an essence in each one of us that can't be touched, that's beyond death and decay. We know it's real when one person reaches out to another in pain. We hear it in music that stirs memory. We feel it when we find ourselves suddenly awash with thankfulness at the beauty of the day. Truth is, we are held in the arms of the Beloved. We are one with all that is.

SO BE IT. AMEN.

Prayer

O Beloved, one who holds us fast, may our diminishing powers teach us faith, may our tired flesh show us the way to trust. May we treasure the days we are given, and use them well. Keep us young in spirit so long as we live, and may our eyes stay bright from the light within. AMEN.

Benediction

May your years teach you wisdom; may you grow old in love.

Heaven: What It's Like and How to Get There

DECEMBER 6, 1992

It can in no sense be said that heaven is outside of any one; it is within . . . and a [person] also, so far as [that person] receives heaven, is a recipient, a heaven, and an angel.

—Emanuel Swedenborg, *Arcana Coelestia*

WHEN I FIRST ARRIVED in Portland to begin my ministry, the *Oregonian* ran an article about me, and I am quoted as saying: "The kingdom of God is here on earth. In many churches, there's talk of heaven and hell. We don't put a lot of energy into that. We do put a lot of energy into making this world a better place." My topic this morning? "Heaven: What It's Like and How to Get There." Never say never. I can only justify my topic by saying that I am intrigued with the idea of heaven—I thought it would be fun to do a sermon on the subject.

I want to begin by sharing with you part of an article by a David Heim, who has been researching the subject for the past few years for gospel radio, the *National Enquirer*, the *Sun*, and the *Weekly World News*. Here are the answers to some questions that may have been gnawing at you.

What does God look like? He is tall and has a white beard. He wears a robe. We know this from the *National Enquirer*. Michael Jackson says that God appears to him onstage during his concerts. Jackson describes him as "a giant figure" who dances in time to the music.

What does God's voice sound like? It's like "a hundred baritones and a symphony orchestra rolled into one." A *Weekly World News* article says that a Russian space probe recorded God's voice. He was rather territorial, saying, "Heaven is mine. You must stay away." Maybe this just means God is an environmentalist and doesn't want us to muck up space. The article did not say what language God spoke.

Where is heaven located? It's at the exact center of the Milky Way. The *Weekly World News* published a photo taken by a space probe. A computer-enhanced enlargement reveals a number of Greek temples at its center.

Will there be romance in heaven? I know that's an important issue for you since the Pope recently proclaimed there will be no sex in heaven—which I have to say kind of took the wind out of my sails. An article in the *Sun* disagrees. Yes, there will be romance in heaven. Strangers will fall in love. Divorced people will reunite. (That's a bit unnerving!) Married couples can find new partners.

Can people in heaven communicate with those back on earth? Yes. And now they can use electronics. In one impressive case, a woman got a message from a relative who had been dead two years. First a voice said, "This is the long-distance operator. I have a collect call." You'd think that heaven would have a WATS line.

Enough of this. I actually did some more scholarly research and found some fascinating information on the history of heaven—or at least a history of Judeo-Christian concepts of heaven. As it turns out, each era has its own version of heaven, one that fits its own particular cultural needs. It seems we project onto our visions of heaven all we especially enjoy on earth—and a healing of all that is frustrating or painful in our earthly lives.

The early Christians of course drew much from Jewish history and tradition. The assumption that God rewarded the good helped make up for their persecution in the earthly life, and they believed that when the suffering of this world was done, they would be able to fully experience the divine. In our own country, black spirituality developed out of much the same rationale: I may be suffering now, but one day I'll be in glory.

During the medieval period, three new cultural concepts dominated: the city, the intellect, and love. So writers began to speak of heaven, not as a garden, but as an urban area. Medieval theological systems included intricate intellectual speculation on heaven. This was your basic "how many angels can dance on the head of a pin" discussion. And the courtly love tradition born at that time was translated religiously—especially by nuns—into rapturous mystical union with Christ. For example, Dame Julian of Norwich wrote, "God wants to be thought of as our lover."

The Renaissance, with its emphasis on the pleasures of this world, put forward a paradise that was human-centered rather than God-centered. Renaissance art pictured heaven as a place where unclad men and women relax in the grass, swim, or simply stroll about, a place of "leisure and loving in a natural setting" (in the words of Colleen McDannell and Bernhard Lang, in *Heaven: A History*).

The Puritans were after perfect knowledge in heaven. The Victorians—you guessed it—were skeptical about the flesh. As the Presbyterian John Kerr explained, "Sensual pleasures shall not attach to our perfect and renovated nature." With the Victorian emphasis on the family, heaven became one big family holiday: going for walks, playing games, discussing pious topics.

The first person who introduced us to a modern heaven was a man way ahead of his time. He was the 18th-century figure Emanuel Swedenborg, an engineer, mathematician, and scientist who began having visions of heaven and gave up his career with the Royal Board of Mines to begin recording his dreams. By the time he died in 1772, he had produced sixteen books and five volumes of a spiritual diary. Now what made his heaven modern? Heaven is no longer just a place of "eternal rest," but the inhabitants experience spiritual progress—the journey to God does not end, but goes on eternally. Sounds a little tiring to me, just like modern life. Onward and upward! Improve! Grow! Produce! Myself, I'm still back there in the Renaissance relaxing in the grass and swimming in the lake.

Another man who was ahead of his time was Friedrich Schleiermacher, who found comfort not in the hope of a future life, but rather in the experience of the divine in the present. He said, "In the midst of finitude to be one with the Infinite and in every moment to be eternal is the immortality of religion." In his thinking he prefigured the modern symbolist thinkers Niebuhr, Tillich, and Bultmann, who speak of the "eternal now" in the context of the theory of relativity, where time and space are not static but fluid and dynamic. *The eternal now.*

This ends my quick overview of heaven through the ages. One thing I noticed in my study is that through all times and cultural shifts, certain themes kept emerging and re-emerging. Perhaps these themes help us to understand some of the deepest longings of the human heart. Perhaps they even help us to understand the peculiar pain and joy that coincide with being human. One of these themes was the hope of being rejoined with loved ones, a belief in the eternal nature of love. Another was the desire for perfect knowledge: "For now we see through a glass, darkly; but then face to face: now I know in part; but then shall I know even as also I am known" (1 Corinthians 13:12). A third theme—which I will explore today—is the longing to escape the confines, the limitations, of earthly life and to experience the wholeness of the ultimate, the divine.

> *We are the only creature given the dual knowledge of what perfection might be and the distance we fall from it every day.*

Our flesh does limit us terribly, doesn't it? Little things become irritating to me—like having to floss your teeth every single day. Don't you get tired of that? Waking up day after day after day and flossing your teeth. Or worrying about your intake of cholesterol, since every bite of your breakfast egg now whispers, "Early death!"

We are the only creature given the dual knowledge of what perfection might be and the distance we fall from it every day—the only creature who longs for completeness and lives daily with partiality. Our knowing is both blessing and curse. In a beautiful film called *Wings of Desire*, two angels—who look just like ordinary men but are invisible to humans—are seen going about their rounds ministering to people in various stages of hurting or despair. They hover near and place a comforting arm around the suffering: a would-be suicide, a man dying after an automobile accident, a poor person riding a train. One of the angels then falls in love with a beautiful trapeze artist and decides he will give up eternal life and accept the pain and loss that will ultimately be his as a mortal. It is the price he is willing to pay for love, for real rather than angelic relationship. Perhaps it is the very transient nature of our existence that gives the depth, the poignancy, to our love.

I was very much moved by that film. First, my imagination was caught up with the idea of these angel protectors, these caring beings, floating around. And then it occurred to me that we do have angel visitors from time to time, and mostly they come in the guise of other human beings. Sophy Burnham in *A Book of Angels* tells the story of Hugh Hildesby, rector of the Church of Heavenly Rest. Hugh says one of his parishioners is an angel. He is also a messenger, says Hugh. His name is Phil, and he is a street person. Schizophrenic and homeless, Phil refuses to stay in a shelter. He sleeps in doorways. In the daytime, or when the weather is cold, he sits in the church. He dresses in rags. He is filthy and never washes. He smells. Once the funeral of a prominent lawyer was in session. Phil sat in a pew in back of the church, dirty, smelly, not a pretty sight. The law partner of the deceased came up to the minister, Hugh, and said with quiet disdain, "Can you get him out of here?"

I was crying because of some deep memory of every other loss I had ever experienced.

Hugh said, "I understand completely. Yes, I can get him out. You should know, however, that if he leaves, I'll go with him. He belongs here. He's been a member of this parish for ten years."

The lawyer looked at him, startled. "I think I understand," he said. "I'm sorry I asked that." Burnham writes, "In that way Phil—this homeless man—stands as a beacon of what we're supposed to be."

One night of a Christmas week a few years ago, this same church had a Christmas party after a service. The congregants were in the parish hall having cookies and coffee, when out of the church rose a magnificent voice singing "O Holy Night." It was a trained voice, radically beautiful. Everyone listened, awestruck, then rushed to see who was there. "It was Phil and God," said Hugh. We have these moments of heavenly grace sometimes, moments when a spark of divinity shines through the ordinariness of our days. These moments, which give us a sense of unity with all that is, act as a touchstone for us as we imagine perfect unity, perfect love.

Such a moment came for me just before I moved to Portland. A congregant of mine in Cincinnati—a beautiful African American woman with a smile that won't wait—lay in the hospital critically ill. Gayle is her name, and she is the head usher at First Unitarian there in Cincinnati. Gayle has liver cancer, and had had 80 percent of her liver removed. Apparently, you can survive quite well with such radical surgery, but the remaining part of the liver must "kick in," as her doctor said, and start functioning. Gayle's liver didn't kick in. For weeks she lay there, the yellow in her face telling the story of her condition. She was put on dialysis. Still the liver refused to function properly.

I saw Gayle almost daily. Usually friends and family were there, and we didn't have much of a chance to talk. Many times she was in great pain. I would hold her hand and read to her, and at the end of my visit she always said, "Now let's all pray together." Whoever was there took hands in a circle of love, and I prayed. I prayed for all I was worth. For indeed Gayle had become quite a special person to me. At church her smile radiated such warmth and love that people were already blessed, even before they had been seated for the service.

Gayle asked me several times when I was leaving town. She didn't want me to go, and I didn't want to go. But finally the day came when I had to leave. For whatever reason, nobody else was with Gayle that day, and she and I had the leisure to talk. She said, "Let's talk about whatever you want to talk about," and smiled up at me. "Well, what do you want to talk about?" I asked. She looked thoughtful then said, "My grandmother." She told me all about this strong, good woman who had raised her. I told her that my grandmother had raised me, too. Then she said, "My grandmother's favorite hymn was 'Precious Memories.' Do you know that hymn?"

"Oh, my gosh," I said. "Yes, sure I do. That was my grandmother's favorite hymn, too!" Then I told her a little bit about my grandmother. It was about that time that I began to weep. Now this is not my usual bedside manner. It's not professional, I know. But I couldn't help it, and I didn't even want to help it. Big silent tears kept pushing their way out of my eyes. I wasn't sure why I was crying. It was a mixture of things, I think. I was crying because of some deep memory of every other loss I had ever experienced. I was crying because I loved Gayle and felt so helpless to do anything for her. I was crying because I had to leave her, knowing she might die. As though she were reading my mind, Gayle looked at me and said,

"Marilyn, I know that I'm going to be all right. I'm going to be all right if I live, and I'm going to be all right if I don't live."

"Yes, you're going to be all right," I answered, feeling keenly the truth of what she said. She gave me a gift that day. She showed me that faith goes way beyond any reassurances about an afterlife. It's enough to know that whatever is, will be all right. The good news is that Gayle is out of the hospital and is healing. I talked with her last Thursday, and she tells me that this very Sunday will be her first day to usher again at First Unitarian.

And the good news for every one of us is that we're going to be all right. I know that's not very definitive, not very specific, for a sermon entitled "Heaven: What It's Like and How to Get There," but quite honestly it's the best I could do. What it's like is being all right—completely all right. And how to get there? You don't have to wait for the afterlife. Just open your heart to loving right now. You'll have all the heaven you'll ever need. And that's a promise.

SO BE IT. AMEN.

Prayer

O Spirit of Life, we long for the wholeness and the goodness that seem to escape us everywhere we turn. Help us to accept ourselves as we are, in all our brokenness. It seems that all our lives, we are losing things we love, people we love. Help us to know the eternal nature of love. Sometimes we feel afraid and alone in our fears. Let us live in the faith that we are all right, now and forevermore. AMEN.

Benediction

May heaven manifest itself in your hearts and in your hands. Go now and be angels unaware.

The Seven Deadly Sins of Unitarian Universalism

APRIL 17, 1994

When I have to choose between two evils, I like to choose the one I haven't tried yet.

—Mae West

W E ARE HERE TODAY to talk about sin—the seven deadly sins. We could talk about the seven cardinal virtues instead: wisdom, justice, temperance, courage, faith, hope, and love. A good list to live by—but not nearly so interesting as the seven deadly sins. Why is it that evil is so much more interesting than goodness? I mean, how many of you really think that Luke Skywalker is as interesting as Darth Vader?

Back to the seven deadly sins. I'll wager there are not ten people here who can name them all. In fact, when I was preparing this sermon, I met with the Portland downtown ministers for our regular monthly breakfast—the Baptist, the Lutheran, the Congregationalist, and so on—and none of them could come up with the whole list. The waitress was serving our oatmeal, and we were saying things like, "Is lust on the list?" It was a strange conversation. OK, are you ready for these? If you're making notes, now's the time to start writing. The seven deadly sins are, yes, lust—lust did make the list. Surprise, surprise. Lust is followed by gluttony. After gluttony come pride, envy, anger, avarice, and sloth.

Now a cursory look at this list tells us that it is not suitable for Unitarian Universalists. These are just not our big sins. In fact, we could do with a little more of some of these. Take lust, for example. We could be more embodied, more incarnational, more passionate, more lusty. Can you imagine anyone saying of us, "Now those Unitarians, they're a lusty lot." Maybe the Universalists, but not the Unitarians. And how about anger? We're big on repressing our anger. We wouldn't want to appear unseemly, impolite, out of order. But some things are worthy of our anger. Anger that honors what is right, anger that fuels action, is honest and good.

It is the mother of all sin and the one unforgivable sin. That sin is pride. Another of the seven that we could use more of is sloth. Sloth—what an appealing sin! I wish I could be lazy, but every time I try, I just become paralyzed with guilt. We are worker bees, with one project after the next. I think our busy-ness is how we handle our anger, actually.

So I just don't find this original list that helpful. Except for one. It is the deadliest of all the deadly sins. It is the mother of all sin and the one unforgivable sin. That sin is pride. *Pride.* And, my friends, I hate to say this—but we've got it in spades.

Most of these pride-based problems, I have to say, apply more to Unitarianism than to Universalism. Early Unitarians, upper-class folk, were characterized by their reason and intellect; Universalists, middle-class folk, were characterized by their warmth and tolerance and belief in universal salvation. We joined together as one denomination in 1961. Although the theology of the two groups was similar, Thomas Starr King—the famous early minister of the San Francisco church—explained the chief difference this way: "The Universalists believe that God is too good to condemn them to hell; the Unitarians believe that they are too good for God to condemn to hell."

Are you ready now for our list of sins? Let's begin with "Staying Stuck in the Negative." Deciding what we don't believe, but never moving to embrace the positive values of what we do believe. Many Unitarian Universalists are rebels without a cause. But you can't build a life on "no," and you can't invite others to join a "no"-based movement.

Did you hear about the Unitarian Universalist who was shipwrecked on a desert island? He survived there alone for 25 years before he was found by a passing ship. His rescuers marveled at the house he had built for himself out of the simplest of materials—branches and leaves and bark. "This is a beautiful home you've made for yourself—so aesthetically pleasing. What good taste you have!" said the ship's captain. "Thank you," he replied. "And what is this shack off to the side?" asked the captain. "That's my meditation hut," said the man. "I see. And what is that huge, magnificent, stupendous structure up on the hill?" asked the captain. "Oh, that," replied the man. "That's where I *don't* go to church."

Now it's true that we are a church of heretics, that we were founded by people who questioned authority. I have no problem with that. But consider: the word "heretic" is from the Greek root *haireti-kos*, meaning "able to choose." One who is able to choose, not one who merely rejects. Our first martyr was Servetus, a theologian who questioned the concept of the Trinity. He chose to be burned at the stake with a copy of his heretical book strapped on his thigh. He chose.

Some of our churches do things that seem more stupid than heretical. When Unitarian Universalists are featured in the national news, it's usually because somebody has done something outrageous. The press expects us to provide good copy. For example, there's the U.U. fellowship that had a program on the sacredness of the flesh and invited a stripper to—well, strip—during the Sunday morning service. The press went crazy with that one. When I was in Berkeley, a U.U. student started an organization called the International Society for Religion and Animal Rights. When her dog Wind-of-Fire died, she held a funeral service and invited all the other pets in the neighborhood. I quote from a news article:

> [The service] was graced by the solemn trappings of religion, including the sharing by animals and humans of a communion ritual. They took the "bread of life," served from a makeshift altar below the pulpit. The animals took communion first, and some choked a bit on the "bread of life" soaked in grape juice, but none barked or balked.

We allow dissent—and the price we pay is that we sometimes invite the ludicrous.

The second deadly sin of Unitarianism is intellectualizing—you know, head-tripping, living from the neck up. We do like to hear the sound of our own voices. I like the question Roy Blount, Jr., poses: "Has any religious group ever expressed concern that they were boring God?" It's a question worth asking ourselves when we run from experience and lose ourselves in endless talk. The menu is not the meal.

I heard Neil Postman, the heretic of the communications scholars, talk about his book *Technopoly: The Surrender of Culture to Technology*. He said, "The fact is there are very few political, social, and especially personal problems that arise because of insufficient information." Instead of amassing more information, he said, what we need is a narrative, a story, that pulls us forward through the tough times and gives our lives meaning. Our culture has no such story. I thought to myself, perhaps that is the central purpose of the church—to suggest such a narrative. We don't so much need more facts and figures: we need a story to live by.

The third sin is connected with the second: failing to embrace our faith with passion. Ralph Waldo Emerson, in his famous Divinity School Address, explained why he left the Unitarian ministry. He called us "corpse cold." That is changing with the infusion of spirituality into our movement in the last ten years or so, but it's still a concern.

A few years back our Association asked distinguished leaders of other faiths to speak to the topic "Why I Am Not a Unitarian Universalist." Harvey Cox, a professor at Harvard Divinity School best known for his book *The Secular City*, had this to say:

> When you're raised in an evangelical Baptist church, there's a certain kind of urgency and life or death quality about the preaching and about repentance and about baptism . . . there's something at a very profound feeling level that goes beyond even the most persuasive kinds of arguments and reasonable reflection. . . . I think I might miss in the Unitarian church a willingness [to use] some of the more traditional, gutsier symbols. Unitarians don't like to talk about blood and we Baptists talk about blood all the time. I find some of the Unitarian language—the hymns, for example—appalling. . . . I also have another thing that keeps me a Baptist despite everything, and that is the Baptist church is a church of poor ordinary people in this country. Eighty percent of the black people in this country are Baptists and an awful lot of very poor white folks.

Now you may not want to sing "The Old Rugged Cross" every Sunday, but Cox makes us think about what might be missing. How seriously do we take our faith?

Our lack of passion for our faith shows up in our giving levels in this denomination. Though we have the highest socioeconomic level of any denomination, we give about half as much as members of other faiths. When Bill Creevy, the minister of the Presbyterian Church down the street from our church, made it known that he was against Ballot Measure 9, the anti-gay measure that came before our voters, he lost two pledges, one for $35,000 a year and the other for $65,000. I told my congregation, "We'd have to lose a couple hundred of you to lose that kind of money!"

What we need is a narrative, a story, that pulls us forward through the tough times and gives our lives meaning.

The fourth deadly sin is self-righteousness. Some of us flat-out don't believe in evil, not in others and certainly not in ourselves, in spite of in-your-face evidence such as the Holocaust, for example. We take that soft, mushy liberal attitude that if we all had good parents and warm milk at bedtime, there would be no ill will or violence in this world. In his essay "The Current Crisis in Remorse," Garrison Keillor writes from the viewpoint of the Director of the Remorse Department in a modern American city: "We in [the] remorse [field] are a radical minority within the social-work community. We believe that not every wrong in our society is the result of complex factors such as poor early-learning environment and resultant dissocialized communication. Some wrong is the result of *badness*. We believe that some people act like jerks."

Yes, sometimes you act like a jerk; sometimes I act like a jerk. That used to be called sin. It used to call for repentance. It used to depend on mercy. But that would make us dependent and childlike, wouldn't it? Yes. All the better. We need to recognize our dependency. We need to say "I'm sorry," and start over with a clean slate. How long has it been since you got down on your knees to pray? Maybe we should cultivate a little humility in our spiritual gardens instead of choking out blessings with the weeds of self-righteousness.

Sin number five is elitism. The danger for Unitarian Universalists is regarding the church as an organization where the elite meet, an organization to meet the needs of a superior social group. We are not a social club or a civic organization. We are a church, and we need to open our doors to all who would enter in need of spiritual food, to all who share our religious values.

So much sin and so little time! Moving right along to number six. Number six is failing to recognize our interdependence. Although one of our "Purposes and Principles" includes honoring the interdependent web of all existence, we by and large hate to see ourselves as needing anything from anyone else. Ask us to help others, we're OK with that—but don't ask us to accept help. I remember when I first came to First Unitarian, I went to the hospital to visit a woman who had been struck with sudden paralysis in her legs. I walked in, and the patient gasped, "Oh my gosh, I'm worse off than I thought!" If we are a community, then we have to admit that we need one another. We have to be willing to accept as well as to give.

Some of us flat-out don't believe in evil, in spite of in-your-face evidence such as the Holocaust.

The final sin on my list is, as I said, the BIG ONE: pride. It takes into account most of the others I have suggested, including staying stuck in an anti-institutional, negative place; believing we can think our way to salvation instead of depending on mercy and grace; self-righteously disregarding our own moral and ethical failings; thinking of ourselves as elite, better than others; and being unwilling to receive, lest we might appear weak. Number seven is the one unforgivable sin because it is the only sin that irrevocably separates us from God—it is the sin of putting ourselves in the place of God.

Note that these sins are not just ordinary sins—they are deadly sins. Deadly because they deaden our lives, drain us of love and human connection. Theologically, the opposite of sin is salvation. And what is salvation? To save. It's from the same root as "salvage"—to rescue that which is lost, sunk in the murky depths, to bring it back up into the light, to restore it to its full value. We're talking about spiritual rescue. Salvation is that which connects us to others and to God (or to our highest values), that which gives us new life and transforms us.

And why do we need that new life? We're not talking about a ticket to heaven here, we're not talking about fire insurance. We need this spiritual salvaging both for ourselves and for the larger world. For ourselves, because we're not going to find any peace elsewhere. The words of St. Augustine keep coming back to me: "My heart is restless until it rests in thee." Until it rests in the absolute love that holds us and keeps us.

And the larger world needs us. We Unitarian Universalists are a very special people, unique in the world of religion. Where else do you find a religious people who understand that faith cannot be coerced, that belief has to have intellectual integrity, that each person is precious beyond measure? Who know that truth is where you find it and no place else, and that each one of us is struck through with divinity? Where else do you find a religious people like this? There are so many hungering for spiritual food, and we are called upon at this time in history, with thousands upon thousands pouring into the Portland area, to invite them to the table—the welcome table.

We are a greatly gifted people, blessed beyond measure. We can't afford to be blind and prideful. We are too much needed. Let us walk among others with humility and with thanksgiving. Let our minds continue to create, but also let our hearts be broken open, that we might walk in a new kind of wholeness and know the meaning of obedience.

SO BE IT. AMEN.

Prayer

Help us this morning to take stock. We like to think we're above it all. We like to think we can handle things. But there are some things we can't manage, can't control—like our lives, sometimes. Help us to get on our knees when we need to, to ask for forgiveness. Help us to walk in humility and in thanksgiving all the days of our lives. AMEN.

Benediction

Go now and covet goodness, lust after righteousness, envy the saints.

Is There Life Before Death?

MAY 1, 1994

All sins are attempts to fill voids.

—Simone Weil

*I*N "THE SUMMER DAY," Mary Oliver asks: "Tell me, what is it you plan to do with your one wild and precious life?" Her question is a haunting one. She says to kneel down in thankfulness. Know that you are blessed. Death will come all too soon, she says. Live your life.

Her dictum sounds simple. But in fact it is a profoundly counter-cultural statement. Is there life before death? Will you live before you die? If you do, you will have to make that an intentional choice—for you see, in the script for this culture, there is a lot of death before death. You can see deadness in the eyes of the people at the supermarket, pushing their carts down the aisle of 2,000 boxes of Crispy-Kiks or Sugar-Pops, or counting out carefully clipped coupons at the check-out stand. You can sense numbness at the mall as shoppers vaguely peruse the sale goods.

What are the dominant messages of our culture? How are we admonished to live? We are told to buy. Anything, just buy. Last year's dress is not good enough this year. We are told to make widgets for 30 years so we can pay our mortgage payments—that is, if you can even get a job at the widget factory these days. You might have to settle for being a temp widget-maker. We are told we are not lovable unless we are young and thin. We are told we should compete because there is not enough of anything, and we need to get ours. We are told that children and those who care for children are not very valuable human beings. We are told the poor want to be poor, that they are separate from and not like us. We are told that art doesn't matter, but armaments do. We are told that we own land and water and air. These messages are lies—not just white lies, but deadly lies, for they deaden our spirits, make our lives small.

In the face of such assumptions, how are we to respond? Sometimes I like to imagine that I would do my own ad campaign, plastering the truth up on billboards and having the truth interrupt our TV shows. "We interrupt this program to tell you not to buy anything new this week. Share your money with the poor." Or how about this one? "Take time today to give thanks for the swan and the black bear and the grasshopper. Get down on your knees in the grass." Or what about a billboard that proclaims, "You're beautiful just because you're a human being. You don't need to change a thing about yourself." Can you imagine what it would be like to be bombarded with truth from the media?

Seriously, I think that in the face of our cultural messages, we have to be outrageous. We have to thumb our noses and go our own way. Against all good advice, refuse to make widgets in order to buy clothing you don't need to go on a vacation away from your boring job making widgets. You are made for something more. Dare to look inside yourself and ask what you really want in this world. Each of you, for one thing, is a creator in your own right. To claim that power, without censoring yourself, is to open up all kinds of possibilities. Do you want to paint or teach or organize or build? Find a way to do that, and to support yourself economically at the same time. It's *Your Money or Your Life*, as one recent book puts it. To create, to birth, brings joy, for it connects you with the very primitive impulse to give new life. Yet to the culture at large, your choice might be impractical, sophomoric—outrageous.

Another big influence on the choices we make is our gender role. There's nothing new about gender roles—every culture has them, and this kind of human sorting has a cultural efficiency to it. The problem is that all human beings don't fit easily into their designated roles. Our particular culture is becoming more and more flexible with gender assumptions, and thankfully, that has led to more freedom for the individual. I have a brother who is 6 feet, 7 inches, and his hobby is decorating birthday cakes. He's right out of the South—he shoots, he fishes—and he decorates cakes. Why not? I know a man who became a lawyer and hated his work. His wife loves her work as a civil servant, so he stays home with the two children, cleans house, and cooks; she gets up at 6 a.m. every day and walks out of the house with a briefcase. I believe it's harder for men to buck gender stereotypes than for women, because they don't get much support for doing "women's work," which is generally degraded in our society. But I believe it's crucial for both men and women to choose according to their own desires and abilities, and not to blindly follow cultural norms.

A related warning: choose substance and spirit over form every time. Since cultural expectations are givens that we are hardly conscious of, it is easy to choose a form that seems right on the surface, but is empty of any life-giving quality. I remember a time when I was applying for a job. I badly needed this job because I was an unemployed single mother at the time—but I had a gut feeling that the job was not a fit for me. I ignored that feeling, looked the director of the agency right in the eye, and said, "I really want this job," which was a boldfaced lie. Just at that moment a light bulb fell out of a fixture onto my head and crashed into a thousand pieces. I took the job anyway, and it was a disaster.

Dare to look inside yourself and ask what you really want in this world.

There was another, much more significant time when I chose form over substance and spirit. That was when I decided to get married. I was 28, and no self-respecting Southern woman could get much past 25 without being called an old maid in those days. So when I happened across a good man, someone who would make a good living, someone who would be a good father, I married him. It was time. He wanted my heart, but I couldn't give it. Sadly, I found I could have no integrity within that empty form, and so I had to leave.

Somebody asked me the other day if I support marriage. Do I support the concept of marriage—or for gays and lesbians, holy union? Yes, of course. Nothing stirs my heart more deeply than to hear two people who love say their marriage vows, each to the other, and promise to enter into the mystery of that sacred union. But do I respect the form of marriage when the substance, the spirit, is not there? No, I do not. I support love. I support life. Not empty form, which denies and deadens.

I want to say a word now about whining and moaning. It's not good for you. Now I'm not talking about genuine sorrow, genuine grieving, which has a clean, purposeful feel to it. No, whining and moaning are in quite another category. They signal excuses to avoid joy, to avoid relationship. They deal in stereotypes and negatives. Whiners and moaners say the same thing over and over again, and their friends get tired of hearing it. "I can't find a relationship, because all women are _____." (You fill in the blank.) Or "I'll always be a failure because my father was _____." (You fill in the blank again.) You know, you *can* decide—on a very intentional, conscious level—to say "yes" to life.

Choose substance and spirit over form every time.

You may need some help to get over your woundedness. But redemption is possible. The dead do come to life. I've seen it happen. You've seen it happen. There is fire in everything. Where is the fire in you? Where is the passion?

We are meant to stand there "shining and willing," in the words of Mary Oliver. We must accept life on its own terms, and that means accept what we do not and cannot ever understand—all the suffering and loss that we encounter in our living. We cry when we come into this world, and we continue to weep. We could interpret that weeping to mean we are not loved—or we could come to understand that we weep precisely because we do love. We all know absolute love and safety from the beginning of our existence—in the womb of our mother. We know what love is like—and I believe that deep memory stays with us all the days of our lives, and each time we are led to weep, we weep because we know love and we mourn our loss.

To live well means to live with courage, to be present with whatever is your reality. *Whatever.* Depression—not clinical depression, which may be a chemical imbalance—but your garden-variety depression, which many of us experience to a greater or lesser extent, has to do with keeping the lid on. In order to say "yes" to life, you have to acknowledge your pain, your frustration, your fear, your anger. Neurosis is created and fed by our trying to escape legitimate pain. Yes, there is life before death—but it all ain't pretty. You don't get to pick and choose; if you would live fully, you've got to feel it all.

To live well means to give yourself to something larger than yourself. Nothing is more boring than living just for yourself. Give yourself, and be all used up with the giving. Let me tell you about Siegfried and Roy, from Las Vegas. They wrote a letter to *Time* magazine that read like this:

> Our concern for the virtual extinction of the white tiger . . . led us more than a decade ago to create our own breeding foundation to help preserve that beautiful species. Our animal family has grown to 27, including five snow-white tigers. We have dedicated our lives —as well as the resources of our estate—to perpetuating this endangered species.

That letter struck me: they have dedicated their lives and their resources to the white tiger. That's impressive. At least on one level, they are leading passionate lives.

To live well means to risk loving. And yet of all the risks we take in this world, perhaps this is the most difficult. Some of you saw the film *Shadowlands,* which portrayed writer and scholar C. S. Lewis as he moved from being a smug intellectual to being a man who allowed himself to love, who became willing to pay the price of love. He wrote,

> To love at all is to be vulnerable. Love anything, and your heart will certainly be wrung and possibly be broken. If you want to make sure of keeping it intact, you must give your heart to no one, not even an animal. . . . It will not be broken; it will become unbreakable, impenetrable, irredeemable.

To live well is to love well, to open your heart, to offer yourself daily for redemption.

Today I have asked a lot of you—and of myself. You might ask, "How? How is it that I can live in love, live with courage, live for purposes larger than my own? How is it I can live imaginatively, refusing cultural mandates that would deny me deep joy and celebration?" There is no easy answer, no quick trick. But I do know a starting place. And that is an intentional commitment to live a life grounded in the Spirit; to make an internal shift that allows you to put soul at the center. This way you will have a partner, a covenanted relationship with the Holy. You already have within yourself the answers you need. But they may be covered over with fear and distrust, or with pride.

Just one word of warning. You think the message is not urgent. You think you have time. You don't. Time has you. We zone out, living in our familiar, our comfortable ways, knowing vaguely that something is wrong, maybe terribly wrong. Not stopping to reflect because of what we might find, or not find. Feeling helpless. Not believing that redemption is possible. You don't have time for a minute more of this. Stop. Turn yourself around. *Tell me, what is it you plan to do with your one wild and precious life?*

SO BE IT. AMEN.

Prayer

O Spirit of Life, forgive us for being careless with the hours and days we have been given. Too often, we lend ourselves to unworthy ends and waste the stuff of life. Help each one of us to know that our life is precious, and our choices do matter, to ourselves and to one another. May we shake off the old garments that no longer fit, and may we dare to ask what does. Love us and lead us, for we want to live before we die. AMEN.

Benediction

May your heart open like a flower, and may you be a blessing to all you come upon.

How Could I Not Be Among You?

APRIL 3, 1994

*Death builds bridges as long as we still hear the living
words, the song.*

—Margaret Randall

ABOUT SEVEN YEARS AGO I got a letter from an old friend
of mine named Julia, a woman I taught with in New
Orleans. I hadn't heard from her for a while, so I was happy, pleased
as I tore open the envelope. As I looked at the hastily scribbled lines,
my body tightened and froze.

"At 4:30 p.m., January 8, my life changed," the letter read. "After
a routine physical, I was told the bad news: I have an advanced malig-
nancy. It's in my right breast. 'We don't have much time,' the doctor
said. 'We have to get you into surgery right away.'"

Five days later she had the operation—a radical mastectomy, that
is, the removal of her breast and the lymph nodes, where the cancer
had spread. She was told she had a 50-50 chance of survival. The good
news is that she is just fine—now, ten years later, she has had no recur-
rence.

But I remember my reaction on the day I received that letter. First
I felt shock that this could have happened to my friend. Julia was a
widow who raised two children alone and was nearing retirement.
She planned to travel and to write. And then I felt angry. How unfair
to have this happen to her now, after her lifetime of hard work! I felt
sadness that she should have to go through this agony of mind and

body, with no one, no family nearby. For several days I left the open letter on my breakfast table, just as a way of being with my friend.

I called, of course. And she sounded good—strong and vital. I asked her in the course of our conversation, "Is there anything I can send you?" And knowing I had been postponing work on a novel, Julia answered, "No, just write your novel. Do what it is that you really want to do, while there's still time. Write your novel, Marilyn. That's what you can do for me."

She gave me a gift that day, and I pass it on to you today. Do what it is you are called to do, without hesitation, without delay, for "time is not on your side." Not for any of us.

We humans are cursed in the sense that we are animal creatures who instinctively reach for life and avoid pain and death—and at the same time, unlike other animals, we are conscious that we will die one day. For most of us, that acknowledgment is difficult. At some level, we think death is going to come to everyone else, but not to us. We are surprised, astounded, to find that we, too, will join all the others who have gone before. We can scarcely conceive of our own "non-being," to use Paul Tillich's terminology.

We are moved to ask ourselves, What happens to us after death? Do we in any sense remain alive? There are those who believe that we go to heaven, if we're good; and heaven, through the ages, has been defined as each specific culture conceives of the good life. What would that mean in terms of contemporary American culture? Will there be MTV in heaven? Will there be "virtual reality"? If so, please count me out. Other traditions believe in reincarnation, that we keep doing life over and over again until we get it right. Still others say that our soul merges with some kind of world soul. And some of course believe that this business about a soul is something we made up to help us get through the night—that our existence has about as much eternal quality as that of a cockroach.

I don't know what comes after death, if anything. Sorry, I can't give you definitive answers this morning. But I have been impressed by the work of Dr. Elisabeth Kubler-Ross in the area of death and dying all during her career. Her latest thinking has been surprising to the hardcore scientists who saw her as one of them: she believes there is life after death, an opinion based on the many accounts of near-death experiences she has heard related by her clients and others. Dr. Carol

Zaleski, who is a scholar of religion at Harvard University, confirms many of Kubler-Ross's findings in her book *Otherworld Journeys*.

Dr. Zaleski examined many eyewitness accounts of life after death from medieval to modern times. Across the centuries and across cultural lines, the accounts are remarkably similar. First, the soul, or self, leaves the body and hovers nearby, observing the scene. Commonly, the disembodied self watches as doctors or others try to give help or to resuscitate the body. Second, there is a review of the person's life. Then, third, there is a guided journey through a dark mist or narrow passage or locked gate into a peaceful realm of brightness and timelessness. Of course, there are variations—in South Asia, one person traveled on the back of a cow, while a New Yorker hailed a taxi for his trip. But the general path remains the same.

Do what it is you are called to do, without hesitation, without delay, for "time is not on your side."

From one prominent researcher in the field of near-death experience, a professor of psychology named Kenneth Ring, comes a typical description. These are the recorded words of a 33-year-old man named—would you believe—Tom Sawyer, who had been working under his truck when the supports gave way, causing his chest to be crushed. His 9-year-old son called the paramedics, and Tom was rescued. In the following passage, he tells about the light he saw after traveling through a dark tunnel:

> The next sensation is this wonderful, wonderful feeling of this light. . . . It's almost like a person. It is *not* a person, but it is a being of some kind. It is a mass of energy. It doesn't have a character like you would describe another person, but it has a character in that it is more than just a thing. It is something to communicate to and acknowledge. And also in size, it just covers the entire vista before you. And it totally engulfs whatever the horizon might be. . . .
>
> Then the light immediately communicates to you. . . . This communication is what you might call telepathic. It's absolutely clear. The first thing you're told is, "Relax, everything is beautiful, everything is OK." You have a feeling of absolute, pure love. It's the warmest feeling. Then the thing is, the light communicates to you and for the first time in your life . . . is a feeling of true, pure love. It can't be compared to the love of your wife, the love of your chil-

dren; even the most beautiful moment in life couldn't even begin to compare. If you can imagine what pure love would be, this would be the feeling that you'd get from this brilliant white light.

The second most magnificent experience . . . is you realize that you are suddenly in communication with absolute, total knowledge. It's hard to describe. . . . You can think of a question . . . and *immediately* know the answer to it. And it can be any question whatsoever. It can be on any subject. One of the religious-orientated questions [I asked] was in regards to an afterlife and this was absolutely answered. . . . Upon entering that light . . . the atmosphere, the energy, it's total pure energy, it's total knowledge, it's total love, pure love—everything about it is definitely the afterlife, if you will. As a result of that [experience], I have very little apprehension about dying my natural death.

People who have had a near-death experience and a vision of the afterlife, whether they are medieval monks or contemporary atheists, do not think they were hallucinating. They believe the experience was real. They come back to earth transformed. They feel privileged, and they want to share what they know with others. Also—and I think this is significant—they are no longer afraid to die. They don't go out and kill themselves, because they understand that they have things to accomplish before their time comes to die. But they are not afraid to face that time when it does come.

These gestures of love are passed from one of us to another, and they are passed down to generations that will follow.

Now I know these accounts have been criticized by some as being merely tricks of the brain, some little evolutionary pacifier to comfort us as we near death. My own response to these stories is that they seem to make sense. As I see it, the universe is dynamic, ever fluid, ever changing. Nothing is lost; energy is changed into another form, and everything is remade anew. This is the lesson of modern physics. This is the lesson of spring. I don't know what comes after death, but to believe that something in the essence of a human being lives on in some other form, transformed, as pure spirit, the mind of God—however you want to put it—makes sense to me.

And there is another way in which I believe all human beings live on: that is in the memory of others they leave behind. That memory is conscious, in part, but it is also unconscious. The conscious memory is easier to recognize. You know how stories are often told after someone dies? Friends and family sit around and swap tales about the one who is gone, holding that remembrance among them like the treasure that it is, for it gives them courage and strength to live their own lives well; it helps to confirm their own ethical codes; it sustains them as they face their own decline and death.

The unconscious memory is more subtle and more diffuse. I mean by this all the daily interactions with one another that teach us who we are and how we are to live. Think of us as one vast spider web: whatever affects one part of the web carries an influence throughout the whole structure. A kind word here, a touch there, a truthful response, righteous anger at an injustice, lifting a child up to see a parade, bathing one who is bedridden: all these very human gestures, some so small as to be completely unobserved, make up the unconscious memory that holds us, that protects us and gives us direction. These gestures of love are passed from one of us to another, and they are passed down to generations that will follow. Have you ever noticed how a son may have the deep, steady voice of his father? Or how a daughter may make a certain gesture reminiscent of her mother? Things of the spirit are "passed down" in the same way, as one life touches another, and that life touches still another, in an endless stream. The dead say to us, with so much certainty, "How could I not be among you?"

Rufus Jones, teacher, writer, and founder of the American Friends Service Committee, described an experience shortly after the death of his 11-year-old son Lowell.

> When my sorrow was at its most acute stage, I was walking along a great city highway, when suddenly I saw a little child come out of a great gate, which swung to and fastened behind her. She wanted to go to her home behind the gate, but it would not open. She pounded in vain with her little fist. She rattled the gate. Then she wailed as though her heart would break. The cry brought her mother. She caught the child in her arms and kissed away the tears. "Didn't you know I would come? It is all right now." All of a sudden I saw with my spirit that there was love behind my shut gate. Yes, where there is so much love, there must be more.

Where there is so much love, there must be more. I stand here today to affirm that love is stronger even than death. That is what Easter is about—that is what the resurrection story is about: that the source and substance of the universe is love, and that love never passes away. Death is a passageway to the union with the absolute that will embrace us as we have never before been embraced. Let us live fully until we die, and let us not fear the journey to come. "For now we see through a glass, darkly; but then face to face: now I know in part; but then shall I know even as also I am known. And now abideth faith, hope, love, these three; but the greatest of these is love" (1 Corinthians 13: 12–13).

SO BE IT. AMEN.

Prayer

O God of invincible spring, we know that each of us one day must give up this earthly body. That knowing is hard for us, and we are afraid. Give us the courage to live each day that is given us as the precious gift it is. Help us to love well those we are given to love. Be with us on the path, wherever it leads, and give us the faith to know that at last it leads us home. AMEN.

Benediction

Go now and live fully every moment of the life you have been given. Live with praise and with thanksgiving. Go in peace.